POWER
CARS

POWER CARS

HIGH-PERFORMANCE MACHINES

GENERAL EDITOR: CRAIG CHEETHAM

Grunye BOOKS

This edition first published in 2003 for Grange Books
An imprint of Grange Books plc
The Grange
Kingsnorth Industrial Estate
Hoo, nr Rochester
Kent ME3 9ND
www.grangebooks.co.uk

A catalogue record for this book is available from the British Library.

ISBN 1-84013-582-4

Produced by
Amber Books Ltd
Bradley's Close
74–77 White Lion Street
London N1 9PF
www.amberbooks.co.uk

Printed in Italy

This material was previously published as part of the reference set *Hot Cars*

CONTENTS

Introduction

If ever an era was defined by the cars people drove it was the late 1960s. Power was everything—and without a street scoop poking out of the hood a car was nothing.

As the excesses of fins and chrome finally gave way to integrated and much neater car design, a new and exciting form of self-expression was formed across the USA.

It came in the shape of ultra-powerful versions of otherwise ordinary saloon cars and coupés. By shoehorning enormous V8 engines into the unitary-construction shells of family runabouts, America's biggest and boldest car manufacturers gave birth to a new era in performance motoring. The muscle car had arrived.

It's difficult to pin down when this revolution started. Some will argue it was the Ford Mustang that was first to get the ball rolling, appearing in 1964 and offering Thunderbird style at prices to suit the working man. Or was it the Thunderbird itself that was the first incarnation of a power car? It appeared a decade before the Mustang, had incredible performance and was one of the most powerful machines that a sensible amount of money could buy. But then again, the Chevy Corvette

appeared even earlier, and that offered incredible performance for the money. Depending on your definition, this could be the inception point, but many will argue there are other cars that mark the birth of the performance revolution.

Sure, the Mustang and Thunderbird were fine automobiles, but were they really the ultimate power icons?

Ask a General Motors fan and they'll immediately set you straight. The Pontiac GTO, they will tell you, is the original and best muscle car, as GM was the first to truly modify a stock saloon and sell it through Pontiac dealerships.

There's certainly no denying the GTO was a legend in its own lifetime, and when a bout of political correctness forced GM to drop it from the line-up, rebellious Pontiac dealers continued to build and sell 'unofficial' GTOs by selling the modification parts needed and fitting them to customers' cars.

So is the GTO the definitive muscle car? We wouldn't like to say. As well as the manufacturer editions, several were created by their owners as the custom car scene started to take off—and it's impossible to define strictly whether a muscle car should be an untampered original or even a

The 1963 Chevrolet Corvette Stingray became America's favorite sports car.

heavily modified standard saloon.

So rather than argue over the fine points of when the muscle car came into being and when it finally died, we have instead created a book dedicated to celebrating an era of American culture when the car was king. There are powerful machines here to suit all tastes, whether you believe a muscle car is a factory build model or hot rod special, and regardless of when it all started. The only criteria for selection were that each one was a significant car in its own right, had performance to rival the sports cars of today, boasted an imposing road presence and could truly claim to be an icon.

The book centres mainly on the mid to late-1960s, however, when the street racing scene was at its height and nearly every family car was also offered in a racing paint scheme with an enormous engine and chromium wheels. It celebrates the peak era, before environmental legislation and political responsibility made car makers switch from brute and brawn to green and clean.

In the process, our aim is to give you a personal

Carroll Shelby designed the AC Cobra for sheer performance, installing a huge Ford V8 engine into an AC Ace chassis.

experience of some of the finest Detroit iron ever to grace America's blacktop. Each car is examined in detail, from the technical nitty gritty to the original pricing, image and performance figures that meant so much to those who bought them.

You'll also find hundreds of fascinating facts about every car's production history, plus the finer details of each model that make it stand out from the pack.

With behind-the-wheel driving impressions and spectacular photography, this book will take you back to a time when powerful cars were seriously cool and it didn't matter a jot that they looked like Mom's old Pontiac Tempest. Climb into the bucket seats, listen to that V8 thumping and slot the stick-shift into first gear—because you're about to take a ride on Thunder Road. Welcome to an era that will never again form part of the over-sanitised motor industry—when there was simply no substitute for cubic inches...

AC COBRA

When Texan racing driver Carroll Shelby wanted a real performance sports car, he put a Ford V8 into AC's Ace chassis and produced a legend—the mighty Cobra. Engines grew, power outputs soared and the Cobra reached supercar status.

"...oozing raw power."

"Turn the key and the huge V8 rumbles into life, shaking the car and oozing raw power. The driving position and seats are comfortable, which is just as well because you'll be working hard. The Cobra is almost all engine and the chassis had to be strengthened to take the 7-liter V8. Despite the wider tires of the 427, there's still a huge surplus of power over grip. Power oversteer is available whenever you want it. When 100 mph can come up in 10 seconds it's hard to breathe."

Hang on tight! Hair raising performance is what the Cobra is all about. The interior is comfortable, but very windy at 150 mph.

Milestones

1962 Carroll Shelby installs a 260-cubic inch Ford V8 into an AC Ace chassis to create the first Cobra, shown at the New York Motor Show, and production begins.

Cobra was based on the AC Ace.

1963 The original 260 V8 engine is replaced with 289 V8 that makes 271 bhp.

1964 Shelby builds the Daytona coupe and a prototype 427 Cobra. Having outgrown the Venice facility building Cobras, Shelby Mustangs and Sunbeam Tigers, Shelby American moves to the Los Angeles airport.

Massive performance made the Cobra a natural for racing.

1965 The Daytona Cobras win the World Sports Car Championship ahead of Ferrari. This is the first championship of its kind won by an American car. The 427 Cobra goes into production.

1966 Shelby American liquidates its Cobra inventory at its famous 'fire sale' and closes its doors in February.

UNDER THE SKIN

Beef it up

To take the bigger engine and its massive power output, the two main longitudinal chassis tubes were replaced by larger diameter, thicker section tube. Suspension pick-up points were strengthened. Original 260 and 289 Cobras retain the Ace's leaf-sprung rear end, but the MkII versions gained more sophisticated coil-sprung suspension which improved handling.

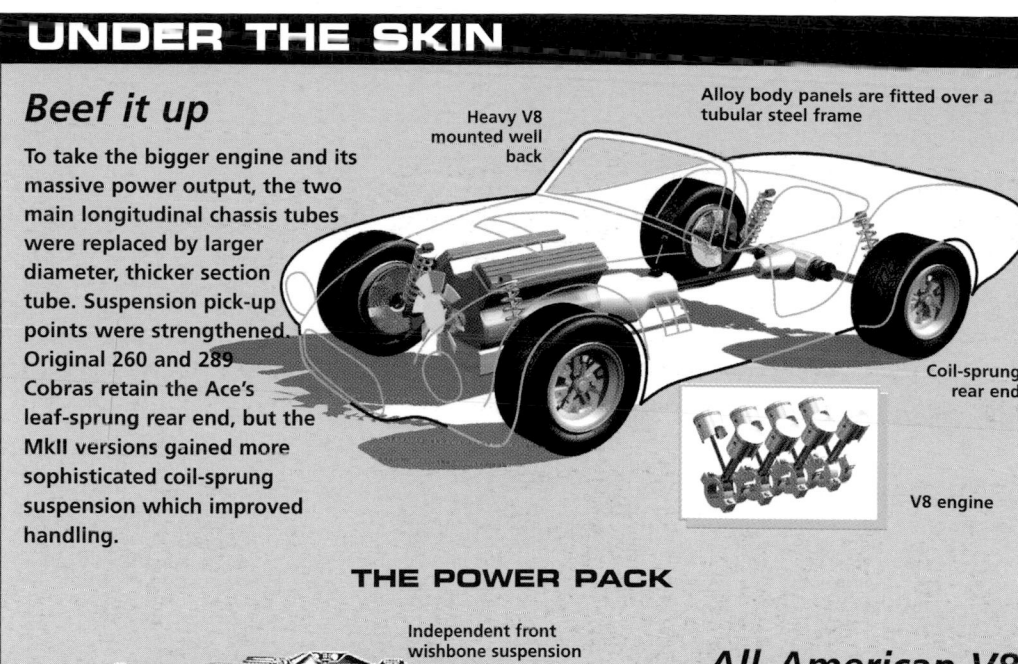

Heavy V8 mounted well back

Alloy body panels are fitted over a tubular steel frame

Coil-sprung rear end

V8 engine

THE POWER PACK

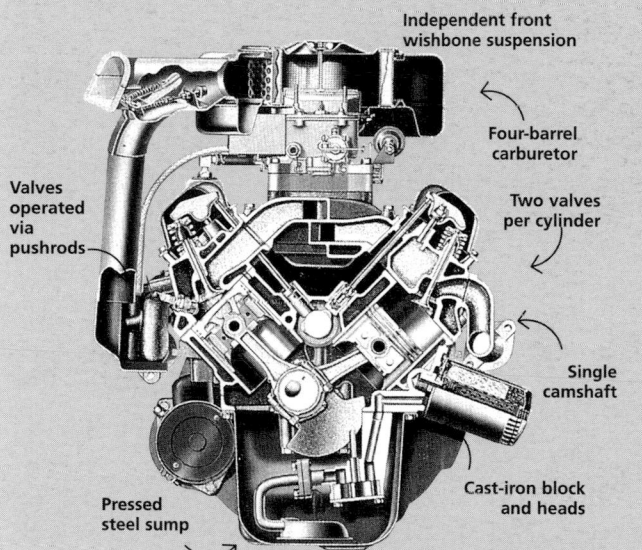

Independent front wishbone suspension

Four-barrel carburetor

Two valves per cylinder

Valves operated via pushrods

Single camshaft

Pressed steel sump

Cast-iron block and heads

All-American V8

All Cobras have American Ford V8s, first the 260 cubic inch, then the 289 and biggest of all, the full-blown 427, which was originally a NASCAR racing engine. All are traditional, simple V8 engines with cast-iron block and heads and a single camshaft, mounted in the vee of the engine, operating the valves via pushrods and rockers. The impressive power and torque outputs are due more to the engine's sheer size rather than clever tuning.

Baby Cobra

It's not as powerful as the 427 and it uses the leaf-spring chassis, but the early Cobra 289, built from 1963 is capable of 138 mph and 0-60 mph in 5.7 seconds. Because the body is so light, the little car had no problem getting the power to the ground.

Not as powerful as the 427, the 289 still has enough performance to thrill.

AC **COBRA** 🇬🇧

Brash and completely over the top, the 427 looks like a caricature of a sports car. Thanks to Shelby American and Ford's massive American V8 engines, the Ace finally has an edge to be competitive in road racing.

Flared wheel arches

To cover the much larger wheels and tires of the 427 model, the wheel arches are drastically flared rather than the whole body being redesigned.

427-cubic inch big block V8

The 427 engine is 97 lbs. heavier than the 289 but much more powerful. Its this engine that gave the Cobra its legendary status.

Side exhausts

Side exhausts make the 427 look even more muscular. They are a feature of the 427 S/C (Street/Competition) models, which are basically racing models sold as road cars.

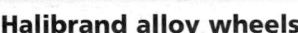

Halibrand alloy wheels

These wheels were very popular in the U.S. where the Ace was transformed into the Cobra. Although the original Cobras run on wire wheels, they cannot handle the power of Ford's potent 427 engine.

Tubular steel chassis

The Cobra's chassis features two main tubular steel chassis members connected by cross braces.

Quick-release fuel filler

Practical as well as stylish, the big alloy fuel filler cap can be opened in a split second for refueling during a race.

Roll-over hoop

This 427 has a roll-over hoop to protect the driver in the event of an accident, but standard Cobras do without it.

Wide track

When the Ace first appeared it was a small and quite narrow car, but the track was widened for the Cobra conversion to fit its massive wheels and tires.

Alloy bodywork

To be as light as possible, all Cobra bodies are made of alloy, and were hand-built at AC's Thames Ditton factory.

Coil spring suspension

The leaf-spring chassis of the original Cobra was updated for the 427 model and more modern coil-spring suspension is installed at the front and rear.

Specifications
1965 AC Cobra 427

ENGINE
Type: V8
Construction: Cast-iron block and heads
Valve gear: Two valves per cylinder operated by single block-mounted camshafts via pushrods and rockers
Bore and stroke: 4.24 in. x 3.78 in.
Displacement: 427 c.i.
Compression ratio: 10.5:1
Induction system: Holley 750 CFM four-barrel carburetor
Maximum power: 425 bhp at 6,000 rpm
Maximum torque: 480 lb-ft at 3,700 rpm

TRANSMISSION
Borg-Warner four-speed manual

BODY/CHASSIS
Tubular steel ladder frame with cross braces and alloy two-door, two-seat convertible

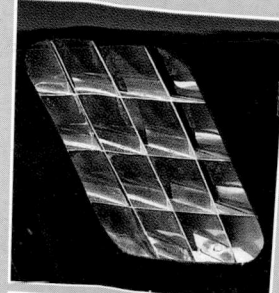

SPECIAL FEATURES

Large chrome side grill vents hot air from the 427's crowded engine compartment.

Quick-release fuel filler cap was a style as well as practical feature.

RUNNING GEAR
Steering: Rack-and-pinion
Front suspension: Double wishbones with coil springs and telescopic shocks
Rear suspension: Double wishbones with coil springs and telescopic shocks
Brakes: Discs, 11.6 in. dia. (front), 10.8 in. dia. (rear)
Wheels: Alloy 15 in. x 7.5 in.
Tires: 7.3 in. x 15 in. (front), 7.7 in. x 15 in. (rear)

DIMENSIONS
Length: 156 in.　　**Width:** 68 in.
Height: 49 in.
Wheelbase: 90 in.
Track: 156 in. (front), 56 in. (rear)
Weight: 2,530 lbs.

AMC **AMX**

American Motors struggled to establish the sort of market identity that the other manufacturers had gained. Its 'character' car, possibly aimed at the Chevrolet Corvette, was the curious AMX two-seat coupe.

"...serious performance."

"Turn the V8's starter motor and your senses awaken—this really sounds like a muscle machine. The deep reserves of torque make driving very easy, and there is plenty of power for fast takeoffs. Add in the optional quick-rack power steering, front disc brakes and limited-slip differential and you have a serious performance machine that is just as capable of tackling twisty mountain roads as taking part in a traffic light drag race."

The dashboard is trimmed with wood grain trim which was very stylish in the late 1960s.

...ones

...-season,
...es its new compact
...e with a choice of
...engines.

Another of AMC's compact muscle cars of the period was the Hurst SC Rambler.

1969 This year the
AMX remains very much as the previous year.

1970 A mild restyle
includes moving the spotlights to the front grill and adding a prominent hump to the hood. The standard engine expands to 390 cubic inches and power outputs rise. This is the last year of AMX sales.

Due to its design, many thought the AMX was supposed to compete with the Corvette.

1971 The AMX name is reduced
to an option package on a larger and curvier Javelin. After 1973 it is more show than go.

UNDER THE SKIN

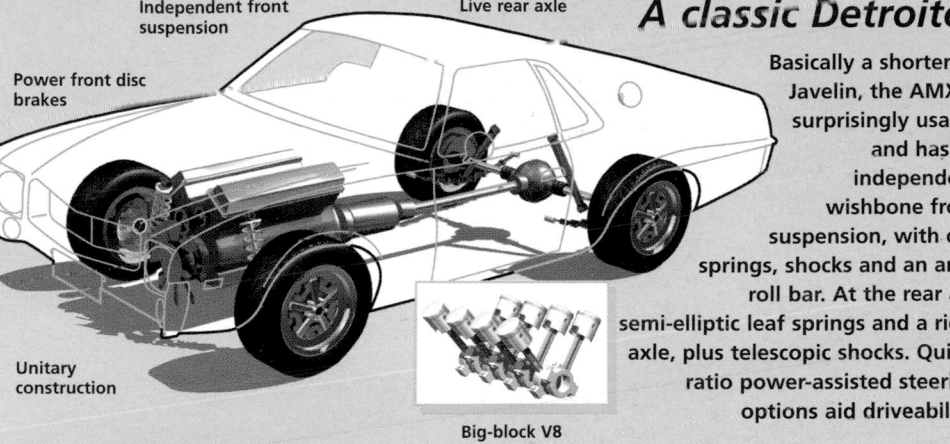

Independent front suspension

Live rear axle

Power front disc brakes

Unitary construction

Big-block V8

A classic Detroiter

Basically a shortened Javelin, the AMX is surprisingly usable and has an independent wishbone front suspension, with coil springs, shocks and an anti-roll bar. At the rear are semi-elliptic leaf springs and a rigid axle, plus telescopic shocks. Quick-ratio power-assisted steering options aid driveability.

THE POWER PACK

Muscle car V8

The standard engine in the AMX is a 225-bhp, 290-cubic inch V8, although larger 343 and 390-V8s were optional. The 390 has a forged steel crankshaft and connecting rods, and a Carter AFB four-barrel carburetor. Its 315 bhp power output is more than adequate and the 425 lb-ft of torque gives it pulling power which modern cars can only dream of. Though very underrated, this two-seat machine is one of the most potent cars to ever have seen action on American pavement.

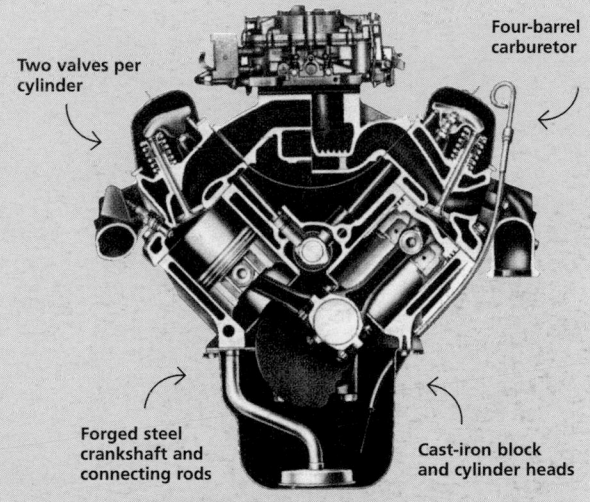

Two valves per cylinder

Four-barrel carburetor

Forged steel crankshaft and connecting rods

Cast-iron block and cylinder heads

Super rare

Few changes occurred in 1969, but the 1970 AMX received a new grill with air vents, plus an improved interior, revised graphics and optional 15-inch wheels. Just 4,116 of the 1970 model were built, making it the rarest and most desirable of all AMXs.

The 1970 AMC AMX muscle cars are the most sought-after by collectors.

AMC **AMX**

By shortening the Javelin, AMC produced a cheap all-American two-seater sports coupe. Just 19,134 AMXs were built, making it a highly desirable muscle car today.

Bulging hood
A popular and sporty option on the AMX was the performance hood complete with dual air scoops. In 1968 the hood bulge was only decorative, but in 1970 the 'Go' package included a fully functional ram air system.

Sporty rear styling
The rear end is styled to give the car a smooth side profile but a ridged-out appearance from behind.

Chrome sills
With AMC's move toward flashier styling, the AMX featured chrome-plated sill covers. Later, these sills gained mock vents, mimicking a side-mounted exhaust.

Short wheelbase
Riding on a 97-inch wheelbase, the AMX is 12 inches shorter than the Javelin. This is even shorter than the Corvette, and qualified the AMX as one of the most compact American cars on the market at the time.

Two-seat interior
Shortening the bodyshell of the 2+2 Javelin means the AMX has room for just two passengers sitting on bucket seats, although there is a large space behind the seats for extra luggage.

Racing paintwork

The typical paint scheme for the AMX in its first two years was twin racing stripes running down the center. Late 1970 models lose the hood stripes but have side stripes instead.

V8 power

Emphasizing its sporty role, the AMX was only ever sold with V8 engines. It was the only AMC at the time not to be offered with a straight-six engine as standard.

Specifications
1968 AMC AMX

ENGINE

Type: V8

Construction: Cast-iron block and cylinder heads

Valve gear: Two valves per cylinder operated by a single camshaft, pushrods and rockers

Bore and stroke: 4.16 in. x 3.57 in.

Displacement: 390 c.i.

Compression ratio: 10.2:1

Induction system: Single four-barrel carburetor

Maximum power: 315 bhp at 4,600 rpm

Maximum torque: 425 lb-ft at 3,200 rpm

TRANSMISSION

Three-speed automatic or four-speed manual

BODY/CHASSIS

Integral with two-door steel coupe body

SPECIAL FEATURES

AMX meant something special after AMC showed a stunning mid-engined sports car with the AMX badge.

The 390-cubic inch V8 was AMC's biggest engine in the late 1960s.

RUNNING GEAR

Steering: Recirculating ball

Front suspension: Wishbones with coil springs and shocks

Rear suspension: Rigid axle with leaf springs and shocks

Brakes: Drums (front and rear)

Wheels: Steel, 14-in. dia.

Tires: E70 x 14 in.

DIMENSIONS

Length: 177 in.   **Width:** 71.5 in.

Height: 51.7 in.   **Wheelbase:** 97 in.

Track: 58.8 in. (front), 57 in. (rear)

Weight: 3,400 lbs.

AMC REBEL MACHINE

After the overachieving little SC/Rambler of 1969, AMC returned to the muscle car market with the Rebel Machine. It still sported loud graphics, but thanks to a 390-cubic inch, 340-bhp V8, it was more than capable of outshining the competition and backing up its flashy appearance.

THE MACHINE

"...built to be a performer."

"It may have a horizontal-sweep speedometer, but a four-on-the-floor and bucket seats assure you that this car was built to be a performer. The 390-cubic inch V8 is a lot more tractable than some others in everyday driving, and although throttle control is required to really get the Machine moving, the end result is worth it. Through corners, the AMC feels quite nimble for its size, with much less understeer than you would expect."

A four-speed transmission with a cue-ball shifter is nestled between the front seats.

Milestones

1968 American Motors releases

photographs of a menacing mid-size Rebel. It has semi-gloss dark paint with matching bumpers and wheels. Called the Machine, it is intended for production in 1969, but none are actually sold.

The SC/Rambler was American Motors' first serious muscle car.

1969 With help

from Hurst Performance, AMC stuffs its biggest engine in the compact Rogue, resulting in the Hurst SC/Rambler. Packing 315 bhp and capable of 14.3-second quarter miles, 1,512 of these patriotic-looking cars are built.

The two-seater AMX could also get the big 390-c.i. V8.

1970 Replacing the

SC/Rambler is a new, larger Rebel Machine. Packing 340 bhp from a 390 V8, it is a potent performer too, but lasts for only one model year.

UNDER THE SKIN

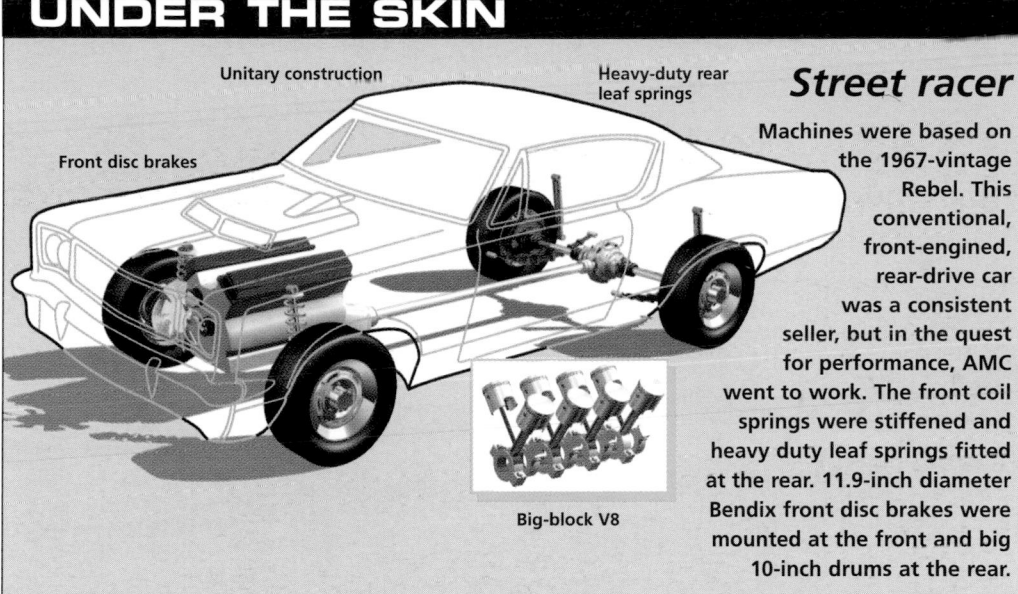

Unitary construction

Heavy-duty rear leaf springs

Front disc brakes

Big-block V8

Street racer

Machines were based on the 1967-vintage Rebel. This conventional, front-engined, rear-drive car was a consistent seller, but in the quest for performance, AMC went to work. The front coil springs were stiffened and heavy duty leaf springs fitted at the rear. 11.9-inch diameter Bendix front disc brakes were mounted at the front and big 10-inch drums at the rear.

THE POWER PACK

AMC's biggest

In order to compete with the big three, American Motors realized that the best way was to stuff its largest engine in a mid size car. The 390-cubic inch mill that powered all Machines is an enlarged version of the 343 unit. It followed customary practice with a cast-iron block and heads, plus two valves per cylinder. Where the 343 has cast-iron rods and crankshaft, the 390 has forged-steel items and larger bearings. The 390 is a moderate performer, producing its 340 bhp at 5,100 rpm.

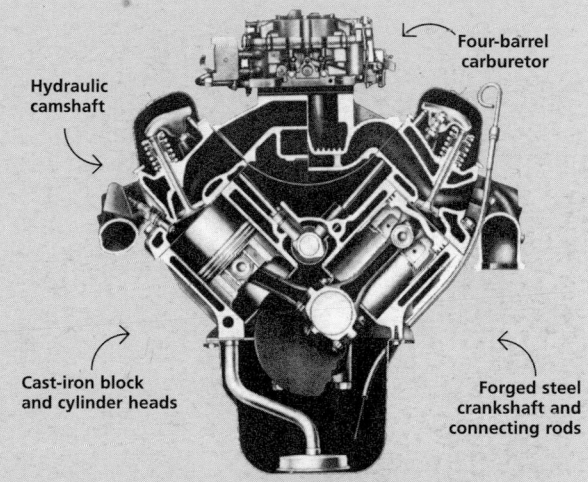

Hydraulic camshaft

Four-barrel carburetor

Cast-iron block and cylinder heads

Forged steel crankshaft and connecting rods

Patriotic

Rebel Machines were offered for only one year, and with a production total of 2,326 are not exactly common. The first 1,000 cars built had a special white, blue and red color scheme, making them particularly sought-after in AMC circles.

Later Machines could be ordered in any Rebel factory color.

AMC REBEL MACHINE

Although AMC stated 'The Machine is not that fast,' the car could give many muscle cars from the big three a run for their money, particularly with an experienced driver behind the wheel.

King of the cubes

In 1970, the 390-cubic inch V8 was the biggest engine offered by American Motors. With a big four-barrel carburetor and functional hood scoop, it produces a credible 340 bhp and 430 lb-ft of torque, good enough for mid-14-second ¼-mile ETs.

Strong transmission

Like the AMX and Javelin, the Machine was offered with a Borg-Warner T-10 four-speed manual transmission and a Hurst shifter. This enabled lightning-quick getaways from the lights.

Twin-Grip

Transmitting power to the rear tires is a Twin-Grip differential with standard 3.54:1 final drive. Steeper gearing was offered over the counter—up to an incredible 5.00:1 for hardcore drag-racer types.

Power steering

Manual steering was standard, but many buyers considered it too heavy and thus ordered the optional power setup. It was, however, boosted and contemporary road testers wrote that it was 'grossly over-assisted.'

Stiff suspension

Rebel Machines rode on some of the stiffest suspension from Detroit. Fitting the Rebel wagon's heavy-duty rear leaf springs gave a street racer stance, and although handling is good for a muscle car, the jacked-up rear results in severe wheel hop if the gas is floored from a standing start.

Hood scoop

Besides having an interesting look, the vacuum-operated hood scoop is functional too, forcing cooler, denser air into the engine. The scoop assembly also contains an integrated 8,000-rpm tachometer, which can be difficult to read in harsh sunlight or rain.

Specifications

1970 AMC Rebel Machine

ENGINE
Type: V8
Construction: Cast-iron block and heads
Valve gear: Two valves per cylinder operated by pushrods and rockers
Bore and stroke: 4.17 in. x 3.57 in.
Displacement: 390 c.i.
Compression ratio: 10.0:1
Induction system: Four-barrel carburetor
Maximum power: 340 bhp at 5,100 rpm
Maximum torque: 430 lb-ft at 3,600 rpm

TRANSMISSION
Borg-Warner T-10 four-speed manual

BODY/CHASSIS
Steel unitary chassis with two-door coupe body

SPECIAL FEATURES

In 1970, the 390 was the largest engine in AMC's inventory.

The functional hood scoop houses an integrated tachometer.

RUNNING GEAR
Steering: Recirculating ball
Front suspension: Unequal-length A-arms with coil springs, telescopic shock absorbers and stabilizer bar
Rear suspension: Live axle with semi-elliptic leaf-springs, telescopic shock absorbers and stabilizer bar
Brakes: Discs front, drums rear
Wheels: 7 x 15 in. pressed steel
Tires: Goodyear Polyglas E60-15

DIMENSIONS
Length: 199.0 in. **Width:** 77.2 in.
Height: 56.2 in. **Wheelbase:** 114.0 in.
Track: 59.7 in. (front), 60.0 in. (rear)
Weight: 3,650 lbs.

Buick RIVIERA GRAN SPORT

Bigger and heavier for 1971, Buick's personal luxury coupe also got dramatic new styling—especially at the rear, which gave rise to its 'boat-tail' nickname. Some saw it as the ultimate land yacht, but the GS™ model's 330 bhp made for fast, executive-style driving.

"...easy and effortless ."

"When viewed from the outside, the Riviera looks positively huge, but take your place behind the wheel and it feels much smaller. Easy and effortless to drive, this big Buick is at its best on long, straight roads, but with the GS package it will corner hard, ultimately only let down by its tires and sheer girth. The V8 is another matter; with the GS option it packs 330 bhp and 455 lb-ft of torque. This car will reach 60 mph quicker than many other personal luxury cars of its era."

A radiused gauge cluster and close-mounted console garnish the Riviera's lavish interior.

Milestones

1971 Replacing the 1966 vintage
Riviera is a new, larger model, with a wheelbase three inches longer and swoopy styling. Weighing about 100 lbs. more, sales drop to 33,810 due in part to its controversial rear end.

The Riviera was reborn as a personal luxury coupe in 1963.

1972 Chrome side spears
and a new grill mark the 1972 model. The Gran Sport package is still around, though power is down because of its low-lead, 8.5:1 compression ratio. The big 455-c.i. V8 makes 225 bhp—250 in GS tune.

1974 saw the heaviest Riviera yet, weighing in at 4,572 lbs.

1973 A bigger front bumper
and toned down rear deck styling give the Buick's personal luxury car a less distinctive look. Sales creep up slightly to 34,080.

UNDER THE SKIN

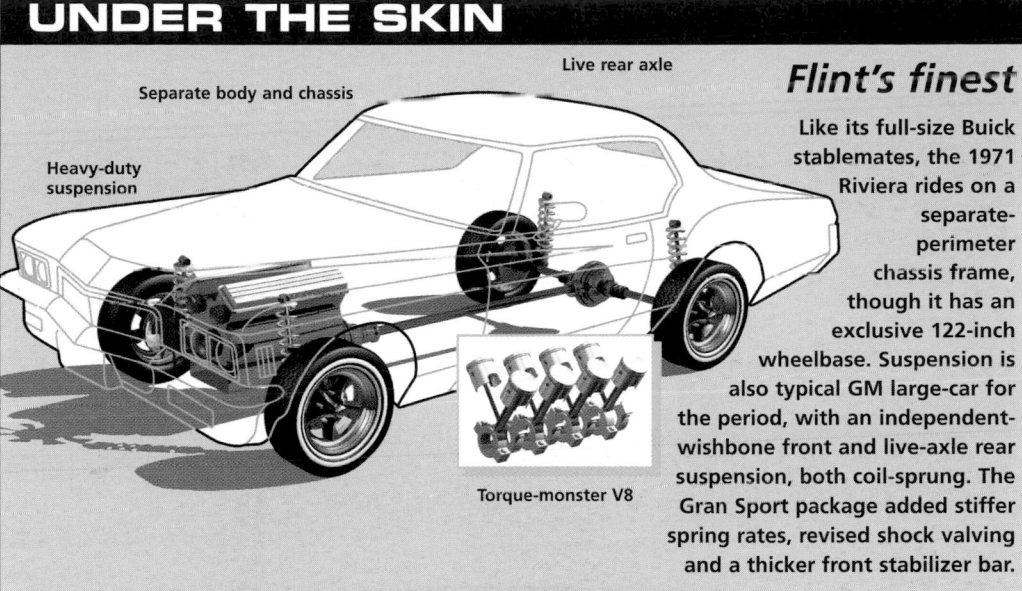

Separate body and chassis

Live rear axle

Heavy-duty suspension

Torque-monster V8

Flint's finest

Like its full-size Buick stablemates, the 1971 Riviera rides on a separate-perimeter chassis frame, though it has an exclusive 122-inch wheelbase. Suspension is also typical GM large-car for the period, with an independent-wishbone front and live-axle rear suspension, both coil-sprung. The Gran Sport package added stiffer spring rates, revised shock valving and a thicker front stabilizer bar.

THE POWER PACK

Mammoth motor

With fuel selling for around 30 cents per gallon in 1971, the Riviera naturally came with Buick's largest V8. Displacing 455-cubic inches, it was an outgrowth of the 1967 430. A very long (3.90-inch) stroke makes it a torque monster; it thumps out a whopping 455 lb-ft at just 2,800 rpm. Driving such a car as the Riviera Gran Sport, it is possible to entice drivers of smaller and lighter muscle cars to a traffic light duel. Though it has a lot of torque, the engine is still well behaved and will provide relaxed high-speed cruising.

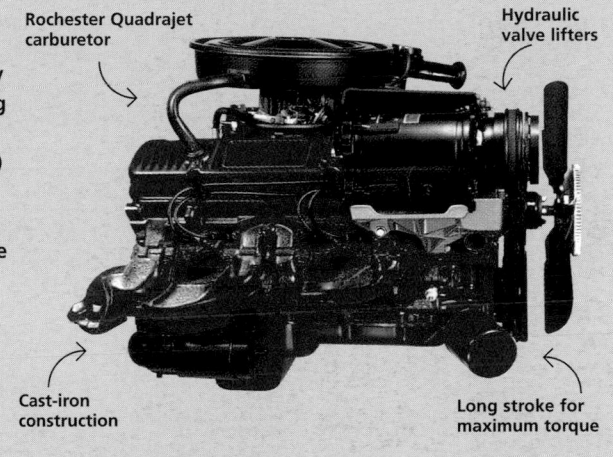

Rochester Quadrajet carburetor

Hydraulic valve lifters

Cast-iron construction

Long stroke for maximum torque

Speed boat

Although large and unique, the boat-tail Riviera does have a following. The 1971-1972 models have the unusually styled rear end, which was toned down for 1973. The 1971 GS is also the most sporty version and luckily can still be bought at reasonable prices.

1971 is the pinnacle year for boat-tails in terms of styling and performance.

Buick RIVIERA GRAN SPORT

Penned by Jerry Hirschberg, the 1971 Riviera was a unique design because it broke away from the conservative luxury so often associated with Buick cars. This is what elevated this short-lived car to cult status in later years.

Giant V8

Powering one of the largest and heaviest Rivieras is Buick's largest passenger car engine. Displacing a monster 455-cubic inches, this giant packs 330 bhp in Gran Sport trim and 455 lb-ft of torque. The Riviera GS was the perfect street sleeper for those who were looking for something different.

Heavy-duty suspension

Ordering the Gran Sport package in 1971 brought with it stiffer coil springs and shock absorbers, plus a thicker stabilizer bar. It made for one of the most sporty luxury coupes then on sale.

Body-on-the-frame construction

Rivieras in 1971 had their own E-body chassis but shared their separated chassis structure with the other GM B- and C-body full-size cars.

Boat-tail deck styling

Riviera stylist Hirschberg gave the new Riviera a very dramatic rear deck style which extended right to the bumper. This necessitated an offset rear license plate bracket.

Cornering lights

Costing just $36 in 1971, cornering lights are mounted in the front fenders. These come on with the turn signals. At night, the front and side signals flash alternately instead of in time.

Dual exhaust

Initially, Rivieras had dual exhaust, each with individual mufflers. This system prevailed until 1975, when the adoption of a catalytic convertor necessitated the need for a single setup.

Counterbalanced hood

Like most U.S. cars of the period, the 1971 Riviera has a counterbalancing hood. When opened, heavy-duty hinges support it, eliminating the need for a prop rod. The hood latch is located in the front-grill assembly.

Specifications

1971 Buick Riviera Gran Sport

ENGINE

Type: V8

Construction: Cast-iron block and heads

Valve gear: Two valves per cylinder operated by pushrods and rockers

Bore and stroke: 4.31 in. x 3.90 in.

Displacement: 455 c.i.

Compression ratio: 8.5:1

Induction system: Rochester Quadrajet four-barrel carburetor

Maximum power: 330 bhp at 4,600 rpm

Maximum torque: 455 lb-ft at 2,800 rpm

TRANSMISSION

GM TurboHydramatic 400 three-speed automatic

BODY/CHASSIS

Steel-perimeter chassis with separate two-door coupe body

SPECIAL FEATURES

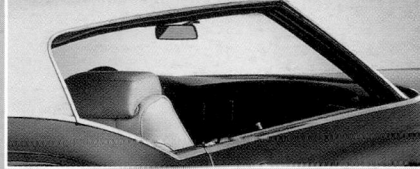

Pillarless styling is a feature of Rivieras built up to 1974.

1971–72 models are the only true boat-tail-styled Rivieras.

RUNNING GEAR

Steering: Recirculating ball

Front suspension: Unequal-length A-arms with coil springs, telescopic shock absorbers and stabilizer bar

Rear suspension: Live axle with coil springs and telescopic shock absorbers

Brakes: Discs (front), drums (rear)

Wheels: Steel 7 x 15

Tires: G70-15 in.

DIMENSIONS

Length: 217.4 in.　　**Width:** 79.9 in.

Height: 56.4 in.　　**Wheelbase:** 122.0 in.

Track: 60.4 in.

Weight: 4,325 lbs.

Chevrolet **CAMARO Z28**

General Motors' answer to the Ford Mustang needed plenty of power to compete with the original pony car. The Z28 performance option on the Chevrolet Camaro was the answer. It dramatically improving handling and power.

" ...factory built race car."

"Designed to compete in Trans Am racing, the high-revving Z28 is a factory built race car. Underrated at 290 bhp, the over-square 302 V8 engine is peaky and nothing much happens until the engine revs past 4,000 rpm. Suddenly the tachometer needle is pointing to 7,000 rpm and the car really comes to life. It's upper end power like this where the Z28 gives you easy 120 mph performance. Complementing the overabundance of high end power, the Z28 is garnished with a four-speed transmission, seven-inch rims and competition suspension."

The interior of this race-modified Z28 uses bucket seat, roll cage and a fire extinguisher.

Milestones

1966 First Camaro
appears based on the Chevy II frame. The standard powertrain is only a 230-cubic inch six cylinder.

Only 602 Camaro Z28s were built in its first year, 1967.

1967 Regular
production option Z28 is introduced with a 302-cubic inch engine, just inside the 305-cubic inch limit set for Trans Am racing. Z28s finish third and fourth at the Sebring 12 Hours, winning the Trans Am category.

1968 Z28 dominates
Trans Am, easily winning the championship with the Roger Penske-prepared cars. Driver Mark Donohue wins 10 out of the 13 rounds.

The Camaro's styling was radically altered for 1970.

1969 Crossram
induction is made available, but is put in only 205 cars.

1970 Model restyled
to be longer and heavier with egg-crate type grill, but the Z28 option lives on and is still found on today's hottest Camaros.

UNDER THE SKIN

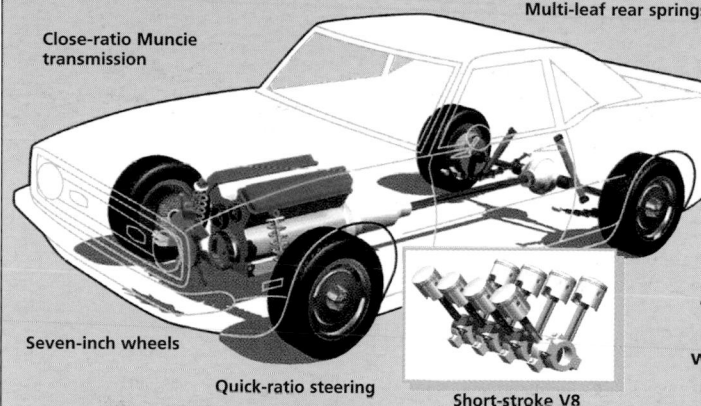

Close-ratio Muncie transmission

Multi-leaf rear springs

Seven-inch wheels

Quick-ratio steering

Short-stroke V8

Tightened up

Detail changes transformed the basic and simple Camaro. The steering ratio was improved to give 'quicker' steering. It also had harder brake linings, stiffer rear multi-leaf springs, and revalved shock absorbers were fitted all around. There was a host of other options to add to the Z28 package, such as even quicker steering and a Muncie M-22 close-ratio four speed transmission.

THE POWER PACK

Hybrid V8

For the Z28, GM used the 327 cast iron block to give a four-inch bore and added a forged crankshaft (similar to the 283) with a three-inch stroke to make a rev-happy, over-square 302-cubic inch V8.

It operated a high (11.0:1) compression ratio, had 'Camelback' cylinder heads fitted with large 2.02-inch intake and 1.60-inch exhaust valves and had very radical valve timing. The engine is designed to give loads of top end performance with its maximum power not coming in until 6,000 rpm.

Holley carburetor

2.02/1.60 valves

Shorter-stroke crankshaft

11.0:1 compression ratio

Longer, sleeker

The distinctive egg-crate grill is a definitive feature on the second-generation Camaro and was included on the Z28. It may not be the original, the rarest, or the most collectable Camaro variant, but it has a more obvious, overtly-sporting image. This shape remained in production, largely unchanged, until 1974.

The 1970 Camaros are more streamlined than first generation cars.

Chevrolet CAMARO Z28

To compete in the prestigious Trans Am championship, the rules required that Chevrolet had to build 1,000 suitable cars ready for sale to the public to homologate the car for racing. The result was the Z28, a racing car for the road.

Performance V8

Chevrolet originally rated the Z28's short-stroke V8 at 290 bhp. Some critics thought its potential was being deliberately underrated, and it could really produce something nearer to 350 bhp at well over 6,000 rpm.

Coupe-only body style

You could not order the Z28 package with the convertible body because Chevrolet only needed to homologate the coupe for Trans Am racing.

Vented disc brakes

Z28s are heavy cars, so with the performance available they have to have vented front disc brakes. Even with the harder pads though, the Z28's braking isn't its strongest feature.

Close-ratio transmission

Standard Z28 transmission was an automatic but for $184 a Muncie four-speed manual was available that could also be ordered with close-ratio gears.

Harder brake linings

Although the Z28 carries rear drum brakes, just like stock Camaros, the linings are a harder compound to improve performance under sustained high-speed braking.

Rear spoiler

The rear spoiler is as much about adding just a touch of style to the rear of the Camaro as managing the airflow over the car to improve rear downforce.

Wide tires

The Z28 used Goodyear WideTread tires on relatively wide (for the time) seven-inch rims.

Stiffer rear springs

The one major suspension change was the switch to multi-leaf instead of the stock single-leaf rear springs which were 25 percent stiffer than standard. Despite this change, the front spring rates did not need to be altered at all.

1967 Chevrolet Camaro Z28

ENGINE

Type: V8
Construction: Cast-iron block and heads
Valve gear: Two valves per cylinder operated by single block-mounted camshaft via pushrods and hydraulic lifters
Bore and stroke: 4.0 in. x 3.0 in.
Displacement: 302 c.i.
Compression ratio: 11.0:1
Induction system: Single four-barrel 800-cfm Holley carburetor
Maximum power: 290 bhp at 5,800 rpm
Maximum torque: 290 lb-ft at 4,200 rpm

TRANSMISSION

Three-speed automatic or four-speed manual

BODY/CHASSIS

Unitary steel construction with two-door coupe body

SPECIAL FEATURES

The 302-cubic inch engine was new for the Z28. It combined 327 block with a 283 crank to achieve a capacity of less than 305 cubic inches for SCCA racing.

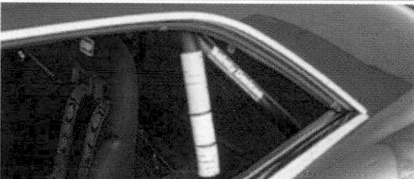

This car has been fitted with a roll cage to comply with SCCA racing regulations.

RUNNING GEAR

Steering: Recirculating ball
Front suspension: Double wishbones with coil springs, telescopic shocks and anti-roll bar
Rear suspension: Live axle with multi-leaf semi-elliptic springs and telescopic shocks
Brakes: Front vented discs, 11 in. dia., and rear drums, 9 in. dia.
Wheels: Steel disc, 7 in. x 15 in.
Tires:: Goodyear WideTread E70-15

DIMENSIONS

Length: 184.7 in.   **Width:** 72.5 in.
Height: 51.4 in.   **Wheelbase:** 108 in.
Track: 59.6 in. (front), 59.5 in. (rear)
Weight: 3525 lbs.

Chevrolet CAMARO ZL-1

GM supported the Automotive Manufacturers Association (AMA) ban in the 1960s by only using its 400 cubic-inch and larger engines in full size cars and Corvettes. Through the Central Office Production Order system Vince Piggins, one of Chevrolet's officers, found a loop hole with the ban and created the ultimate Camaro—the ZL-1.

"...the apex of Chevy muscle."

"This is the apex of Chevy's muscle cars. In the driver's seat the car resembles a typical six-cylinder Camaro. When you start it up and listen to the aggressive engine you soon realize you've slid behind the wheel of a true factory-built racer. With the addition of tubular headers, drag slicks and a super tune, one of these nasty Camaros could run the ¼ mile in 11.68 seconds at more than 120 mph. Few cars come close to offering the level of thrill that a ZL-1 can."

Most ZL-1s had stripped cabins, but this one has a deluxe interior with woodgrain trim.

Milestones

1967 In response to the Mustang,
Chevrolet launches the Camaro. The most powerful engine available is the 375 bhp, 396 V8. Because of the AMA ban, GM's intermediates weren't available with engines larger than 400 cubic inches. Meanwhile, a handful of Chevy dealers were installing 427 V8s into these cars, especially Camaros.

In 1967 car dealers were installing 427 V8s into new Camaros.

1968 Don Yenko of
Yenko Sports Cars becomes the largest dealer converting these Camaros. GM's Vince Piggins takes notice. Later that year, Piggins and Yenko get together to offer the conversion package from GM's COPO (Central Office Production Order) department for 1969.

Don Yenko's YSC Camaros got the ball rolling for the ZL-1.

1969 A few hundred COPO Camaros
are built. While most come with cast iron 427s, 69 versions known as ZL-1s are built with aluminum big-block engines. Tuned ZL-1s made 500+ bhp and could cover the ¼ mile in just under 12 seconds.

UNDER THE SKIN

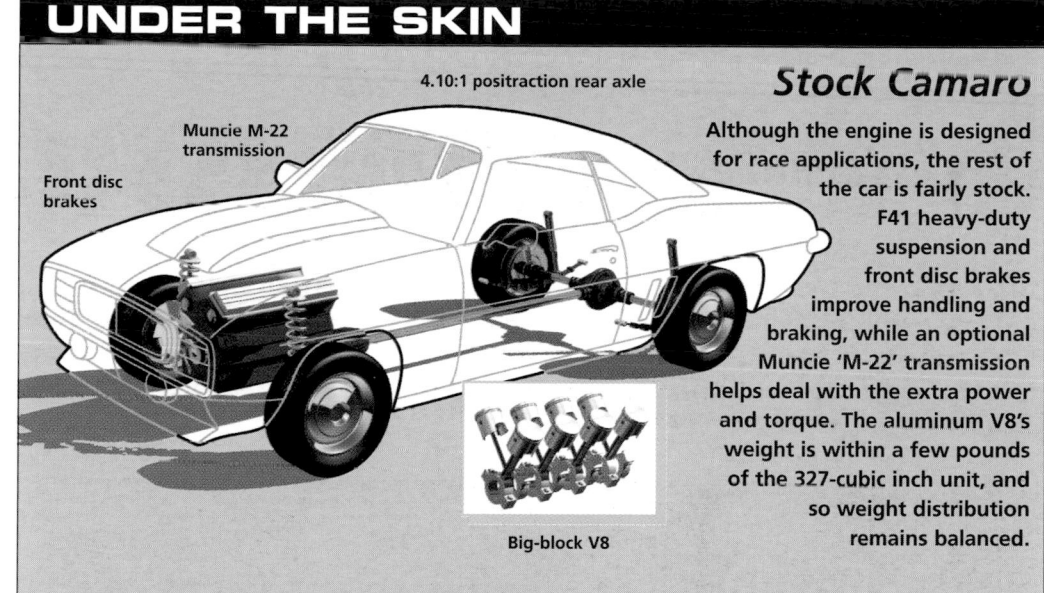

Muncie M-22 transmission

4.10:1 positraction rear axle

Front disc brakes

Big-block V8

Stock Camaro

Although the engine is designed for race applications, the rest of the car is fairly stock. F41 heavy-duty suspension and front disc brakes improve handling and braking, while an optional Muncie 'M-22' transmission helps deal with the extra power and torque. The aluminum V8's weight is within a few pounds of the 327-cubic inch unit, and so weight distribution remains balanced.

THE POWER PACK

Exotic big-block

The ZL-1 was unlike any other engine that GM made at that time. The engine is roughly equivalent to the L88 Corvette racing V8 but has an aluminum instead of cast-iron block. The reciprocating assembly consisted of a forged steel crankshaft, forged pistons that slide in steel cylinder liners and four-bolt main bearing caps. The aluminum cylinder heads have closed chambers and rectangle intake ports. A Holley 850-cfm four-barrel carburetor fed the massive engine the fuel it required.

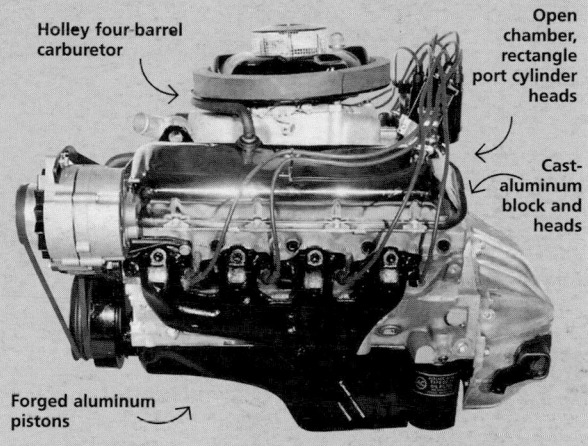

Holley four-barrel carburetor

Open chamber, rectangle port cylinder heads

Cast-aluminum block and heads

Forged aluminum pistons

Pure racer

ZL-1s are ranked with the Hemi Cuda convertible and Ram Air IV™ GTO® as one of the most desirable muscle cars ever produced. With only 69 built with the all-aluminum engine, they attract a premium price and often trade hands for $150,000 or more.

To this day, Chevrolet hasn't built a more powerful production car than the ZL-1.

Chevrolet CAMARO ZL-1

Most ZL-1s had plain bodies with skinny steel wheels—they didn't even have any badging to designate their model or engine size. This unique ZL-1 has the RS appearance package, vinyl top and 427 badging.

ZL2 cowl hood

All ZL-1s came with cowl induction hoods. It forced cool air into the engine from the high pressure area just below the windshield.

Expensive engine

You had to have a healthy bank account to be able to afford a ZL-1 Camaro. The engine's all-aluminum construction saved 160 lbs. over the cast-iron 427. Because it is virtually hand built, the engine alone cost $4,160—more than most cars of the period.

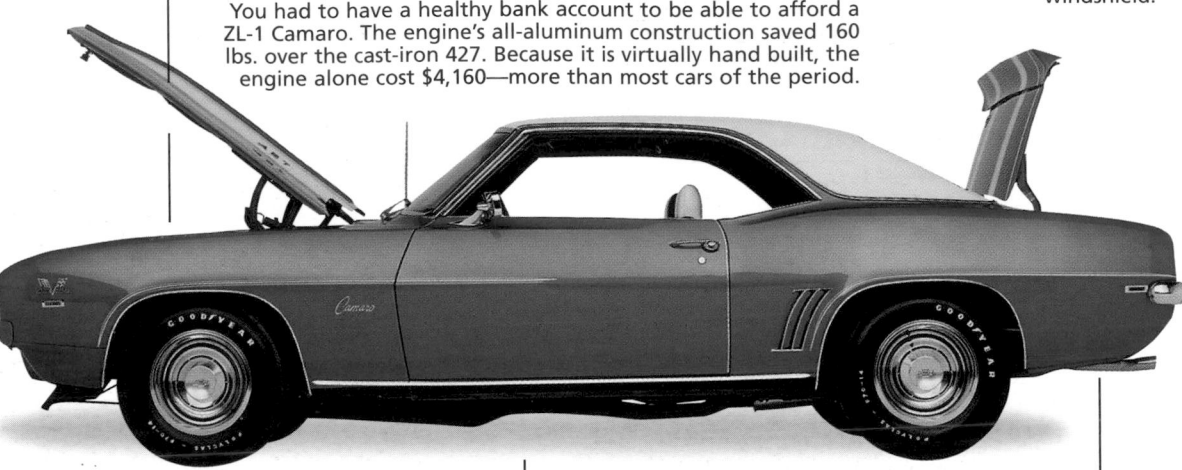

Better balance

Although it is a big-block unit, the ZL-1 engine weighs about 500 lbs. which is roughly the same as a 327, and so these special Camaros actually handle better than the stock SS 396™. However, these cars were designed for use in NHRA Super Stock drag racing events.

Standard exhaust system

ZL-1s left the factory with lots of mismatched parts because the owners were expected to do a lot of race development themselves. The stock exhaust manifolds restrict the flow of exhaust gases and were usually among the first items to be replaced.

The ZL-1 option package

All ZL-1s began life as SS 396s, but the engine and Super Sport™ option were deleted. Instead, the special cars received the ZL-1 option package which included the aluminum engine, F41 suspension, front discs and a cowl induction hood.

Heavy duty suspension components

All ZL-1s were equipped with the heavy duty F41 suspension and front disc brakes. To better handle the 450 lb-ft of torque from the powerful engines, ZL-1s were equipped with 12-bolt rear ends with 4.10 gears.

Performance transmission

Only two transmissions were strong enough to cope with the ZL-1 V8: the Muncie M-22 'Rock Crusher' four-speed or the equally stout TurboHydramatic 400 automatic.

Specifications

1969 Chevrolet Camaro ZL-1

ENGINE

Type: V8

Construction: Aluminum block and cylinder heads

Valve gear: Two valves per cylinder operated by a single camshaft

Bore and stroke: 4.25 in. x 3.76 in.

Displacement: 427 c.i.

Compression ratio: 12.0:1

Induction system: Holley four-barrel carburetor

Maximum power: 430 bhp at 5,200 rpm

Maximum torque: 450 lb-ft at 4,400 rpm

TRANSMISSION

Muncie M-22 four-speed manual

BODY/CHASSIS

Unitary steel chassis with two-door hardtop coupe body

SPECIAL FEATURES

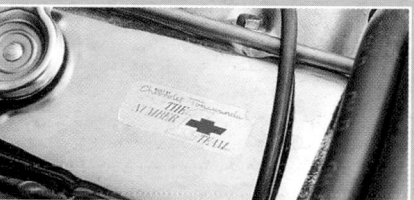

Each ZL-1 engine has a special sticker on the valve cover.

Most ZL-1s have exposed headlights, but this car has the RS package.

RUNNING GEAR

Steering: Recirculating ball

Front suspension: Double wishbones with coil springs, telescopic shock absorbers and anti-roll bar

Rear suspension: Live axle with semi-elliptic leaf springs and telescopic shock absorbers

Brakes: Discs (front), drums (rear)

Wheels: Steel, 6 x 15 in.

Tires: Goodyear Wide Tread GT, E70-15

DIMENSIONS

Length: 186.0 in.   **Width:** 74.0 in.

Height: 51.0 in.   **Wheelbase:** 108.0 in.

Track: 59.6 in. (front), 59.5 in. (rear)

Weight: 3,300 lbs.

Chevrolet CHEVELLE SS 454

In 1970, Chevrolet introduced the ultimate powerhouse for its midsize muscle car. It was also the year GM lifted its displacement ban on all of its midsize cars. For the Chevelle, it meant 450 bhp from a stout LS-6 454 V8 for the Super Sport model. Today, it is regarded as one of the most fearsome muscle cars of all time.

"...all-out performance."

"This is not a toy—it's an LS-6 Chevelle SS. It's one of those cars GM built just to show up Ford and Mopar. For years, the SS used semi-powerful 396 V8s, but when Chevy® released the LS-6 454, the competition shuddered. The all-out performance engine has a factory rating of 450 bhp—no other muscle car production engine had a higher rating. The LS-6 Chevelle's only limitation was its tires. But even with the stock tread, the SS could be power shifted to 13.7 seconds in the ¼ mile."

While most Chevelle Super Sports were ordered with custom buckets, this one has a bench seat.

Milestones

1969 SS is an option

package. Top-of-the-line engine continues to be the L78 396 with 375 bhp. However, Vince Piggins, GM's performance products manager, had 323 COPO (Central Office Production Order) Chevelles built with L72 427 V8s. They produce 425 bhp, and run the ¼ mile in 13.3 seconds at 108 mph.

Earlier Chevelles had much boxier styling.

1970 General Motors

unleashes its wildest muscle cars yet, with revised styling. The LS-5 (360 bhp) and LS-6 (454 bhp) 454 V8s join the 396 in the Chevelle SS line up as a regular production order.

In 1970, the smaller-engined SS 396 was still available.

1971 The SS 454

returns, though the LS-6 option is dropped. The less powerful LS-5 actually gains 5 bhp, to 365. Only 9,402 SS 454s are built. A new Chevelle arrives for 1973.

UNDER THE SKIN

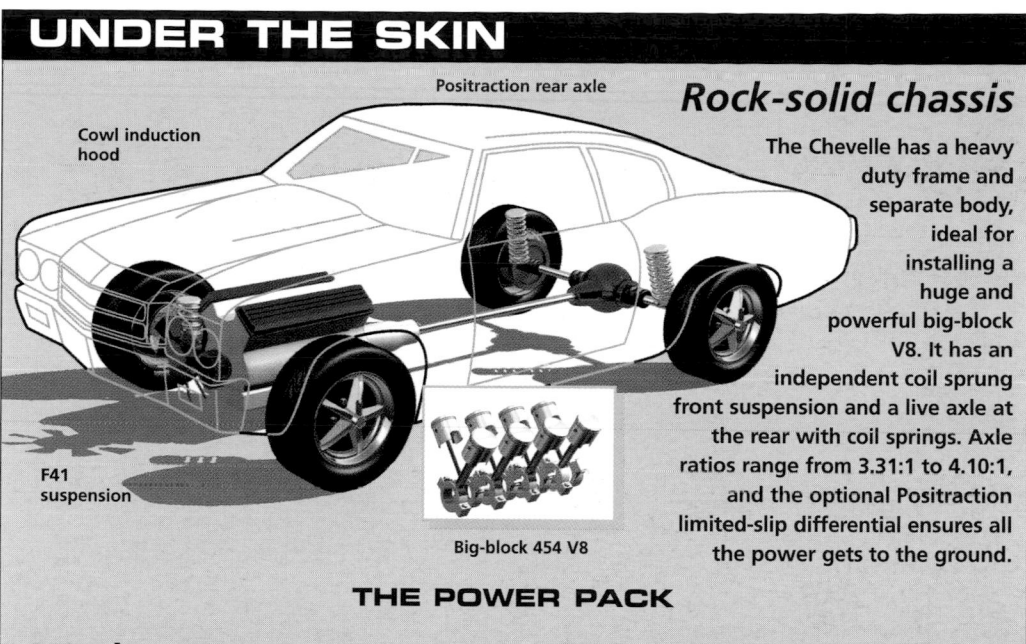

Positraction rear axle

Cowl induction hood

F41 suspension

Big-block 454 V8

Rock-solid chassis

The Chevelle has a heavy duty frame and separate body, ideal for installing a huge and powerful big-block V8. It has an independent coil sprung front suspension and a live axle at the rear with coil springs. Axle ratios range from 3.31:1 to 4.10:1, and the optional Positraction limited-slip differential ensures all the power gets to the ground.

THE POWER PACK

Hard-core power

The lightning and thunder raging under the hood of the highest performance Chevelle SS—the infamous LS-6—produces 450 bhp and 500 lb-ft of torque. The block shares the same 4.25-inch bore as the 427 V8, but the stroke was increased to 4.00 inches. The longer stroke helps produce gobs of low end power. The powerful LS-6 uses high (11.25:1) compression forged pistons, steel crankshaft, high-lift camshaft with mechanical lifters and closed-chamber, rectangle-port cylinder heads. It uses an aluminum intake manifold and a Holley 800 cfm carburetor. This engine means business.

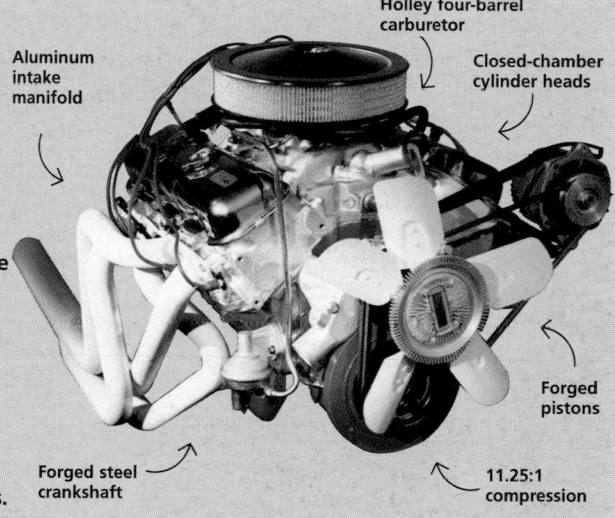

Aluminum intake manifold

Holley four-barrel carburetor

Closed-chamber cylinder heads

Forged pistons

11.25:1 compression

Forged steel crankshaft

Collector's cars

The 1970 Chevelle Super Sport was restyled from the 1969 model and again in 1971. A 1970 SS with the LS-6 is as rare as it is powerful. Only 4,475 of these venomous vehicles were produced, making them popular and valuable among auto collectors.

Not many muscle cars come close to the tire-shredding power of the LS-6 SS.

Chevrolet CHEVELLE SS 454

The LS-6 Chevelle was one of the most powerful muscle cars ever produced. It combined Chevrolet's largest engine with its sporty midsize car to give outrageous results.

LS-6 454-cubic inch V8

The biggest performance option in 1970 was the LS-6 engine. It produces 450 bhp at 5,600 rpm and 500 lb-ft of torque at 3,600 rpm. It has high compression pistons, rectangle port cylinder heads, and solid valve lifters. Few other muscle machines could rival the power of the LS-6.

Body stripes

By 1970 style was every bit as important as performance, and SS Chevelles were available with twin stripes running over the hood and rear decklid.

M-22 'Rock crusher' transmission

With 500 lb-ft of torque, only two transmissions were strong enough to cope with the LS-6 engine. This one has a Muncie M22 'Rock crusher' four-speed. This stout unit has a 2.20:1 straight-cut first gear.

Magnum 500 wheels

Magnum 500 steel wheels were used on all 1970 Chevelle Super Sports. The Polyglas F70x14 could barely handle the engine's torque.

Hardtop body

While all LS-6 engines were supposed to be installed in hardtops only, it's rumored that a few found their way into convertibles.

Upgraded suspension
The SS package included the F41 suspension which has stiffer front springs to compensate for the weight of the big-block engine.

Dual exhaust
A full-length 2.5-inch dual exhaust system enables the LS-6 to optimize the engine's performance.

Cowl induction hood
A vacuum-controlled flap at the top of the hood draws air in from the high-pressure area at the base of the windshield to help the engine exploit its power. This is known as cowl induction.

SS
454

Specifications

1970 Chevrolet Chevelle SS 454

ENGINE
Type: V8
Construction: Cast-iron block and heads
Valve gear: Two valves per cylinder operated by pushrods and rockers
Bore and stroke: 4.25 in. x 4.00 in.
Displacement: 454 c.i.
Compression ratio: 11.25:1
Induction system: Holley four-barrel carburetor and aluminum intake manifold
Maximum power: 450 bhp at 5,600 rpm
Maximum torque: 500 lb-ft at 3,600 rpm

TRANSMISSION
Manual four-speed, close-ratio M-22

BODY/CHASSIS
Steel body on separate steel chassis

SPECIAL FEATURES

All Chevelle Super Sports came with Magnum 500 steel wheels and Polyglas F70x14 tires in 1970.

These NASCAR-style tie down hood pins were a popular item and helped keep the hood from lifting at high speed.

RUNNING GEAR
Steering: Recirculating ball
Front suspension: Independent with wishbones, anti-roll bar, coil springs and telescopic shock absorbers
Rear suspension: Live axle with coil springs and telescopic shock absorbers
Brakes: Disc, 11-in. dia. (front), drum 9-in. dia. (rear)
Wheels: Magnum 500, 14-in. dia.
Tires: Polyglas F70x14

DIMENSIONS
Length: 189 in.   **Width:** 70.2 in.
Height: 52.7 in.   **Wheelbase:** 112 in.
Track: 56.8 in. (front), 56.9 in. (rear)
Weight: 4,000 lbs.

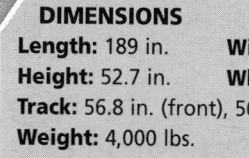

Chevrolet CORVETTE

Chevrolet was the first major car company in the world to dare to make a regular production car out of fiberglass. It was a crude affair at first but the sleek body and throaty engine captured the hearts of the American public, kick-starting the Corvette legend.

"...impressive in its day."

"You forget the modified sedan car origins of the Blue Flame Special six-cylinder engine when the throttle is floored and it roars to life. Despite the handicap of the two-speed Powerglide automatic, its 11 second 0-60 mph time is impressive for the day. Dynamically, the Corvette was closer to its traditional British sports car rivals than anything else made in the U.S. at the time, with stiff springs and a taut ride."

The interiors on early Corvettes were a bit confined and had a simple dashboard Layout.

Milestones

1952 The first full-size plaster model of the Corvette is presented to the GM president Harlow Curtice by Harley Earl. Curtice likes it and the Corvette is all set for production.

By 1957 the Corvette's V8 had gained optional fuel injection.

1953 The public sees the Corvette

for the first time at the GM Motorama Show. Production begins later in the year and all cars are painted Polo White. Changes are made for the 1954 model year with more colors and increased power.

A major facelift came for the Corvette in 1961.

1954 For the 1955 model

year Chevrolet's proposed facelift is shelved and the car's future is in doubt until the new V8 engine is used.

1955 It's the end of

of the line for the six-cylinder Corvette. The small block V8 is now the preferred power unit.

UNDER THE SKIN

Something old, something new

With the decision made to have a fiberglass body, the Corvette had a separate chassis. It is an X-braced perimeter steel section affair, given extra stiffness once the one-piece fiberglass floor molding is added. Having the semi-elliptic leaf springs for the rear axle mounted outside the chassis rails was a Corvette innovation.

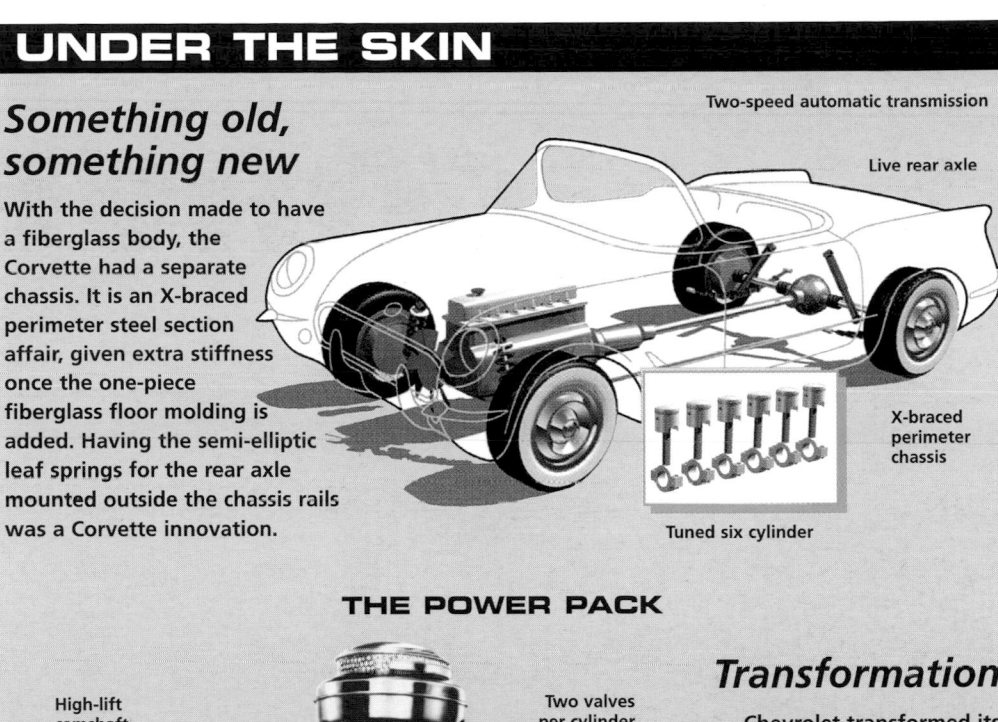

Two-speed automatic transmission

Live rear axle

X-braced perimeter chassis

Tuned six cylinder

THE POWER PACK

High-lift camshaft

Two valves per cylinder

Cast-iron construction

Pushrod valve actuation

Transformation

Chevrolet transformed its existing low powered sedan engine into the Corvette's impressive 3.9-liter Blue Flame Special. A high-lift, long duration camshaft was used in the simple pushrod engine, the cylinder head was modified, compression ratio increased, and double valve springs, along with solid valve lifters, were fitted to deal with higher rpm. Induction was transformed by fitting three Carter sidedraft carburetors on a much improved alloy manifold.

Rare original

Although the six-cylinder Chevrolet Corvettes aren't the best performing examples of the breed, they're now very valuable. Collectors value the 1953 and 1954 cars for their relative rarity, historical importance and purity of shape.

The early six-cylinder Corvettes are highly collectable today.

Chevrolet CORVETTE

Because of poor sales, GM almost gave up on the little sports car. In 1955 it got a husky V8 engine and the car was making the power it lacked. Luckily, sales picked up and the Corvette has been in Chevrolet's line up ever since.

Wishbone front suspension

The Corvette's double wishbone and coil spring front suspension was a modified version of the contemporary Chevrolet sedans, with different spring rates to suit the sports car.

Six-cylinder engine

The first Corvettes used a modified Chevrolet sedan engine. Tuning made it an effective sports car powerplant with 150 bhp.

Whitewall tires

Whitewall tires were very fashionable in the 1950s. One advantage was that they broke up the high-sided look of the tall sidewalls.

Fiberglass body

Although there were a number of fiberglass-bodied specialty and kit cars around in the U.S. in the early 1950s General Motors was the first to make a regular production car out of the material. In production the fiberglass panels used were about half as thick as the prototype's.

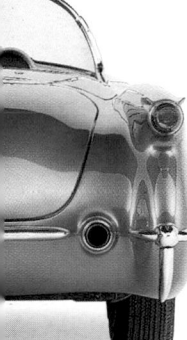

Two-speed transmission

Incredibly, the only available GM transmission which would take the power and torque of the modified engine was the two-speed Powerglide automatic. A three-speed manual became available for the 1955 model year cars.

Wrap-around windshield

The wrap-around style of windshield was popular in the early 1950s. Apart from looking great, it improved three-quarter vision compared with a conventional flat front glass with thick pillars.

Live rear axle

Because it was a limited-production car, the first Corvettes had to use many off-the-shelf Chevrolet components and the engineering had to be as simple as possible.

Specifications

1954 Chevrolet Corvette

ENGINE

Type: Inline six cylinder

Construction: Cast iron block and head

Valve gear: Two valves per cylinder operated by single block-mounted camshaft via pushrods and solid valve lifters

Bore/stroke: 3.56 in. x 3.94 in.

Displacement: 235 c.i.

Compression ratio: 8.0:1

Induction system: Three Carter YH sidedraft carburetors

Maximum power: 150 bhp at 4,200 rpm

Maximum torque: 233 lb-ft at 2,400 rpm

TRANSMISSION

Two-speed Powerglide automatic

BODY/CHASSIS

X-braced steel chassis with fiberglass two-seater convertible body

SPECIAL FEATURES

The first Corvettes have very curvaceous rear ends with subdued fins and prominent taillights.

Stone guards over the front headlights were purely a styling feature and unnecessary on ordinary roads.

RUNNING GEAR

Steering: Worm-and-sector

Front suspension: Double wishbones with coil springs, telescopic shocks and anti-roll bar

Rear suspension: Live axle with semi-elliptic leaf springs and telescopic shocks

Brakes: Drums (front and rear), 11-in. dia.

Wheels: Steel disc, 15-in. dia.

Tires: Crossply 5.5 x 15

DIMENSIONS

Length: 167 in.   **Width:** 72.2 in.

Height: 51.3 in.   **Wheelbase:** 102 in.

Track: 57 in. (front), 59 in. (rear)

Weight: 2,851 lbs.

Corvette STING RAY

When Chevrolet® introduced the Corvette Sting Ray in 1963, it was the quickest roadster Detroit had ever made. Its 327-cubic inch V8 gave the new Corvette serious muscle, and for the first time, an American sports car could out-gun its European rivals.

"America's favorite sports car."

"Off the line, this Vette™ has the kind of low-end grunt that will leave most modern sports cars in a cloud of dust and burning rubber. First you hear the throaty rumble of the big-shouldered 427 V8, then the three two-barrel carbs snarl to life and you can feel the power throb through the chrome shifter. Both the steering and clutch are heavy, while the handling and brakes are crude by today's standards. But that snap-your-head-back lunge of power still makes the Sting Ray America's favorite sports car."

The cockpit is Spartan and functional with a classic hot rod feel often imitated but never quite equaled.

Milestones

1953 The first Motorama Corvette
show car enters production with a six-cylinder engine.

1955 Zora Arkus-Duntov,
father of the Sting Ray, becomes head of the Corvette program, a position he held until retirement in 1982. Under him, manual transmission and the V8 engine are offered as options (1955) and fuel injection becomes available (1957).

1957 The Vette is the fastest
real production car in the world, showing what can be done when conventional engineering is applied well.

The 1963 convertible. Soft top is stored under a panel behind the seats.

1963 The first Sting Ray
production car is built, with all-independent suspension and the first coupe body. Its styling is based on a racing car design originally developed in 1958 by Bill Mitchell.

1965 Big-block
engine and disc brakes are available. The 396-cubic inch V8 with a solid cam is introduced with 425 bhp.

1967 Pinnacle of performance
is the L88 427-cubic inch V8. This also marks the last year of this body style.

UNDER THE SKIN

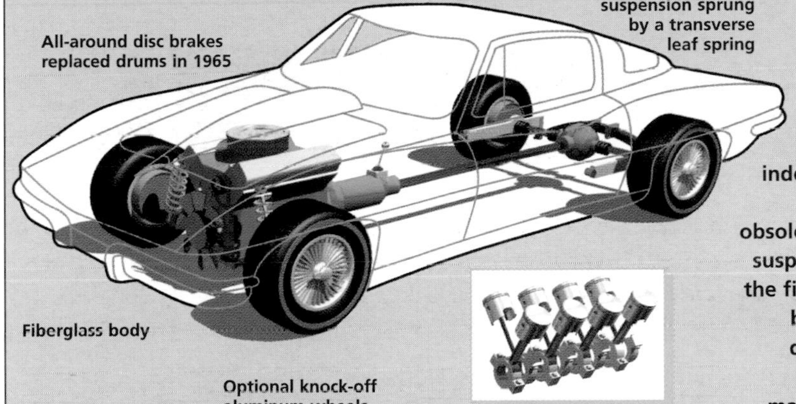

Steel ladder frame

Independent rear suspension sprung by a transverse leaf spring

All-around disc brakes replaced drums in 1965

Fiberglass body

Optional knock-off aluminum wheels

Traditional American V8

Technical advances

The 1963 Sting Ray was the first Corvette to have independent suspension. Earlier cars had used obsolete 1953 Chevy sedan suspension. The 1965 was the first Corvette with disc brakes. The V8 engine drives the rear wheels through a four-speed manual or a three-speed automatic transmission.

THE POWER PACK

Pushrod-operated overhead valves

Solid lifter camshaft

Chevy® V8s

The Sting Ray started out with Chevrolet's famous small-block V8. This 327 engine made from 250 bhp up to 375 bhp with fuel injection. In 1965, the Corvette gained the new Mark IV big-block engine. Power increased to 425 bhp from its 396 V8. In 1966, the engine was enlarged again to 427-cubic inches and made up to 425 bhp. The 435 bhp 427 L88 was offered the very next year.

M-22 manual transmission

Cast-iron block

Split rear window

The most sought-after Sting Ray is the 1963 split rear window coupe model. The designer, Bill Mitchell, intended it to form a visual connection with the central raised sections on the hood. The feature was dropped because it spoiled rear vision. Some later cars have been retro-fitted with the center pillar in an attempt to raise their values.

The split rear window coupe was only available in 1963.

Corvette STING RAY

The Sting Ray was introduced in 1963, 10 years after the Corvette's first appearance. The engine is set well back in the frame, giving nearly 50/50 weight distribution and excellent handling for the day.

Fiberglass body

Like all Corvettes, the Sting Ray has a body made from a number of fiberglass panels mounted on a traditional separate frame.

Disc brakes all around

Vented discs with dual-pot calipers on each wheel were fitted from 1965. While old stocks lasted, buyers could opt for the discontinued drums to save money.

V8 engine

Apart from the very early models, all Corvettes are powered by V8 engines. There is a wide variety of displacements and states of tune.

Optional side exhausts

The Sting Ray's enormous options list included the Side Mount Exhaust System. The side pipes are covered with a perforated shield to prevent the driver or passengers from burning themselves.

No trunk lid

To preserve the contour of the car, there is no trunk lid and access to the luggage compartment is from behind the seats.

Foldaway top

The Corvette's convertible top folds away completely when not in use and is stored beneath a flush-fitting fiberglass panel behind the driver. Optional hard top cost $231.75 in 1966.

Alloy gearbox and clutch housing

To save weight, the Sting Ray was given an alloy clutch housing and an alloy-cased gearbox. This also improved weight distribution.

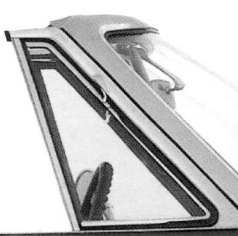

Flip-up headlights

The headlights are rotated by two reversible vacuum operated motors—a postwar first for an American car.

Triple side vents

Side vent arrangement, like many minor details, changed over the years. The 1965 and '66 models like this one have three vents.

Independent rear suspension

Another Corvette first, the Sting Ray has a crude but effective system with a transverse leaf spring mounted behind the differential.

Specifications
1966 Chevrolet Corvette Sting Ray

ENGINE
Type: V8, 90°
Construction: Cast-iron block and heads; Single cam, pushrods
Bore and stroke: 4.0 in. x 3.25 in.
Displacement: 327 c.i.
Compression ratio: 11:1
Induction system: Rochester fuel injection or one/two Carter four-barrel carbs
Maximum power: 375 bhp at 6,200 rpm
Maximum torque: 350 lb-ft at 4,000 rpm

TRANSMISSION
Three-speed automatic (optional four-speed manual)

BODY/CHASSIS
Steel ladder frame with two-door convertible or coupe fiberglass body

SPECIAL FEATURES

Innovative retractable headlights.

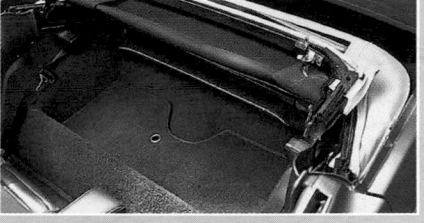

Soft top folds away neatly into compartment behind seats, with luggage space below.

RUNNING GEAR
Front suspension: Double wishbone, coil springs, anti-roll bar
Rear suspension: Semi-trailing arms, half-shafts and transverse links with transverse leaf spring
Brakes: Vented discs with four-pot calipers (optional cast-iron drums)
Wheels: Five-bolt steel (knock off aluminum optional) 6 in. x 15 in.
Tires: 6.7 in. x 15 in. Firestone Super Sport 170

DIMENSIONS
Length: 175.3 in. **Width:** 69.6 in.
Height: 49.8 in. **Wheelbase:** 98 in.
Track: 56.3 in. (front), 57 in. (rear)
Weight: 3,150 lbs.

Chevrolet **EL CAMINO SS454**

Part car, part truck—the El Camino was always an exclusive vehicle. In the late 1960s, however, the horsepower race could not be ignored, and in 1970 Chevrolet released the meanest El Camino of them all—the SS454.

"...Super Sport hauler."

"From behind the wheel you would think you were sitting in a Chevelle™ SS™: the dashboard, front bucket seats and console are identical. It feels the same too, with a throaty growl from the big V8 and instant acceleration. However, with an unloaded bed, great care is needed when cornering and braking because it's easy to bring out the rear end. At the drag strip this particular El Camino is unique—few pick ups are capable of 14-second ¼-mile times."

Sportiness abounds inside, with front bucket seats and full instrumentation.

Milestones

1964 After a four-year

absence the El Camino is relaunched, although it is now based on the midsize Chevelle. A Super Sport package is available, and a big-block 396-cubic inch V8 is optional from 1966.

In 1959, the El Camino was revealed as a stylish pick up.

1968 This year the

El Camino receives a major facelift with softer, more flowing styling. Engines range from a straight-six to the 396-cubic inch V8.

1970 Like the Chevelle SS, the El

Camino is now available with a 454-cubic inch V8 in either 360-bhp or 450 bhp tune.

In 1970, the Chevelle SS rode the same chassis as the El Camino.

1971 The El Camino

SS454 returns, but the 450-bhp LS6 engine is dropped and all V8s have lowered compression; performance and horsepower are also down. A restyled El Camino is still available with the 454-cubic inch V8.

UNDER THE SKIN

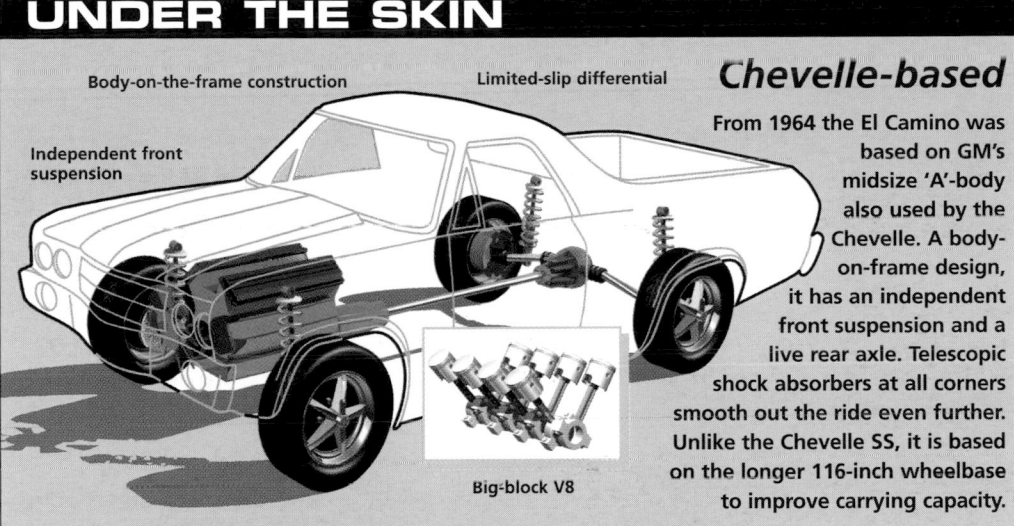

Body-on-the-frame construction

Limited-slip differential

Independent front suspension

Big-block V8

Chevelle-based

From 1964 the El Camino was based on GM's midsize 'A'-body also used by the Chevelle. A body-on-frame design, it has an independent front suspension and a live rear axle. Telescopic shock absorbers at all corners smooth out the ride even further. Unlike the Chevelle SS, it is based on the longer 116-inch wheelbase to improve carrying capacity.

THE POWER PACK

Killer rat motor

SS454s could be ordered with two versions of the 454-cubic inch rat-motor: the LS5 or LS6. Both versions are all-iron, pushrod, short-stroke V8s, although the LS5 has a 10.25:1 compression ratio, hydraulic valve lifters and is rated at 360 bhp. The LS6 features forged-aluminum pistons and forged-steel crankshaft and connection rods. Topped by a huge Holley 850-cfm four-barrel carburetor, it puts out an incredible 450 bhp and 500 lb-ft of torque.

Hydraulic valve lifters

Quadrajet four-barrel carburetor

Cast-iron block and cylinder heads

Forged-steel crankshaft

Power lust

The most desirable of all El Caminos is the 1970 SS454 equipped with the LS6 engine. This monster thumps out 450 bhp and is the quickest of all El Caminos. Only a handful were built and they are now highly sought-after for their performance.

The 1970 LS6-engined El Camino SS454 was only built for one year.

Chevrolet EL CAMINO SS454

The SS454 was the pinnacle of the El Camino's career. It has the perfect combination of style and practicality, together with the sheer power and performance of the big-block V8.

Big-block V8

The Turbo Jet 454 engine was available in two states of tune. The hydraulic lifter LS5 (as fitted to this car) was rated at 360 bhp and the killer LS-6 at 450 bhp.

Bench or buckets

Like the Chevelle, the El Camino could be specified with either a front bench or twin bucket seats. This example has bucket seats with a center-mounted console. The dashboard layout on both models is identical.

Disc brakes

Early El Camino SS models could definitely go, but stopping was more of a problem. By 1970 the Super Sport package offered power front disc brakes, which helped make the monster pickup slightly safer.

Large load area

The El Camino was extremely practical with a load area of 32.14 sq ft.

Positraction differential

The combination of an empty load bed and 500 lb-ft of torque can result in the rear wheels spinning under hard acceleration. An optional Positraction limited-slip differential helps to reduce this.

Close-ratio four-speed

To handle all the torque from the Turbojet LS5 engine, this El Camino uses a Muncie M21 close-ratio four-speed transmission. It is named after GM's transmission plant in Muncie, Indiana.

Dealer-installed tarp

To help protect both the bed and loads, a dealer-installed tarp was available.

1970 Chevrolet El Camino SS454

ENGINE

Type: V8

Construction: Cast-iron block and heads

Valve gear: Two valves per cylinder operated by a single camshaft via pushrods, rockers and hydraulic lifters

Bore and stroke: 4.25 in. x 4.00 in.

Displacement: 454 c.i.

Compression ratio: 10.25:1

Induction system: Single Rochester Quadrajet four-barrel carburetor

Maximum power: 360 bhp at 4,400 rpm

Maximum torque: 500 lb-ft at 3,200 rpm

TRANSMISSION

Muncie M21 (close ratio) four-speed

BODY/CHASSIS

Separate steel perimeter frame with two-door cabin and exposed cargo area

SPECIAL FEATURES

For 1970 only, El Camino SS models were fitted with these Magnum 500 Super Sport wheels.

A special cowl induction hood draws air into the engine at the base of the windshield.

RUNNING GEAR

Steering: Recirculating ball

Front suspension: Double wishbones with coil springs, telescopic shock absorbers and anti-roll bar

Rear suspension: Live axle with control arms, coil springs and telescopic shock absorbers

Brakes: Discs, 11.0-in. dia (front), drums, 9.5-in. dia (rear)

Wheels: Magnum 500, 7 x 15 in.

Tires: HR70-15

DIMENSIONS

Length: 206.8 in.   **Width:** 75.4 in.

Height: 54.4 in.   **Wheelbase:** 116.0 in.

Track: 60.2 in. (front), 59.2 in. (rear)

Weight: 4,270 lbs.

Chevrolet IMPALA SS 427

When Chevrolet put the engine used in the Corvette® in very nearly the same tune into the big Impala SS™, the car's sheer size meant the result wasn't quite as dramatic. It did, however, produce a high-speed cruiser with plenty of power to spare.

"...full-size muscle monster."

"For some, bigger is better, and this is certainly true of the SS 427. The front bucket seats are huge. The monster 427-cubic inch V8 has enough torque to move mountains and motivates the tremendous bulk of the Impala down the road at maximum velocity. It would be natural to think that the SS 427 would plow through corners, but a wide track and well-located rear end ensure this is one of the better behaved full-size muscle monsters of the late 1960s.

The Impala SS has full instrumentation and tremendous interior space.

Milestones

1965 Impalas are redesigned
with smoother, more modern contours and a new perimeter chassis, plus revised suspension. The Impala SS returns with available bucket seats and a new optional Mark IV 396-cubic inch V8 engine. The 409 will be dropped at the end of the year.

The last year for the boxy, square Impala SS was 1964.

1966 Externally, few changes mark
this year's full-size Chevys®. The big news is under the hood. The 396 engine is joined by a larger 427-cubic inch unit available in 390-bhp and 425-bhp versions.

1965 Impala SS models came standard with an in-line six.

1967 A new fastback
roof is grafted to the Impala Sport Coupe.

1969 Having reverted
to an option package in 1968, the Impala SS is retired this year.

UNDER THE SKIN

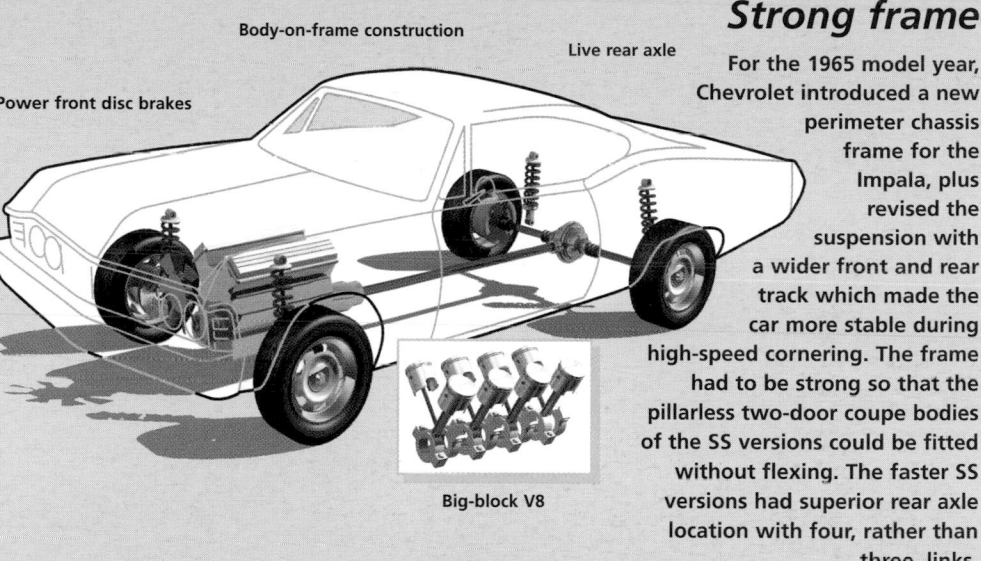

Body-on-frame construction

Live rear axle

Power front disc brakes

Big-block V8

Strong frame

For the 1965 model year, Chevrolet introduced a new perimeter chassis frame for the Impala, plus revised the suspension with a wider front and rear track which made the car more stable during high-speed cornering. The frame had to be strong so that the pillarless two-door coupe bodies of the SS versions could be fitted without flexing. The faster SS versions had superior rear axle location with four, rather than three, links.

THE POWER PACK

The fat rat

In 1966, Chevrolet launched its 427, an enlarged version of the 396-cubic inch V8 which was more common to find in a Corvette than a full-size car. The following year, it was available in full-size cars. The standard 427 engine returned for 1968 with a power output of 385 bhp and a four-barrel carburetor in full-size cars (GM outlawed multi-carb setups in 1967 on all models but the Corvette). The engine continued until 1969, by which time it thumped out 390 bhp.

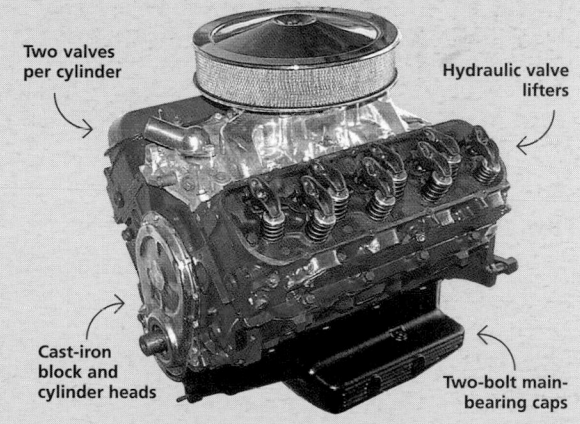

Two valves per cylinder

Hydraulic valve lifters

Cast-iron block and cylinder heads

Two-bolt main-bearing caps

Milestone SS

1967 was a milestone for the SS Impala. The Impala was reskinned with larger, swoopier sheet metal. It was also the first and last year that the SS 427 was a model in its own right. Today, these cars make an interesting alternative to Chevelles and Camaros.

The 1967 Impala SS with fastback styling and the 427 is the one to go for.

49

Chevrolet IMPALA SS 427

'For the man who'd buy a sports car if it had this much room' was how Chevrolet marketed the Impala SS 427. It was a fine machine, with a huge torquey V8, seating for five and a well-engineered suspension.

Four transmissions

The big V8s could be matched to a variety of transmissions: a three- or four-speed heavy-duty manual; Powerglide; or strong TurboHydramatic 400 three-speed automatic.

V8 engine

The fastest of all the Impalas, the SS 427 is powered by the same short-stroke cast-iron 427-cubic inch engine found in the Corvette. Despite its size, it is happy to rev and produces its maximum power at 5,200 rpm with maximum torque coming in at 3,400 rpm. In its highest state of tune, Chevrolet claimed 385 bhp for the Impala engine.

Front disc brakes

Front disc brakes are a necessity for the faster SS models with their high performance and weight. For the SS, Chevrolet made front discs an option, which came with different wheels for $121.15.

Heavy-duty suspension

The best-handling SS Impalas use the optional heavy-duty F41 suspension with its stiffer springs and shocks. At just $31.60, it was a very small price to pay for the extra handling security.

Fastback style

The fastback style was very fashionable in the 1960s and helped give a sporty look to very large cars. The size of cars like the Impala and the Ford Galaxie meant they could have a long sloping rear roof line and still have room for rear passengers.

Front parking lights

The ends of the front fenders contain what look like turn signals. In fact, they are just parking lights, with the turn signals located in the lower grill assembly.

Pillarless construction

Chevrolet gave the Impala its sleek look by the use of two styling features. As well as the long, sloping rear fastback, the car has pillarless construction. This accentuates the side window glass area and makes it appear bigger than it really is.

Specifications

1968 Chevrolet Impala SS 427

ENGINE

Type: V8

Construction: Cast-iron block and heads

Valve gear: Two valves per cylinder operated by a single camshaft with pushrods and rockers

Bore and stroke: 4.25 in. x 3.76 in.

Displacement: 427 c.i.

Compression ratio: 10.3:1

Induction system: Single four-barrel carburetor

Maximum power: 385 bhp at 5,200 rpm

Maximum torque: 460 lb-ft at 3,400 rpm

TRANSMISSION

M21 four-speed manual

BODY/CHASSIS

Box-section perimeter chassis with two-door fastback hardtop body

SPECIAL FEATURES

In 1968, the 427-cubic-inch V8 was offered in 390- or 425-bhp form.

For 1968, all cars sold in the U.S. had to have side marker lights. In addition to the lights the SS also had proper engine identification.

RUNNING GEAR

Steering: Recirculating ball

Front suspension: Double wishbones with coil springs, telescopic shock absorbers and anti-roll bar

Rear suspension: Live axle with four links, Panhard rod, coil springs and telescopic shock absorbers

Brakes: Discs, 11-in. dia. (front), drums, 11-in. dia. (rear)

Wheels: Steel discs, 6 x 15 in.

Tires: 8.25 x 15 in.

DIMENSIONS

Length: 213.2 in.   **Width:** 79.9 in.

Height: 55.4 in.   **Wheelbase:** 119.0 in.

Track: 62.5 in. (front), 62.4 in. (rear)

Weight: 3,835 lbs.

Chevrolet MONTE CARLO SS 454

Super Sport™ is the meaning behind the SS designation, and the big-block Monte Carlo lives up to that name proudly. Grand-touring comfort is backed by a 360-horsepower, 454-cubic inch V8, making this one of the first executive-class luxury performance cars of all time.

"...unbelievable authority."

"Only a light touch of the throttle is needed to get a sneak preview to what lies ahead. When the big Quadrajet is running at wide open throttle, the stout 454-cubic inch big-block makes unbelievable mid-range power. As soon as the tires bite, the engine's 500 lb-ft. of torque will pin you deeply into the back of the seat with unbelievable authority. Yet the ride remains comfortably smooth and the big Monte will cruise happily at 100 mph all day long."

Plenty of room and plenty of comfort. The Monte SS is the ultimate highway cruiser.

Milestones

1970 Chevrolet

enters the personal luxury field with the Monte Carlo—a two-door coupe based on the Chevelle chassis. It boasts the longest hood ever fitted to a Chevrolet. In SS form it is available with the monster 454 V8. The moderate LS-5 makes 360 bhp and the bone-crushing LS-6 puts out 450 bhp.

The big 454 V8 in SS tune was also offered in the Chevelle.

1971 Having proved to be a great success, the

Monte Carlo returns for another season with a revised grill. The muscular SS 454 also returns, but with rising insurance premiums and lower octane fuel it is not popular with just 1,919 built.

A 'new' Monte Carlo SS arrived for 1983. This is a 1986 model.

1972 The Monte Carlo enters its last

season with the original body. The SS 454 is no longer available, but Monte Carlo sales remain strong with 180,819 built.

UNDER THE SKIN

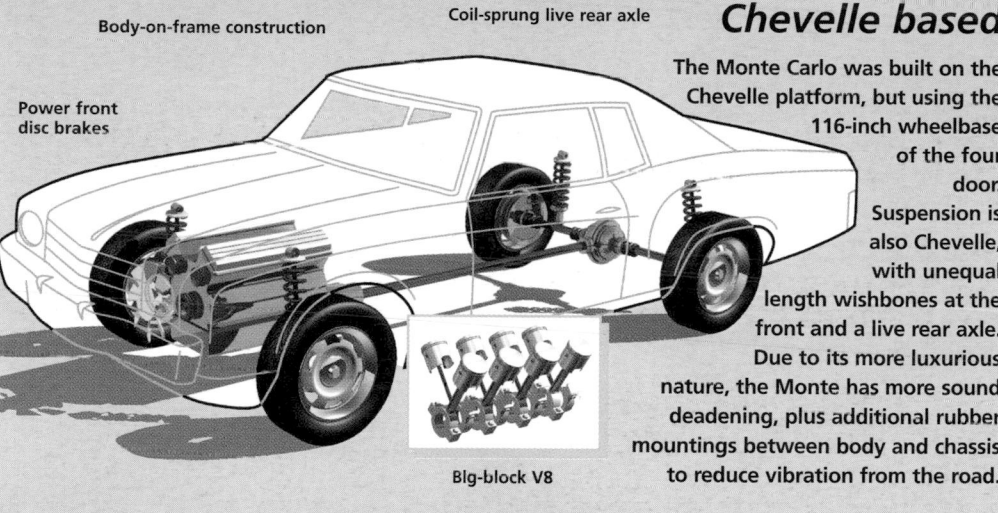

Body-on-frame construction

Coil-sprung live rear axle

Power front disc brakes

Blg-block V8

Chevelle based

The Monte Carlo was built on the Chevelle platform, but using the 116-inch wheelbase of the four door. Suspension is also Chevelle, with unequal length wishbones at the front and a live rear axle. Due to its more luxurious nature, the Monte has more sound deadening, plus additional rubber mountings between body and chassis to reduce vibration from the road.

THE POWER PACK

Biggest stock Rat

Arriving in 1970, the big-block 454 was part of the Mk IV V8 series which were first introduced in Chevrolet passenger cars in 1965. It has a cast-iron block and cylinder heads, plus a forged-steel crankshaft and connecting rods. The LS-5 has a 10.25:1 compression ratio, hydraulic lifters and a single Rochester Quadrajet four-barrel carburetor. It thumps out an impressive 360 bhp at a low 4,400 rpm and a hefty 500 lb-ft of torque. If fitted with the infamous LS-6 it makes 450 bhp in 1970 and 425 bhp in 1971.

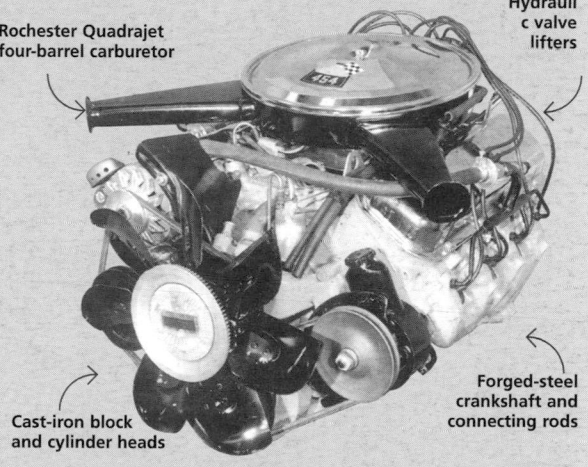

Rochester Quadrajet four-barrel carburetor

Hydraulic valve lifters

Cast-iron block and cylinder heads

Forged-steel crankshaft and connecting rods

Good buy

SS 454 Montes were only built for two years and production totalled just 5,742. Although rare, they are often overlooked. Excellent examples can be picked up for as little as $8,000, making the Monte Carlo 454 one of the best big-block muscle buys.

Few muscle cars could match the performance and luxury of the SS 45.

Chevrolet MONTE CARLO SS 454

To order an SS 454 you had to check RPO Z20 on the options list. Considering the added performance, this option was a bargain at $420.25. Surprisingly, less than 4,000 buyers chose the option in 1970.

Rally wheels

To go with its high-performance image, all SS 454s had G70-15 wide oval white stripe tires fitted on 7x15-inch Rally wheels.

Big-block muscle

The long 4-inch stroke in Chevrolet's famous cast-iron LS-5 big-block V8 is the reason why this 454-cubic inch Rat motor produces 500 lb-ft. of torque at a very usable 3,200 rpm. Its forged crankshaft is nitride and cross-drilled, making the bottom end virtually bullet proof. Big-valve cast-iron cylinder heads and a Rochester Quadrajet carburetor complete the package.

Front-end style

The bold front end sports a pair of single headlights surrounded by wide chrome bezels. The handsome grill has chrome trim and features a special badge in the center.

Vinyl top

To increase appeal for the luxury car buyer, a special vinyl top was made available as an option. For only $126.40, there was a choice of five distinct colors: black, blue, dark gold, green or white.

Distinctive styling

Built only as a two-door hardtop, the Monte Carlo's exterior styling is very European-looking with its long hood and short deck design. The pronounced fender profile that runs front to back is vaguely reminiscent of the old Jaguar XK models.

Special suspension

In addition to GM's normal practice of using unequal length A-arms up front and a solid, live axle at the rear, all SS 454s contained a unique Automatic Level Control system with built-in air compressor.

Optional interior

An optional console could be fitted between a pair of comfortable bucket seats upholstered in soft vinyl. Simulated burred-elm wood inlays were applied to the instrument panel.

Specifications

1970 Chevrolet Monte Carlo SS 454

ENGINE
Type: V8
Construction: Cast-iron block and heads
Valve gear: Two valves per cylinder operated by a single camshaft, pushrods and rocker arms
Bore and stroke: 4.25 in. x 4.00 in.
Displacement: 454 c.i.
Compression ratio: 10.25:1
Induction system: Rochester Quadrajet four-barrel carburetor
Maximum power: 360 bhp at 4,400 rpm
Maximum torque: 500 lb-ft at 3,200 rpm

TRANSMISSION
GM TurboHydramatic 400 automatic

BODY/CHASSIS
Separate steel body and frame

SPECIAL FEATURES

Discreet badges on the rocker panel are the only giveaway of the 454.

All production 1970 SS Monte Carlos were powered by the LS-5 454-cubic inch V8.

RUNNING GEAR
Steering: Recirculating ball
Front suspension: Unequal length A-arms, telescopic shock absorbers, coil springs and anti-roll bar
Rear suspension: Live solid axle with telescopic shock absorbers and coil springs
Brakes: Discs (front), drums (rear)
Wheels: Rally, 7 x 15 in.
Tires: Goodyear Polyglas, G70-15

DIMENSIONS
Length: 206.0 in   **Width:** 76.0 in.
Height: 52.0 in   **Wheelbase:** 116.0 in
Track: 61.9 in. (front), 61.1 in. (rear)
Weight: 3,860 lbs.

Cosworth VEGA 75

A limited production of Vegas received an engine transplant and turned it into a performance machine. It looks good, handles well and has an advanced twin-cam engine designed by British Formula One racing experts Cosworth.

"...exotic twin-cam engine."

"For its time the standard Vega was an advanced car, offering more power than its rivals, and the Cosworth version was even better. Unfortunately, because the U.S. was new at building emission-controlled performance cars, the exotic 2.0-liter, twin-cam engine lacks sufficient torque. The four-speed Muncie transmission offers precise shifts and the steering is responsive. The handling is exceptional and the Cosworth Vega can corner with the best of its rivals."

The interior is very European in character—stark but very functional.

Milestones

1970 Chevrolet® introduces the Vega

as a 1971 model in sedan and coupe forms. Chevy's® import fighter was available with a 2.3 liter engine with up to 110 bhp, but the engine is criticized for its roughness.

Although Cosworth was known for its race engines, the Vega was never raced seriously.

1973 Further improvements make

the Vega quicker, but the appearance of the Cosworth, with a twin-cam engine, sees the fastest Vega yet. Chevrolet plans to build 5,000 for the 1975 model year.

Cosworth later helped Ford with rally cars like the Sierra and Escort Cosworth.

1976 Sales never

reach projected figures and having sold just 1,447 units in the 1976 model year, the Cosworth Vega is discontinued.

UNDER THE SKIN

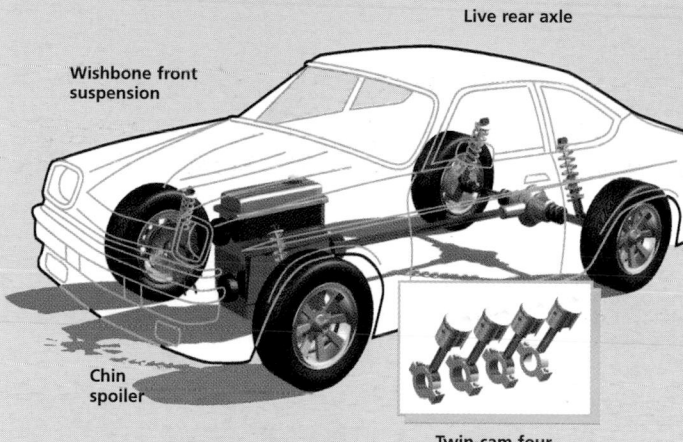

Live rear axle

Wishbone front suspension

Chin spoiler

Twin-cam four

Euro technology

Launched as a 1971 model, the Vega adopted monocoque construction for reduced weight, just like the European imports. Running gear consists of a double wishbone front suspension and a live rear axle, located by control arms and an anti-roll bar. Cosworth Vegas have a quicker steering ratio, and larger radial tires on wide alloy wheels give improved grip.

THE POWER PACK

Hi-tech engine

The standard 140 cubic inch (2.3-liter) alloy block/iron head Vega engine was a disaster, but the Cosworth engine is quite different, with a shorter stroke and smaller, 2-liter displacement. It was an advanced unit, featuring dual overhead cams, four valves per cylinder and electronic fuel injection. The pistons, designed and machined by Cosworth, run in the alloy etched block without the iron plating used in the Chevrolet engine. In stock tune, the small engine produces 110 bhp.

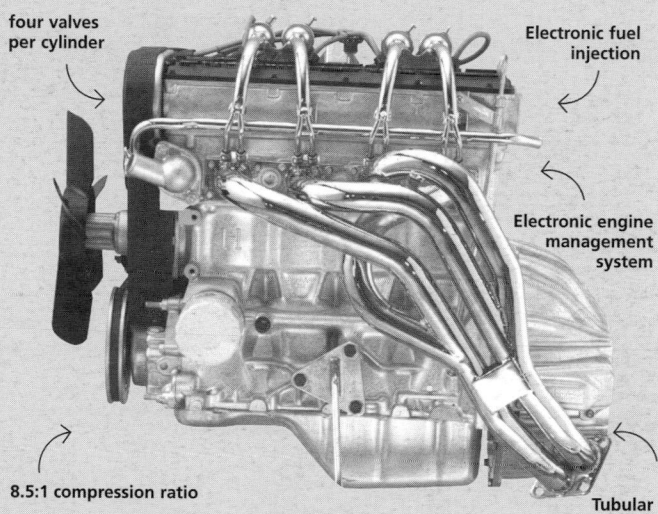

four valves per cylinder

Electronic fuel injection

Electronic engine management system

8.5:1 compression ratio

Tubular header

A hotter Vega

With just 3,508 built over a two-year production run, the Cosworth Vega is a real collector's item. It is also a historically important car, because it was built as an economical performance car when gasoline prices were driven up by the fuel crisis of the time.

The Cosworth is by far the most desirable Vega.

Cosworth VEGA

Using electronic fuel injection and four valves per cylinder in a 2-liter engine might have been normal in Europe during the 1970s, but not in the U.S. It's too bad this high-tech hot rod wasn't more successful.

Wide radials

Due to its better performance, the Cosworth deserves bigger tires so it uses with fatter BR70-13 radials as standard equipment.

High-tech horsepower

Small displacement, overhead cams and electronic fuel injection are common on U.S. cars today. But these features made the Cosworth an exotic high-tech hot rod with 110 bhp from its very small 122 cubic inch engine in 1975.

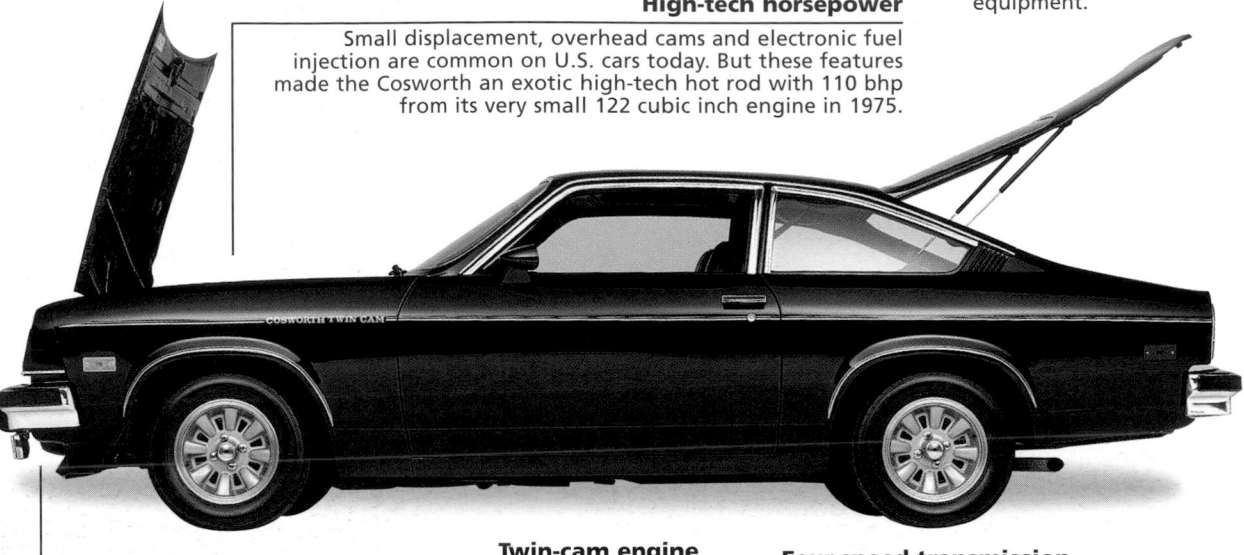

Twin-cam engine

Chevrolet followed the exotic import route and fitted the Vega with a Cosworth-designed twin-cam cylinder head, the first in a U.S. car for many years. When the engine first appeared the power output was an excellent 130 bhp and 115 lb-ft of torque, but in production the figures were much lower.

Four-speed transmission

In attempt to attract buyers of would-be imported small cars, the Cosworth Vega came with a Muncie four-speed transmission.

European styling

Vegas bore styling cues from the larger Camaro®, which was unmistakably European, although this was later marred by big bumpers.

Low rear axle ratio

All 1975 Cosworth Vegas used 3.73:1 rear axle ratios, while in 1976 they used 4.10:1s. The Cosworth's rear suspension is upgraded to handle the engine's power.

Alloy wheels

The standard Vega wheels have been replaced by wider 6-inch alloy wheels.

Specifications

1975 Chevrolet Cosworth Vega

ENGINE
Type: In-line four-cylinder twin-cam
Construction: Light alloy block and head
Valve gear: Four valves per cylinder operated by twin belt-driven overhead camshafts
Bore and stroke: 3.50 in. x 3.14 in.
Displacement: 122 c.i.
Compression ratio: 8.5:1
Induction system: Bendix electronic injection
Maximum power: 110 bhp at 5,600 rpm
Maximum torque: 107 lb-ft at 4,800 rpm

TRANSMISSION
Four-speed Muncie

BODY/CHASSIS
Unitary monocoque construction with two-door coupe body

SPECIAL FEATURES

Each Cosworth Vega has a dash-mounted plaque making it exclusive.

The twin-cam alloy engine is highly exotic for a 1970s American compact.

RUNNING GEAR
Steering: Recirculating ball, 16:1 ratio
Front suspension: Double wishbones with coil springs, telescopic shocks and anti-roll bar
Rear suspension: Live axle with upper and lower control arms, coil springs, telescopic shocks and anti-roll bar
Brakes: Discs, 9.9-in. dia. (front), drums, 9-in. dia. (rear)
Wheels: Alloy, 6 in. x 13 in.
Tires: Radial BR70-13 in. x 6 in.

DIMENSIONS
Length: 170.2 in.   **Width:** 65.4 in.
Height: 47.9 in.   **Wheelbase:** 97 in.
Track: 55.2 in. (front), 54.1 in. (rear)
Weight: 2,639 lbs.

Dodge CHALLENGER R/T SE

As the muscle car movement reached its peak in 1970, Dodge finally got a ponycar of its own. Aptly named Challenger, it offered a huge range of engines and options. Enthusiasts were drawn to the R/T model. In 440 Six Pack form, it could run with the best of them.

"...muscle at its finest."

"There is something really magical about E-body Mopars. The seats may offer little support and the light steering can make the Challenger feel a little unwieldy at times, but take the car for a blast and you cannot help but fall in love with it. The 440 Six Pack engine, coupled to a Pistol Grip four-speed enables the R/T to accelerate like a speeding bullet, accompanied by tremendous tire squealing and a thundering exhaust roar; it is muscle at its finest."

R/Ts got the Rallye Pack instrument cluster. This car has the rare Pistol-Grip shifter.

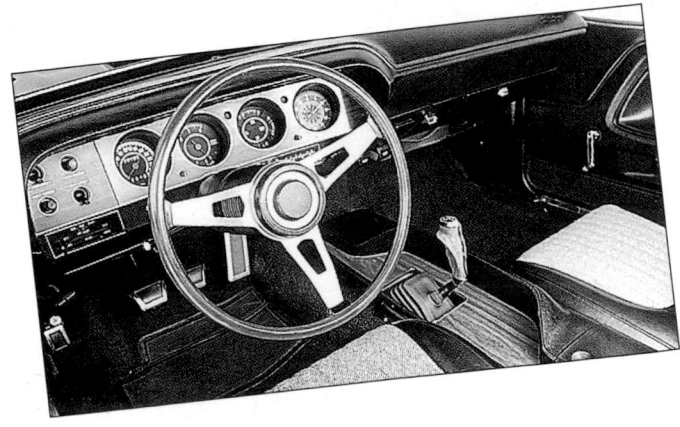

Milestones

1970 Dodge enters the ponycar
war with its new Challenger. It is offered as a coupe or convertible with one of the longest option lists available, including nine engines. An R/T model caters to the performance crowd and was available with a 383, 440 or 426 Hemi engine.

The Challenger shares its firewall and front inner structure with B-bodies like this Charger.

1971 Due to rising insurance
rates, safety issues and emissions regulations, the performance market enters its twilight years. The Challenger returns with just minor styling tweaks, but its sales figures drop by 60 percent—just 4,630 R/Ts are built this year.

The Cuda was Plymouth's version of the R/T. This is a 1971 model.

1972 High-horse-power engines,
convertibles and the R/T package depart, leaving a Rallye 340 as the top performer.

UNDER THE SKIN

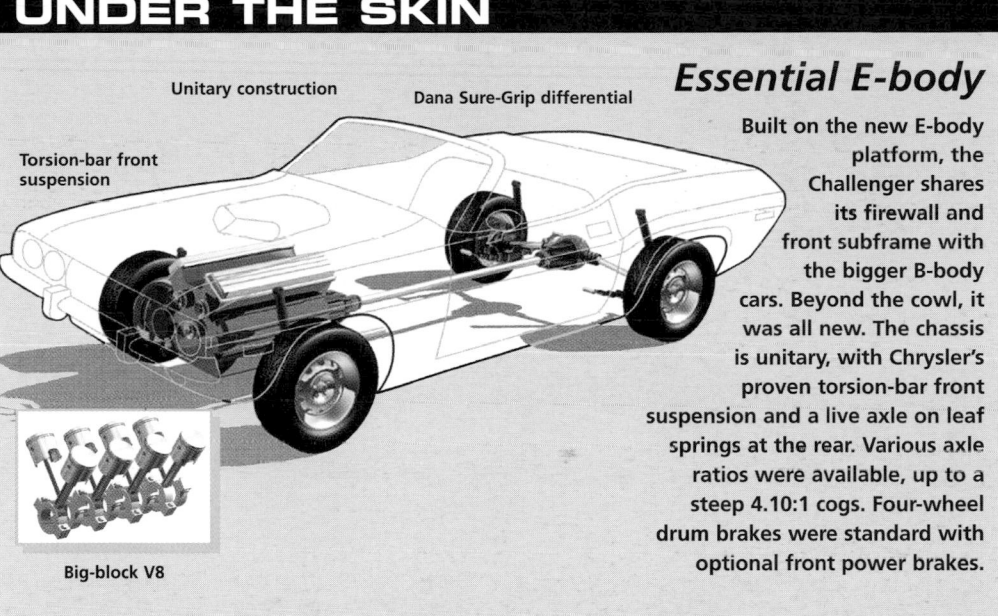

Unitary construction

Dana Sure-Grip differential

Torsion-bar front suspension

Big-block V8

Essential E-body

Built on the new E-body platform, the Challenger shares its firewall and front subframe with the bigger B-body cars. Beyond the cowl, it was all new. The chassis is unitary, with Chrysler's proven torsion-bar front suspension and a live axle on leaf springs at the rear. Various axle ratios were available, up to a steep 4.10:1 cogs. Four-wheel drum brakes were standard with optional front power brakes.

THE POWER PACK

A Six Pack to go

Base Challengers came with the bulletproof but hardly exciting 225-cubic inch Slant-Six, but eight V8s were optional. R/T models got a standard 335-bhp, 383-cubic inch mill, though the mighty Hemi and 440 were available. The 440 is an immensely robust and torquey engine, which cranks out a whopping 480 lb-ft at 3,200 rpm. In Six Pack form, with a trio of Holley two-barrel carburetors, the 440 gets an additional 10 lb-ft of torque.

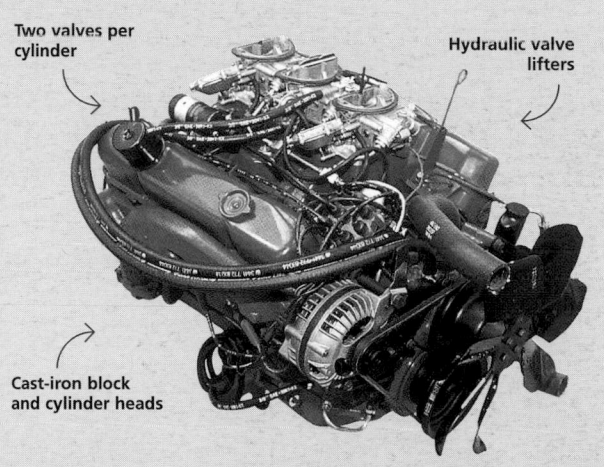

Two valves per cylinder

Hydraulic valve lifters

Cast-iron block and cylinder heads

SE Comfort

As with most Chrysler products, owners were free to order virtually any option on their Challenger R/T. If ordered in the sporty SE guise, these hot Dodges came with soft leather seats, a sporty vinyl top and smaller rear window.

1970 R/T-SEs are very rare: only 3,979 were built.

Dodge CHALLENGER R/T SE

Smoothly styled and an able performer in R/T guise, the Challenger was well received when new, and remains today as one of the most sought-after early muscle cars.

Mopar Power

Although the 383 was standard fare, the big 440 Magnum was an ideal choice for those into serious racing. Adding the Six-Pack option with three two-barrel carburetors resulted in 390 bhp and 490 lb-ft of torque. A good running Six Pack was a threat to just about anything with wheels.

Special Edition

An SE, or Special Edition, package was basically a luxury trim package on the Challenger. It added a vinyl roof with a smaller rear window, upgraded interior appointments and exterior trim. It could be ordered on both base and R/T models.

Manual transmission

Although the standard Challenger transmission was a three-speed manual, R/Ts ordered with the 440 or Hemi got the robust TorqueFlite automatic transmission. A handful were, however, fitted with four-speed manuals, complete with Hurst shifters with a wood-grain Pistol-Grip shift handle.

Standard R/T hood

Most Challenger R/Ts left the factory with a performance hood, which included dual scoops and a raised center section. For $97.30, however, buyers could order a Shaker hood scoop that attached directly to the air cleaner.

Dana Sure-Grip differential

A good way to reduce quarter-mile ETs was to order the Per-formance Axle Package with a 3.55:1 ring and pinion with a Sure-Grip limited-slip differential. Steeper 4.10:1 cogs could be specified as part of the Super Track Pak.

Heavy-duty suspension

As the R/T was the standard performance model, it has a heavy-duty suspension with thicker front torsion bars and stiffer rear leaf springs, plus a beefy front anti-roll bar.

Wide wheels

For the early 1970s, 6-inch-wide wheels were considered large. The Rallye rims fitted to the R/T are only 14 inches in diameter, shod in F-70 14 Goodyear Polyglas tires. Bigger G-60 15 tires and 15-inch Rallyes could be ordered resulting in slightly improved grip.

Specifications

1970 Dodge Challenger R/T-SE 440

ENGINE

Type: V8

Valve gear: Two valves per cylinder operated by a single V-mounted camshaft via pushrods, rockers and hydraulic lifters

Bore and stroke: 4.32 in. x 3.75 in.

Displacement: 440 c.i.

Compression ratio: 10.1:1

Induction system: Three Holley two-barrel carburetors

Maximum power: 390 bhp at 4,700 rpm

Maximum torque: 490 lb-ft at 3,200 rpm

TRANSMISSION

Four-speed manual

BODY/CHASSIS

Unitary steel chassis with steel body panels

SPECIAL FEATURES

All Challengers came with a racing-style fuel filler cap, which is also found on the bigger intermediate Charger.

As it was the performance model, the R/T got a full set of gauges.

RUNNING GEAR

Steering: Recirculating ball

Front suspension: A arms with longitudinal torsion bars, telescopic shock absorbers and anti-roll bar

Rear suspension: Live axle with semi-elliptic leaf springs, telescopic shock absorbers and anti-roll bar

Brakes: Drums, 11.0-in. dia. (front and rear)

Wheels: Stamped steel, 14x6 in.

Tires: Fiberglass belted, F-70 14

DIMENSIONS

Length: 192 in.   **Width:** 76.1 in.

Height: 50.9 in.   **Wheelbase:** 110.0 in.

Track: 59.7 in. (front), 60.7 in. (rear)

Weight: 3,437 lbs.

Dodge CHALLENGER T/A

With the SCCA's Trans Am wars in full swing, Dodge jumped in to the foray with its aptly-named Challenger T/A. Built for only one year and powered by a 340 cubic inch V8, it was conceived as a road racer but became a factory street rod.

"...mindwarping acceleration."

"Unlike its big-block counterparts, the T/A is a better-balanced package with less weight over the front wheels. It therefore offers more nimble handling. The rev-happy 340 V8 engine, with its triple carburetors and the bulletproof TorqueFlite transmission give mind-warping acceleration. For its time, the power-assisted steering is smooth and the brakes firm, but the sound of the V8 blowing through the side pipes is enough to stir anyone's soul."

Full instrumentation and black upholstery give the interior a real sporty feel.

Milestones

1970 Dodge finally

launches its own ponycar—the Challenger. An R/T performance model is offered with standard big-block power. With the popularity of Trans Am racing Dodge develops a homologation special: the Challenger T/A. Street versions are fitted with a 340-cubic inch V8, a fiberglass lift-off hood, side pipes and large rear tires. Only 2,142 are built this year.

In 1969, the top performing Dodge small block muscle car was the Dart GTS 383.

1971 With factory

support in Trans Am racing on the decline, the T/A does not return, although the big-block R/T makes it second and last appearance. Only 4,630 R/Ts are built and Challenger sales in general are less than half those of 1970.

The 1971 Demon is also powered by a 340-cubic inch V8.

1972 Big-block engines

are no longer available and the performance model is a new Challenger 360 Rallye. The Challenger itself lasts until 1974.

UNDER THE SKIN

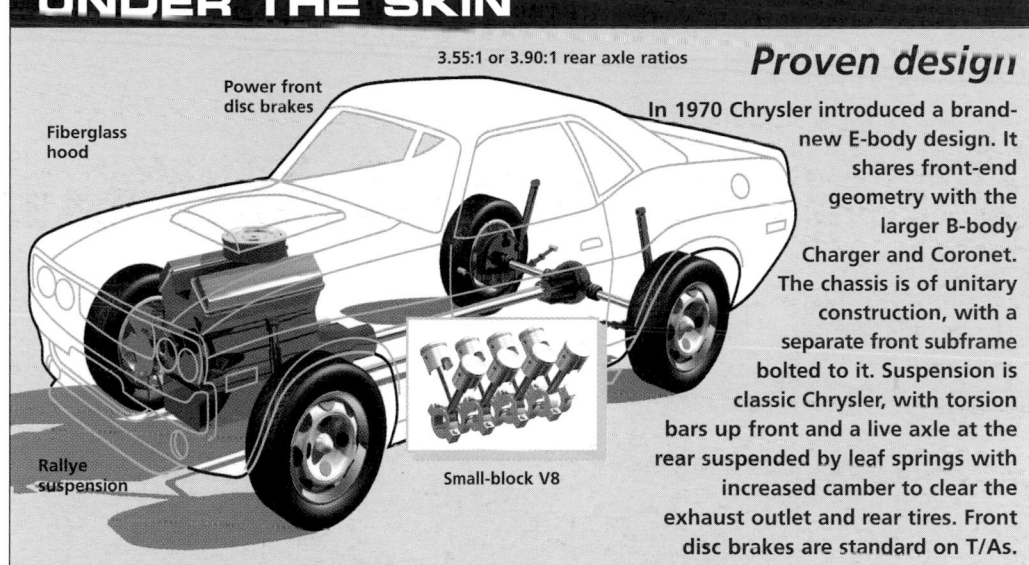

3.55:1 or 3.90:1 rear axle ratios

Power front disc brakes

Fiberglass hood

Rallye suspension

Small-block V8

Proven design

In 1970 Chrysler introduced a brand-new E-body design. It shares front-end geometry with the larger B-body Charger and Coronet. The chassis is of unitary construction, with a separate front subframe bolted to it. Suspension is classic Chrysler, with torsion bars up front and a live axle at the rear suspended by leaf springs with increased camber to clear the exhaust outlet and rear tires. Front disc brakes are standard on T/As.

THE POWER PACK

Rev-happy magnum

The T/A proved that the hemi or the 440 Magnum are not necessary to produce real power. The 340-cubic inch unit used in the Dart Swinger is fitted with a special Edelbrock intake manifold, on which sits three two-barrel Holley carburetors. The advertised output was 290 bhp at 5,000 rpm, although this was purely for insurance reasons. With this engine the Challenger T/A and its AAR 'Cuda twin are a serious threat on the street and hydraulic lifters ensured that they were always ready for action.

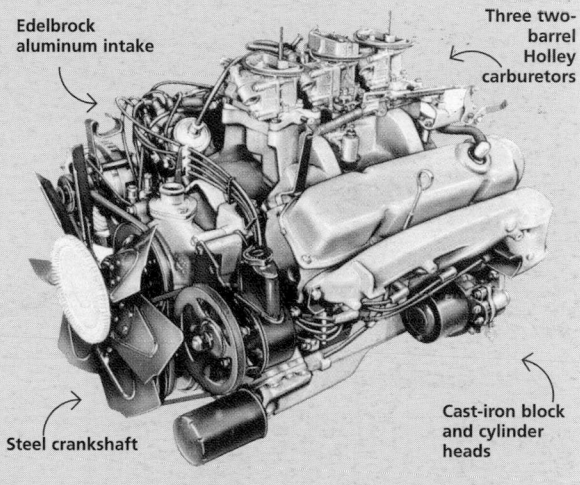

Edelbrock aluminum intake

Three two-barrel Holley carburetors

Cast-iron block and cylinder heads

Steel crankshaft

Loud T/A

In 1970 Dodge finally got serious about SCCA racing and launched its T/A. On the race circuit all cars ran a 305-cubic inch V8 which was nothing more than a destroked 340. To make the street versions more fun, an Edelbrock intake and trio of Holley carbs were added.

The Challenger T/A has handling to match its massive power output.

Dodge CHALLENGER T/A

With its matte black hood and wide stripes, the Challenger T/A might just be one of the most stylish cars Dodge built during the heyday of muscle cars. It was equally at home taking high speed turns or accelerating in a straight line.

V8 engine

When all six barrels of the carburetors are wide open, the 340 has rocket-like acceleration. Though it's a smaller engine than what most Mopar enthusiasts consider to be powerful, the 340 really holds its own against larger-engined cars.

Panther Pink paint

Believe it or not, this color was offered by Dodge. It's called Panther Pink and it's one of the optional High Impact colors.

Limited-slip differential

Despite the larger rear tires, many T/A buyers specified a Positraction limited-slip differential to reduce wheel spin and increase bite.

'Six-pack' carburetors

In order to extract maximum performance out of the 340-cubic inch small-block, Dodge installed three Holley two-barrel carburetors atop the engine. During normal driving only the center carburetor is used, but punching the throttle opens the outboard units and produces astonishing acceleration.

Hardtop body

The Challenger was available in coupe and convertible forms, but all T/A models were hardtop coupes. However, a vinyl roof was available.

Torsion bar suspension

Unlike its rivals, Chrysler used torsion bar front suspension on its cars in the early 1970s. These are more robust than coil springs and result in a smoother ride over rough surfaces.

Big rear wheels

The Challenger T/A was one of the first Detroit production cars to feature different size front and rear tires. At the back are massive G60 x 15 Goodyear Polyglas GTs, which give the T/A excellent straight-line traction.

Four-speed transmission

The standard transmission on the T/A is a Hurst-shifted four-speed with a direct-drive top ratio. The only option was a TorqueFlite three-speed automatic.

Specifications

1970 Dodge Challenger T/A

ENGINE

Type: V8

Construction: Cast-iron block and heads

Valve gear: Two valves per cylinder operated by pushrods and rockers

Bore and stroke: 4.03 in. x 3.31 in.

Displacement: 340 c.i.

Compression ratio: 10.5:1

Induction system: Three Holley two-barrel carburetors

Maximum power: 290 bhp at 5,000 rpm

Maximum torque: 345 lb-ft at 3,200 rpm

TRANSMISSION

TorqueFlite three-speed automatic

BODY/CHASSIS

Unitary steel construction with two-door four-seater coupe body

SPECIAL FEATURES

All Challengers are fitted with this racing-style chromed fuel filler cap.

At the rear, Challengers have a single, large back up light behind the Dodge lettering.

RUNNING GEAR

Steering: Recirculating ball

Front suspension: Double wishbones with longitudinal torsion bars, telescopic shock absorbers and anti-roll bar

Rear suspension: Live axle with semi-elliptic leaf springs, telescopic shock absorbers and anti-roll bar

Brakes: Discs (front), drums (rear)

Wheels: Steel discs, 7 x 15 in.

Tires: E60 x 15 (front), G60 x 15 (rear)

DIMENSIONS

Length: 191.3 in.   **Width:** 76.1 in.

Height: 51.7 in.   **Wheelbase:** 110.0 in.

Track: 60.7 in. (front), 61.2 in. (rear)

Weight: 3,650 lbs.

Dodge CHARGER 500

'Win on Sunday, sell on Monday' was a Detroit mantra in the late 1960s. With Chrysler being trounced by Ford on the super speedways, it needed a worthy contender. The result was the high-performance, limited-production Dodge Charger 500.

"...breathtaking acceleration."

"Turn the key and hear the distinctive starter crank the mighty Hemi. Although it requires premium fuel, the 426-cubic inch V8 powers the Charger around town without stumbling in low revs like some engines, although fast street racing is its call. Planting your foot to the floor brings a howl of delight from under the hood and, combined with the four-speed transmission, the acceleration is breathtaking—the Hemi pulls all the way up to the redline."

Charger 500s came with a stock R/T (Road and Track) interior, and woodgrain trim.

Milestones

1967 A second-generation Charger, with coke bottle fender line, is released for 1968. The R/T model comes with either a 375 bhp, 440-cubic inch or 425-bhp, 426-cubic inch Hemi V8.

The Charger debuted for 1966 with fastback styling.

1968 With Chrysler losing the battle in NASCAR to Ford, Mopar produce the Charger 500. It has a plugged grill with exposed headlights and a flush back window. It is sold as a 1969 model.

Regular Charger R/Ts got a split hidden headlight grill for 1969.

1969 The slippery Charger 500s manage to capture 18 NASCAR victories this year. Unfortunately, Ford's more aerodynamic Talladegas won 30.

1969 A more streamlined Daytona replaces the 500 later this year. It has a pointed nose cone and tall rear wing.

UNDER THE SKIN

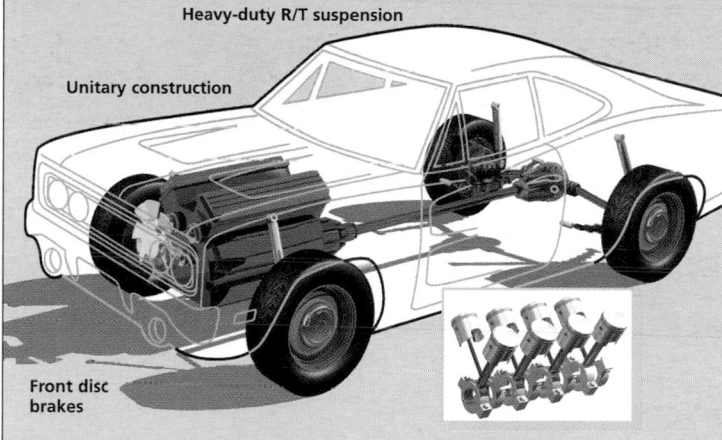

Heavy-duty R/T suspension

Unitary construction

Front disc brakes

426 Hemi V8

Heavy duty

As a member of Chrysler's B-body intermediate line up, the Charger 500 has a unitary body/chassis with a separate front subframe bolted to it. At the rear is a Dana live axle with a Sure-Grip differential, while the front has upper and lower A-arms but with longitudinal torsion bar springs in place of more conventional coils. Front disc brakes were standard, though 11-inch drums are retained at the rear.

THE POWER PACK

Ultimate Hemi

Like the standard Charger R/T, the 500 was offered with just two engines—the 375-bhp, 440-cubic inch Magnum or 426-cubic inch Hemi V8. The Hemi, installed in a mere 32 Charger 500s, was perhaps the ultimate muscle car engine. With 425 bhp, 490 lb-ft of torque and an aluminum intake manifold with twin Carter AFB four-barrel carburetors, it is a fearsome powerplant. Equipped with this engine and 4.10:1 rear gearing, a Charger 500 can zip through the ¼-mile in just 13.7 seconds.

Hemispherical combustion chambers

Dual Carter AFB four-barrel carburetors

Forged steel crankshaft

All cast-iron construction

Rare Hemis

Built as a homologation exercise, the Charger 500 is exceedingly rare. The Hemi V8-engined cars are even more exclusive, with just 32 built. As with all muscle Mopars, these machines are highly sought after today and mint examples can cost $50,000.

Exposed headlights, flush-fit grill and smooth rear window distinguish the 500.

Dodge CHARGER 500

Although marginally faster than the standard Charger on the speedways, the 500 really came into its own on the street. One magazine even went as far as to call it a showroom racer—surprisingly docile on the street circuit.

Hemi V8

Only two engines were available in the limited edition 500. The first was the big 440-cubic inch Magnum, installed in the majority (340) of the cars. The second was the mighty Hemi, which produced an incredible 425 bhp and 490 lb-ft of torque.

Body modifications

To combat problems of turbulence on the second-generation Charger, the 500 was fitted with a flush-mounted grill and smooth rear window. The latter necessitated a shorter trunk lid and an extended rear backlight shelf.

Heavy-duty suspension

All Charger 500s were fitted with the same suspension. This included heavy-duty shocks, stiffer front torsion bars and an extra leaf in the right rear spring, plus a thicker and tighter front anti-roll bar.

Out-of-house conversion

The Charger 500 started life as a 1968 Charger but, besides the nose and window alterations, it got 1969 style taillights and was marketed as a 1969 model. The conversion was undertaken by Creative Industries—an aftermarket car crafter based in Michigan.

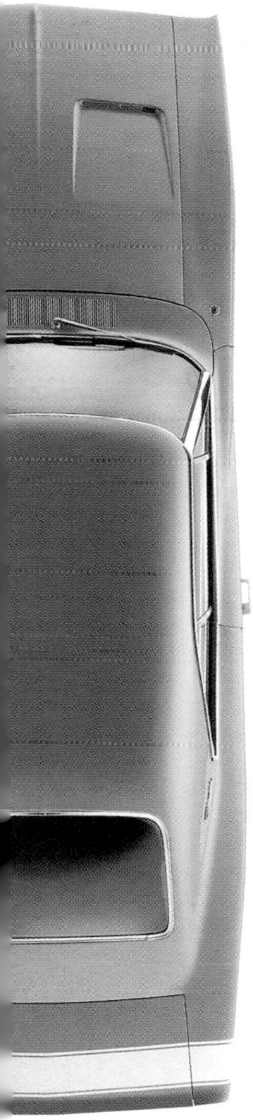

Front disc brakes

Base model Chargers came with four-wheel drum brakes, although R/T models have 11-inch units front and rear. Charger 500s, however, have front discs as standard equipment.

Dual exhaust

Like the vast majority of muscle cars, the Charger 500 needed a large exhaust system. It is fitted with twin full-length 2¼-inch diameter pipes.

Specifications

1969 Dodge Charger 500

ENGINE

Type: V8

Construction: Cast-iron block and heads

Valve gear: Two valves per cylinder operated by a single camshaft with pushrods and rockers

Bore and stroke: 4.25 in. x 3.75 in.

Displacement: 426 c.i.

Compression ratio: 10.25:1

Induction system: Twin Carter AFB four-barrel carburetors

Maximum power: 425 bhp at 5,000 rpm

Maximum torque: 490 lb-ft at 4,000 rpm

TRANSMISSION

Four-speed manual

BODY/CHASSIS

Steel unitary chassis with two-door fastback body

SPECIAL FEATURES

All Chargers from 1968 to 1970 have this racing style fuel filler cap on the left rear quarter panel.

The Charger 500s flush-fit grill was modeled after the 1968 Coronet R/T.

RUNNING GEAR

Steering: Recirculating ball

Front suspension: Unequal length A-arms with longitudinally-mounted torsion bars, telescopic shock absorbers and anti-roll bar

Rear suspension: Live axle with semi-elliptic leaf springs and telescopic shock absorbers

Brakes: Discs, 11-in. dia. (front), drums, 11-in. dia. (rear)

Wheels: Steel discs, 5 x 14 in.

Tires: F70-14

DIMENSIONS

Length: 208.0 in.   **Width:** 76.5 in.

Height: 53.1 in.   **Wheelbase:** 116.0 in.

Track: 59.5 in. (front), 29.2 in. (rear)

Weight: 4,100 lbs.

Dodge CHARGER DAYTONA

There was a street version of the Charger Daytona because Dodge had to build a certain number to qualify for NASCAR racing. With its Hemi-engined 200-mph missile, Dodge went on to win 22 races in 1969.

"...shattering performance."

"You do not notice the aerodynamic aids until you are well past 120 mph, but they really came into play on superspeedways, helping to keep the cars stable as they passed each other at around 200 mph.

It is unlikely you will reach that speed in a street-spec Hemi V8 since it only has 425 bhp; but that is still enough for earth shattering performance and acceleration. Low gearing and light steering do not give an immediate sense of confidence, but it is fairly accurate."

The interior of the street Charger is much more civilized than that of its NASCAR sibling.

Milestones

1969 Race goers at Alabama's Talledega track get the first sight of the racing Charger Daytona. Charlie Glotzbach laps the track at just under 200 mph. Charger driver Richard Brickhouse wins the race, and the Charger Daytona goes on to take another 22 checkers this season.

Plymouth's version of the Charger was the Superbird.

1970 Plymouth builds a sister to the Charger Daytona in the shape of the almost-identical Superbird.

Chargers and Superbirds often went head to head on the track.

1971 Both the Charger Daytona and the Plymouth Superbird are effectively outlawed from racing when NASCAR insists on a reduction in engine size by 25 percent. To prove a point, Dodge organizes a run at Bonneville on the Salt Flats, where Daytona 500 winner Bobby Isaacs reaches over 217 mph.

UNDER THE SKIN

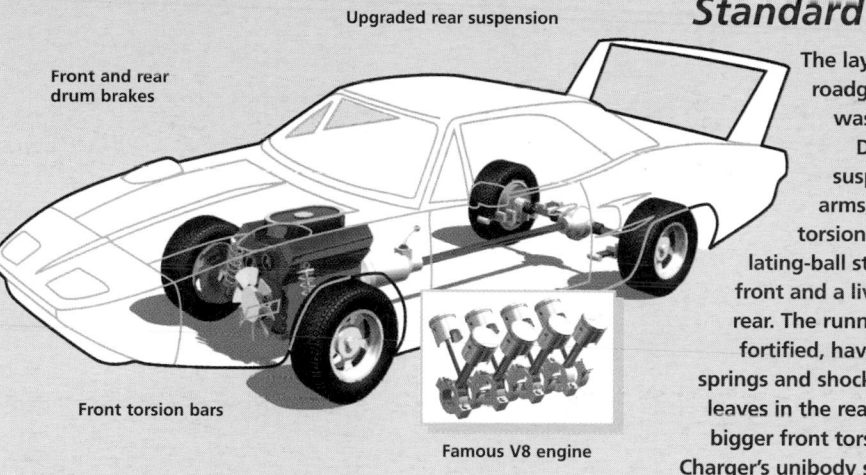

Upgraded rear suspension

Front and rear drum brakes

Front torsion bars

Famous V8 engine

Standard layout

The layout from the roadgoing Charger was kept for the Daytona, with suspension of A-arms, longitudinal torsion bars, recirculating-ball steering at the front and a live axle at the rear. The running gear was fortified, having far stiffer springs and shocks, with extra leaves in the rear springs and bigger front torsion bars; the Charger's unibody structure was made far stronger for the racers.

THE POWER PACK

MOPAR Muscle

The immortal Hemi engine first appeared in 1964, when Chrysler seriously decided to take on Ford in NASCAR. It is an all-cast-iron unit with a single camshaft in the V operating canted valves in highly efficient hemispherical combustion chambers through a combination of pushrods, solid lifters and rockers. It is oversquare with a large bore to allow room for the large valves. With its shorter stroke, it is designed to rev high, up to 7,200 rpm. The 426-c.i. alloy-headed, high-compression race engines gave over 650 bhp when fitted into the front of the Charger Daytona.

Special

The distinctive looks of the Charger Daytona have ensured its status as a cult classic. All cars are supremely powerful, but Keith Black (builder of MOPAR performance engines) prepared a promotional version with hair-raising performance.

The Daytona has one of the most outrageous wings ever seen on a stock car.

Dodge CHARGER DAYTONA

The Charger Daytona's outrageous look was no styling gimmick; the sharp extended nose and huge rear wing really did make the car far more aerodynamic and quicker around the track.

426-c.i. Hemi

The street version of the Hemi gave less power than the higher tuned race engines, with their outputs between 575 and 700 bhp. Also, they ran with iron heads, lower compression ratios, and later hydraulic rather than solid tappets which kept the potential engine speeds lower.

Four-speed transmission

Street versions of the Charger Daytona came with a standard three-speed manual, but the racers were equipped with a close-ratio, four-speed with a Hurst shifter. Customers could specify a four-speed as a no-cost option or opt for the TorqueFlite three-speed auto.

Two four-barrel carburetors

For the street Hemi engine there were two Carter four-barrel carburetors, arranged to open progressively. Just two barrels of the rear carb open at low throttle.

Extended nose

The new nose was made of Fiberglass and was some 17 inches long. It made the car more aerodynamically efficient. The poor fit, that is a feature of all Charger Daytonas and Plymouth Superbirds, clearly had no effect on the aerodynamics of this 200-mph car.

Unitary construction

Although it looks like a classic example of a traditional body-on-frame piece of American design, the Charger Daytona is a unitary vehicle, with the bodywork acting as the chassis.

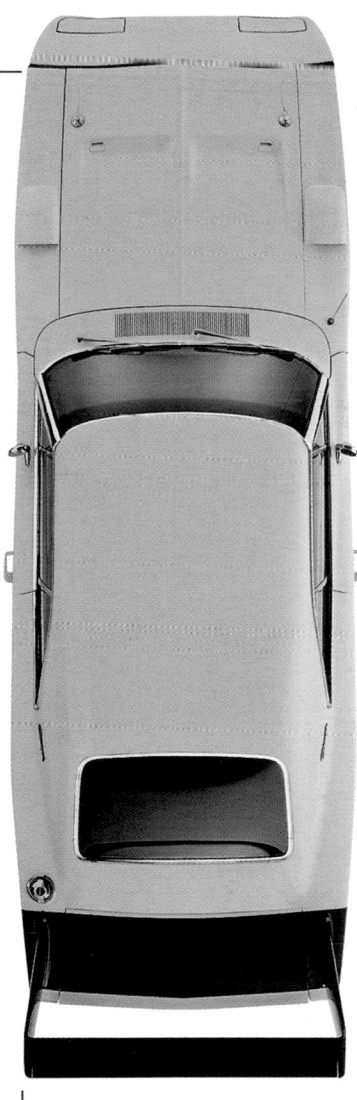

Pop-up lights

With the addition of the sharp extended nose, the standard headlights were covered and had to be replaced by a new arrangement of pop-up light pods, with each having two headlights.

Rear wing

That distinctive rear wing is mounted more than two feet above the trunk lid, so there is room for the trunk to open. But its real benefit is to allow it to operate in clean air.

Specifications

1969 Dodge Charger Daytona

ENGINE

Type: V8

Construction: Cast-iron block and heads

Valve gear: Two valves per cylinder operating in hemispherical combustion chambers opened by a single V-mounted camshaft with pushrods, rockers and solid lifters

Bore and stroke: 4.25 in. x 3.75 in.

Displacement: 426 c.i.

Compression ratio: 10.25:1

Induction system: Two Carter AFB 3084S carburetors

Maximum power: 425 bhp at 5,600 rpm

Maximum torque: 490 lb-ft at 4,000 rpm

TRANSMISSION

Four-speed manual

BODY/CHASSIS

Unitary monocoque construction with steel body panels and fiberglass nose section

SPECIAL FEATURES

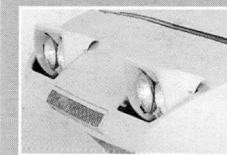

The aerodynamic fiberglass nose houses the unique pop-up headlights.

The black rear wing distinguishes the Charger from the Plymouth Superbird.

RUNNING GEAR

Steering: Recirculating-ball

Front suspension: A-arms with longitudinal torsion bars, telescopic shock absorbers and anti-roll bar

Rear suspension: Live axle with asymmetrical leaf springs and telescopic shock absorbers

Brakes: Drums, 11.0-in. dia. (front), 11.0-in. dia. (rear)

Wheels: Stamped steel, 14 in. x 6 in.

Tires: F70 x 14

DIMENSIONS

Length: 208.5 in.   **Width:** 76.6 in.

Height: 53.0 in.   **Wheelbase:** 117.0 in.

Track: 59.7 in. (front), 59.2 in. (rear)

Weight: 3,671 lbs.

Dodge CORONET R/T

The Coronet R/T was the first mid-size Dodge muscle machine to feature all the performance and luxury features in a single package. With a powerful 440-cubic inch V8, it didn't disappoint.

"...it just keeps on going."

"Unlike previous mid-size Chrysler muscle cars, the Coronet R/T has a more sporty feel. With a distinctive start-up sound, the giant Magnum V8 roars into life. Smooth and refined, the big V8 has plenty of torque. Dropping the pedal launches the car forward and it just keeps on going, daring you to go faster. Watch out for the corners though; the nose-heavy R/T doesn't handle very well and its 480 lb-ft of torque will surely result in oversteer."

The Coronet R/T has standard bucket seats, a center console and full instrumentation.

Milestones

1967 Dodge introduces its Coronet R/T (Road and Track). It is a complete high-performance package and is fitted with a standard 440-cubic inch V8, although the Hemi engine is also available. This year sales figures total 10,181.

The Coronet R/T debuted in both hardtop and convertible forms.

1968 The R/T returns with handsome new sheet-metal on an unchanged wheelbase.

1969 After a major facelift in 1968, changes this year are minor, with a new grill and rear tail panel. Engine choices remain the same.

The race-ready Super Bee was the Coronet's high performance stablemate.

1970 Greater competition in a heavily crowded market takes its toll on the Coronet R/T and sales fall to just 2,615. Only 13 of these cars are fitted with the Hemi V8.

UNDER THE SKIN

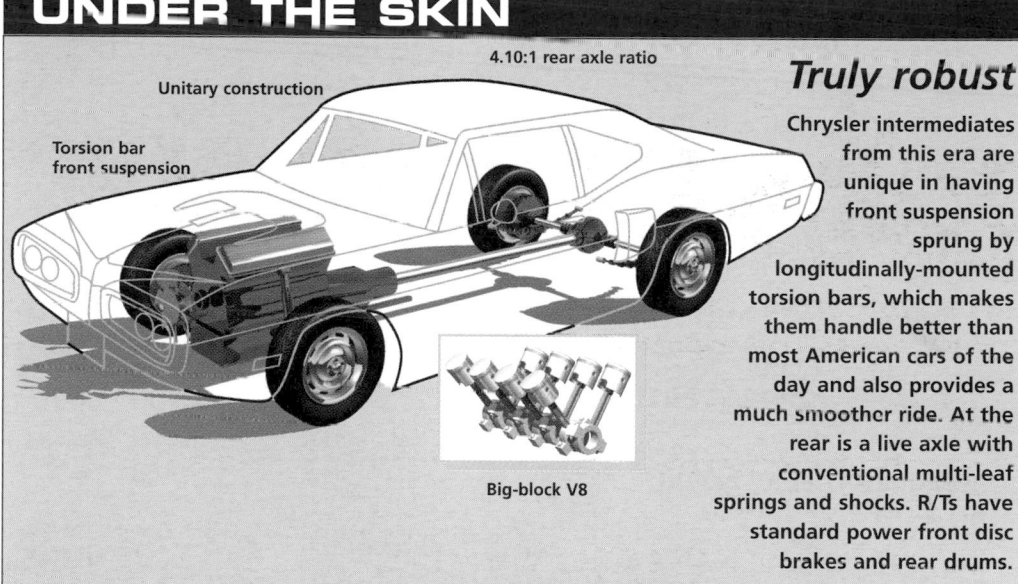

4.10:1 rear axle ratio

Unitary construction

Torsion bar front suspension

Big-block V8

Truly robust

Chrysler intermediates from this era are unique in having front suspension sprung by longitudinally-mounted torsion bars, which makes them handle better than most American cars of the day and also provides a much smoother ride. At the rear is a live axle with conventional multi-leaf springs and shocks. R/Ts have standard power front disc brakes and rear drums.

THE POWER PACK

More reliable

Only two engines were available with the R/T package: the more common 440-cubic inch Magnum and the street-lethal 426-cubic inch Hemi. The Magnum was lifted from the full-size Chrysler line, but in the R/T it has a longer duration camshaft profile, bigger exhaust valves, a dual snorkel intake, a four-barrel Carter carburetor, and free-flowing exhaust manifolds. It produces 375 bhp and 480 lb-ft of torque. By including the 'Six Pack,' the 440 received 3x2 carburetors for 490 bhp.

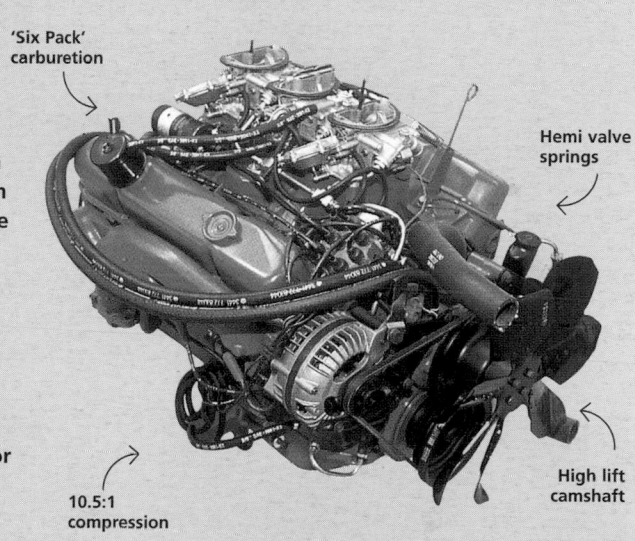

'Six Pack' carburetion

Hemi valve springs

10.5:1 compression

High lift camshaft

Short life

When the Coronet was launched in 1967, its styling was boxy and upright. A new, smoother body was introduced the following year, which was carried over to 1969 with few changes. 1970 models feature an aggressive twin 'horse collar'-type grill.

1970 was the last year for the convertible Coronet.

Dodge CORONET R/T

This peppermint green 1970 Coronet 440 is one of just 2,615 R/Ts built that year. With so much competition in the muscle car arena, sales plummeted in 1970, making this a desirable muscle car today.

Torsion bar suspension

Chrysler was unique in employing torsion bars for the front suspension. Mounted lengthways, they are extremely simple and robust.

Street racer's powerplant

Easier to maintain, more flexible and less temperamental than the Hemi, the 440 delivers plenty of torque and is perfect for drag racing. It is nicknamed the 'Wedge' because of the shape of its combustion chambers.

Bulletproof TorqueFlite

The V8 in this R/T is backed up by the optional 727 TorqueFlite three-speed automatic. This transmission is extremely reliable and has been used in countless Mopars over the years.

Bigger wheels

For 1970 handsome 15-inch Rallye wheels became available on the Coronet R/T. They feature chrome beauty rings and center caps.

Bumble bee stripe

A tail end stripe, usually in black, white or red, was available at no extra cost.

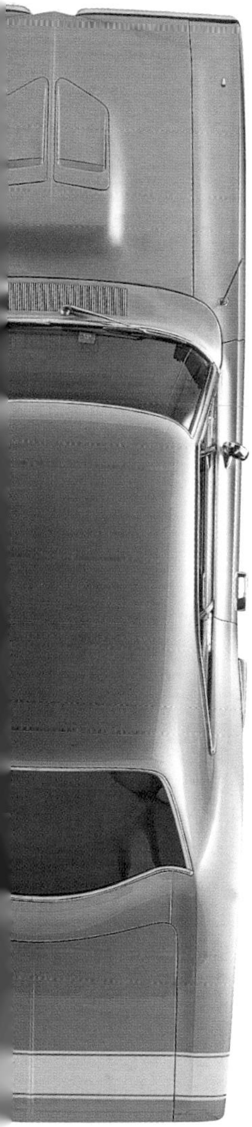

Specifications

1970 Dodge Coronet R/T

ENGINE

Type: V8

Construction: Cast-iron block and heads

Valve gear: Two valves per cylinder operated by pushrods and rockers

Bore and stroke: 4.32 in. x 3.75 in.

Displacement: 440 c.i.

Compression ratio: 10.5:1

Induction system: Single Carter AFB downdraft four-barrel carburetor

Maximum power: 375 bhp at 4,600 rpm

Maximum torque: 480 lb-ft at 3,200 rpm

TRANSMISSION

TorqueFlite 727 three-speed automatic

BODY/CHASSIS

Steel monocoque with two-door body

SPECIAL FEATURES

Side-mounted scoops are only fitted to 1970 Coronet R/Ts and are purely decorative features.

Though the engine in this Coronet R/T makes 375 bhp, it is the base engine. Also available was a 390 bhp version with three two-barrel carbs, and a 426 Hemi that made 425 bhp.

RUNNING GEAR

Steering: Recirculating ball

Front suspension: Longitudinally-mounted torsion bars with wishbones and telescopic shocks

Rear suspension: Live rear axle with semi-elliptic leaf springs and telescopic shocks

Brakes: Discs (front), drums (rear)

Wheels: Steel disc, 15-in. dia.

Tires: Goodyear Polyglas GT F60 15

DIMENSIONS

Length: 207.7 in. **Width:** 80.6 in.

Height: 52.5 in. **Wheelbase:** 117 in.

Track: 58.9 in. (front and rear)

Weight: 3,546 lbs.

Aggressive front

Twin 'horse collar'-type grills are unique to 1970 Coronets and give the car an aggressive appearance. The hood scoops are an R/T-only feature and are non-functional.

Ford FAIRLANE 427

To fight its opposition on the street Ford built the Fairlane 427, which had widened shock towers and larger front coil springs to fit a detuned 427 V8. Unfortunately, the Fairlane 427 was costly to build, so only 70 units were made in 1966 and 200 in 1967. Most went to pro racers for NHRA Super Stock competition.

"...uses a detuned race engine"

"Only a Borg-Warner 'Top-Loader' four-speed transmission was able to handle the 480 lb-ft of torque that the massive engine was capable of making. Though it uses a detuned version of its race engine, the brutal 427, if equipped with dual four-barrel carbs, it 'only' makes 425 bhp. On the street, the Fairlane 427 was very competitive. Only a handful were made and at $5,100 were very pricey, thus giving a slight edge to the competition."

The only indication of power from the vinyl-clad interior was a 9,000 rpm tachometer.

Milestones

1964 After minimal success on the drag strips with the larger Galaxies, Ford creates the Thunderbolt—a specially prepared 427-powered lightweight Fairlane sedan. These factory-built race cars helped Ford secure the NHRA manufacturers' championship.

The first Fairlanes to be equipped with the 427 were the competition-only Thunderbolts.

1966 A new, bigger Fairlane is released, which has plenty of room for 427 FE V8 engines. Only 70 white hardtops and coupes are built to qualify for Super Stock drag racing.

The 1966 Fairlane has similar styling to the 1966-67 Galaxie.

1967 The 427 returns as a regular production option for its second and final season. Only 200 Fairlanes are equipped with the side-oiler 427 and are available in a variety of colors and optional trim packages.

UNDER THE SKIN

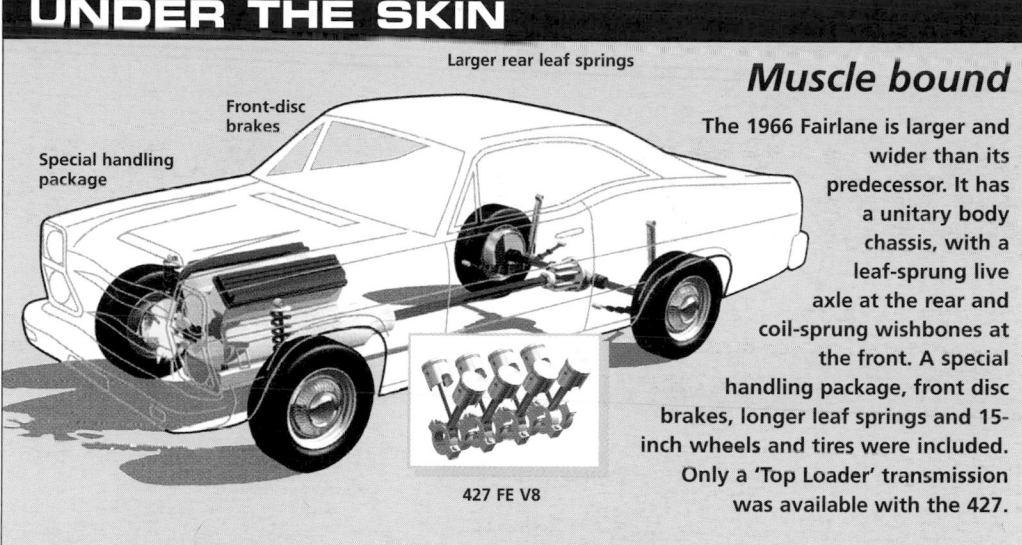

Larger rear leaf springs

Front-disc brakes

Special handling package

427 FE V8

Muscle bound

The 1966 Fairlane is larger and wider than its predecessor. It has a unitary body chassis, with a leaf-sprung live axle at the rear and coil-sprung wishbones at the front. A special handling package, front disc brakes, longer leaf springs and 15-inch wheels and tires were included. Only a 'Top Loader' transmission was available with the 427.

THE POWER PACK

The side-oiler

Oiling was always a problem on the 406 and 427 FE engines, and so in 1965 Ford introduced a new block design known as the 'side-oiler'. It is this version of the 427-cubic inch engine that powers the Fairlane. Instead of routing the main oil gallery down the center of the block, like other FE engines, the side-oiler has the main oil gallery positioned low on the left side near the pump outlet. It is rated at 410 bhp with a single four-barrel carburetor and 425 bhp with a dual carburetor set up.

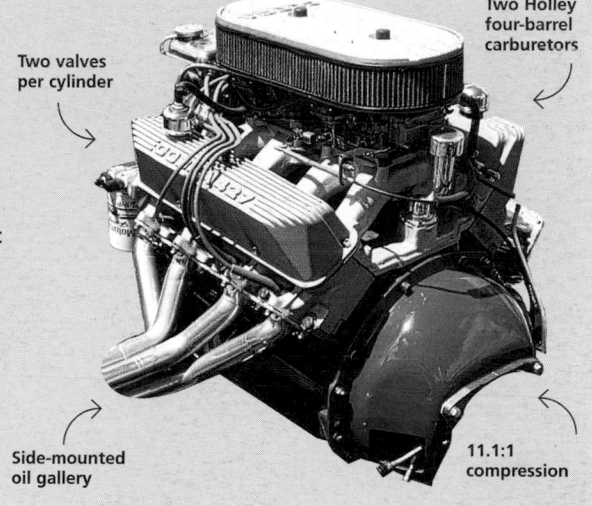

Two valves per cylinder

Two Holley four-barrel carburetors

Side-mounted oil gallery

11.1:1 compression

Rare beast

Although the 1966 models are very rare, this no frills homologation special isn't very refined. For 1967, Ford offered the Fairlane 427 in a variety of colors and exterior trim. The cars still had the potent 427 V8 and also carried the equally potent price tag.

The 1967 Fairlane 427s were a serious threat on the streets and at the track.

Ford FAIRLANE 427

Although it was one of the quickest muscle cars around in 1966, the rarity of the Fairlane 427 prevented it from having the same impact among street racers as a Chevelle SS396 or a tri-power GTO.

Race-derived engine

The 427-cubic inch engine was only available with the base model trim and was never used in the plusher GT/GTA model. After all, it was a thinly-disguised race car and potential purchasers were carefully screened by dealers.

Heavy-duty suspension

To cope with the weight and power of the 427 engine, the standard Fairlane suspension was reworked with stiffer spring rates and larger front coil springs. This unit also took up considerable space, which necessitated relocating the front shock towers.

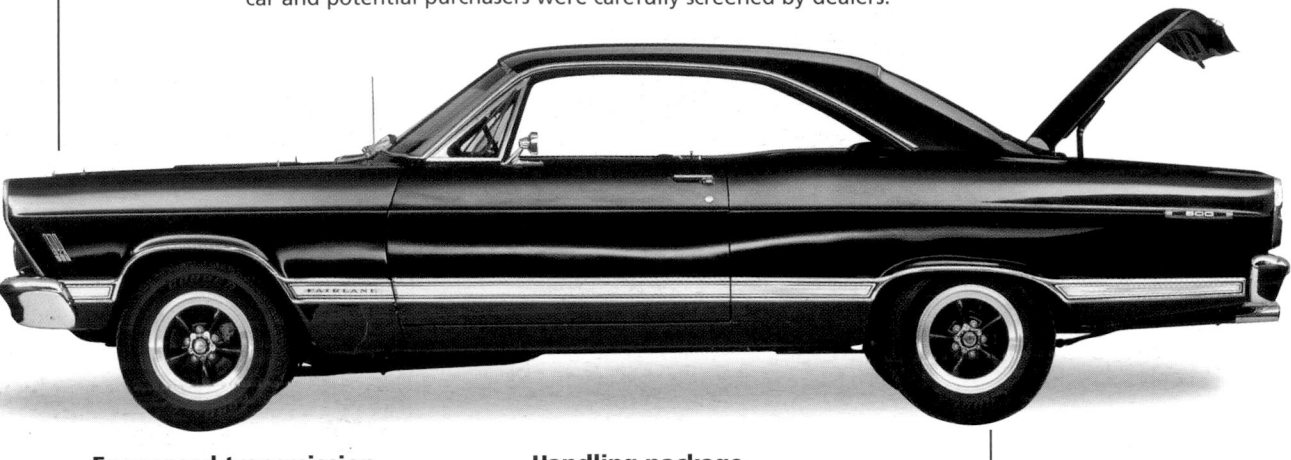

Four-speed transmission

Unlike the Fairlane GT/GTA, the 427 was only available with one transmission: a Borg-Warner 'Top Loader' T-10 four-speed.

Handling package

A special handling package, consisting of manual front disc brakes, longer rear leaf springs and larger blackwall tires, was available. This particular car is one of the very few to be fitted with these items.

Smooth styling

For 1966, the Fairlane hardtop received similar styling to the Pontiac GTO, with stacked headlights and smooth-flowing contours.

Fiberglass hood

In 1966 all 427 Fairlanes were built with a fiberglass lift-off hood with four tie-down pins. For 1967 a steel hood was available alongside the fiberglass unit.

Specifications

1967 Ford Fairlane 427

ENGINE

Type: V8

Construction: Cast-iron block and heads

Valve gear: Two valves per cylinder actuated by a single camshaft via pushrods, rockers and solid lifters

Bore and stroke: 4.23 in. x 3.78 in.

Displacement: 427 c.i.

Compression ratio: 11.1:1

Induction system: Two Holley four-barrel downdraft carburetors with aluminum intake manifold

Maximum power: 425 bhp at 6,000 rpm

Maximum torque: 480 lb-ft at 3,700 rpm

TRANSMISSION

Borg-Warner 'Top Loader' T-10 four-speed

BODY/CHASSIS

Steel unitary chassis with two-door body

SPECIAL FEATURES

Stacked headlights are a feature of 1966-1967 Fairlanes. The lower units are the high beams.

Dual 652 cfm Holley four barrel carburetors are housed beneath an open element aircleaner.

RUNNING GEAR

Steering: Recirculating ball

Front suspension: Double wishbones with heavy duty coil springs, telescopic shock absorbers, anti-sway bar

Rear suspension: Live axle with long semi-elliptic leaf springs and telescopic shock absorbers

Brakes: Discs front, drums rear

Wheels: 14 x 5.5-in.

Tires: 7.75 x 14

DIMENSIONS

Length: 197.0 in.   **Width:** 74.7 in.

Height: 54.3 in.   **Wheelbase:** 116.0 in.

Track: 58.0 in.   **Weight:** 4,100 lbs.

Ford FALCON

In the early 1960s, Ford embarked on its 'Total Performance' sales campaign. It also brought a number of Ford Falcons to Europe for use in racing and rallying, where they performed incredibly well.

"...means business."

"With its full roll cage and gutted interior, you can tell that this Falcon means business. Turn the key and the 289-cubic inch V8 rumbles to life. Thanks to its side mounted exhaust, the sound is impressive. Being fairly compact and light, the Falcon makes the most of its power and pulls hard in all gears. With stiffer springs than stock, a front anti-roll bar, and large tires it tackles sharp corners with enthusiasm, understeering mildly."

Only the bare essentials are retained, with just a single bucket seat for the driver.

Milestones

1960 Ford introduces its new compact car, the Falcon. It proves a tremendous success with 410,876 examples built.

1961 Midway through the year a sporty Falcon Sprint model is revealed with bucket seats and V8 power.

1964 Falcons gained boxier styling than the 1963 car.

1962 Ford begins its total performance campaign and sends race-prepared Falcons to Europe for use in rallying events.

1963 Driving a Falcon, Bo Ljungfeldt achieves a class win in the Monte Carlo Rally.

The Falcon Sprint was also available as a convertible.

1964 Restyled Falcons continue to do battle but are soon replaced in rallying by the sportier Mustang. The survivors continue in use as road racers through the 1960s.

UNDER THE SKIN

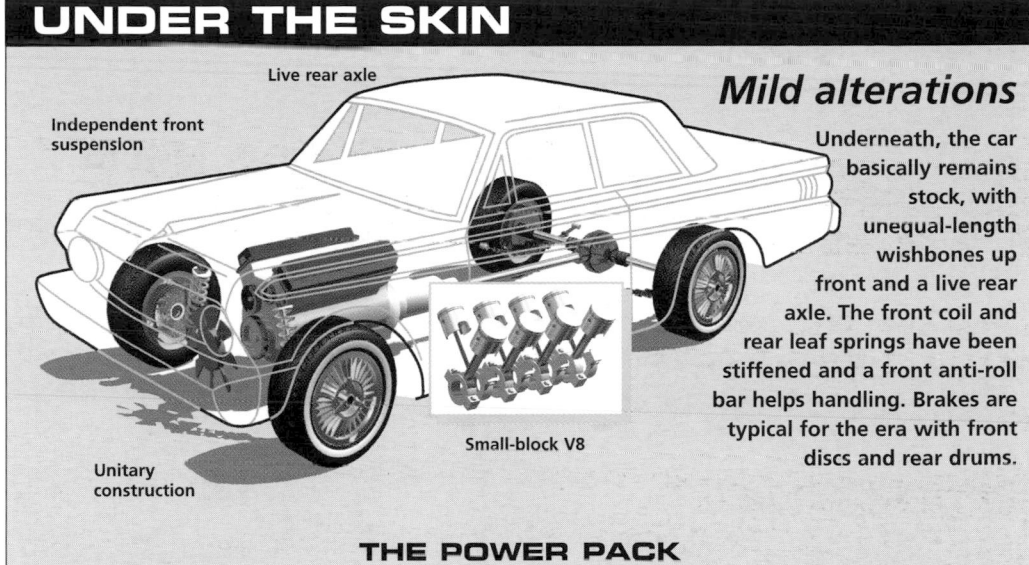

Live rear axle

Independent front suspension

Unitary construction

Small-block V8

Mild alterations

Underneath, the car basically remains stock, with unequal-length wishbones up front and a live rear axle. The front coil and rear leaf springs have been stiffened and a front anti-roll bar helps handling. Brakes are typical for the era with front discs and rear drums.

THE POWER PACK

High Performance

European competition Falcons used the High Performance 289-cubic inch V8. Typical of the times, it was a cast iron unit with two valves per cylinder. It developed 271 bhp, 46 more than the standard unit thanks to a slightly higher compression ratio, increased carburetor velocity, a higher-lift camshaft, and free-flowing exhaust headers. Although potent in this trim, the small-block V8 could be easily tweaked for more power and was the same engine used in the Shelby Mustangs.

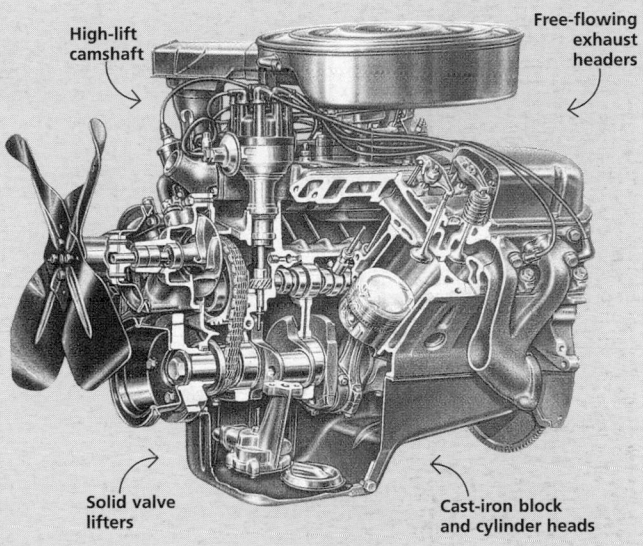

High-lift camshaft

Free-flowing exhaust headers

Solid valve lifters

Cast-iron block and cylinder heads

Falcon Futura

For rallying, Ford campaigned Futura Sprint two-door hardtops with fiberglass body panels and standard 289 V8s. After their rallying career was over, a handful were raced in the British Saloon Car Championship until the early 1970s.

After rallying, a few Falcons raced in the British Saloon Car Championship.

85

Ford **FALCON**

While high performance Falcons were generally used for drag racing in the U.S., the European-spec cars had a more powerful engine and were successfully campaigned as road racers in the 1960s.

Crisper styling

Falcons were restyled for 1964, with squarer, neater lines and a concave grille. This restyle carried over into 1965 with few changes. V8 engines transformed the Falcon's performance image.

V8 engine

This Falcon has considerable go thanks to the 289 cubic inch V8 engine. This was the powerplant that made the cars highly competitive in rallying and circuit racing during the 1960s and continues to do so in historic events today.

Stiffened suspension

For more responsive handling, the springs have been stiffened. Today, Falcons demonstrate excellent poise in FIA historic racing events across Europe.

Original-style brakes

Under FIA rules, even the original braking set up of front discs and rear drums must be retained. Braking ability contrasts sharply with modern machinery.

Fiberglass body panels

In order to reduce weight and increase performance the front fenders, hood and trunk are made from fiberglass.

Specifications

1964 Ford Falcon

ENGINE

Type: V8

Construction: Cast-iron block and heads

Valve gear: Two valves per cylinder operated by pushrods and rockers

Bore/stroke: 4 in. x 2.87 in.

Displacement: 289 c.i.

Compression ratio: 10.5:1

Induction system: Twin four-barrel Holley cfm 600 carburetors

Maximum power: 271 bhp at 6,000 rpm

Maximum torque: 312 lb-ft at 3,400 rpm

TRANSMISSION

Borg Warner T-10 four-speed

BODY/CHASSIS

Steel monocoque with two-door body

SPECIAL FEATURES

Circular taillights are a trademark of early 1960s Fords.

The elastic retaining strap on the hood looks crude but was actually homologated by Ford for racing.

RUNNING GEAR

Steering: Recirculating ball

Front suspension: Unequal length wishbones, coil springs, telescopic shocks and 1-in. dia. anti-roll bar

Rear suspension: Live rear axle with semi-elliptic leaf springs and telescopic shocks

Brakes: Discs to front, drums to rear

Wheels: 7 x 15 Minilite spoked alloy wheels

Tires: 205 60R 15

DIMENSIONS

Length: 180.2 in.   **Width:** 76.6 in.

Height: 52.4 in.   **Wheelbase:** 109.5 in.

Track: 47.5 in. (front), 43.1 in. (rear)

Weight: 2,811 lbs.

Four-speed transmission

Manual transmissions are essential for track racing so this Falcon features an original equipment Borg Warner T-10 four-speed transmission.

Ford GALAXIE 500XL

In the early 1960s Ford waged war on the drag strips as part of its 'Total Performance' campaign. "Win on Sunday, sell on Monday" was the motivational phrase that sparked the heated horsepower wars. This 1963 lightweight Galaxie is one of Ford's finest.

"...dual-purpose dynamo."

"After Tiny Lund won the Daytona 500 in a 1963 Galaxie, with its larger engine now displacing 427-cubic inches, Ford thought it was unstoppable in its Total Performance campaign. In addition to being more competitive in NASCAR, 50 lightweight cars were built for NHRA drag racing. In Super Stock drag trim Gas Rhonda was consistently knocking off 12.07 ETs at 118.04 mph down the ¼ mile. This dual-purpose dynamo succeeded in both forms of racing and helped crown Ford the king in 1963."

Like all 427-equipped Galaxies, this one has a factory installed 4-speed transmission.

Milestones

1962 Ford increases

its 390 V8 to 406 cubic inches. Later this year the 406 becomes available with tri-power carburetion making 405 bhp.

A Galaxie fastback was relaunched in 1963 after a one-year absence.

1963 Again Ford increases

its maximum engine size. The 406 V8 becomes a 427. With a four barrel carb the engine makes 410 bhp, but with the dual quads, it makes 425 bhp. Although Ford dominates NASCAR this year, the 50 lightweight Galaxies that were built to compete in drag racing didn't share the same success.

In 1964 50 427 Galaxies were built for drag racing.

1964 Looking to dominate

drag racing, Ford puts 100 percent of its attention and money into the new lightweight Fairlane. With a special drag package the new cars, known as Thunderbolts, proved to be untouchable and win the season.

UNDER THE SKIN

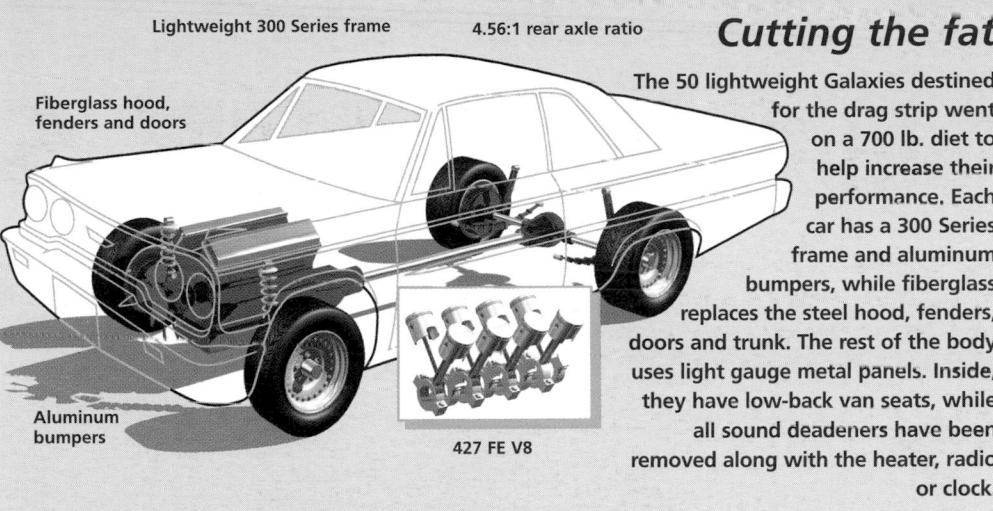

Lightweight 300 Series frame

4.56:1 rear axle ratio

Fiberglass hood, fenders and doors

Aluminum bumpers

427 FE V8

Cutting the fat

The 50 lightweight Galaxies destined for the drag strip went on a 700 lb. diet to help increase their performance. Each car has a 300 Series frame and aluminum bumpers, while fiberglass replaces the steel hood, fenders, doors and trunk. The rest of the body uses light gauge metal panels. Inside, they have low-back van seats, while all sound deadeners have been removed along with the heater, radio or clock.

THE POWER PACK

Ford gets serious

In 1963 Ford unleashed its hottest powerplant yet. The FE Y-block 427-cubic inch V8 features a larger bore than the previous 406, and is built with heavy duty parts. To homologate the 427s for NASCAR racing, many were built using a single four barrel carburetor and 11.6:1 compression. The lightweight drag cars used dual reverse-mounted 600 cfm Holley carburetors and 12.2:1 compression. Single carb versions make 410 bhp while the dual-carburetor motors make 425 bhp.

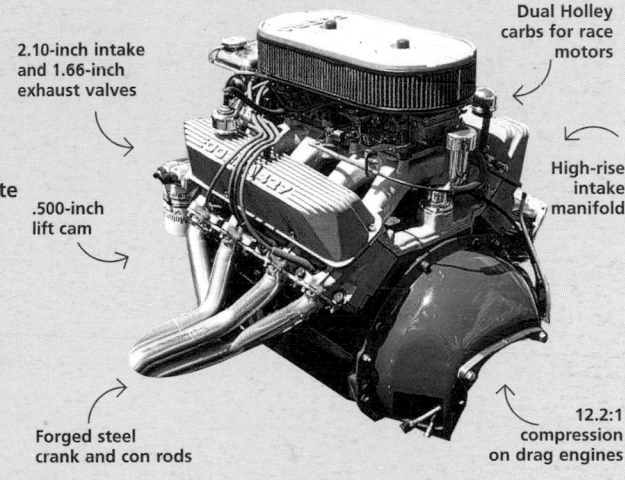

2.10-inch intake and 1.66-inch exhaust valves

.500-inch lift cam

Forged steel crank and con rods

Dual Holley carbs for race motors

High-rise intake manifold

12.2:1 compression on drag engines

Prized Fords

XL titles adorn the big, sporty Fords of the early 1960s. Convertibles always demand higher prices than hardtops and 427-cubic inch Galaxie XL convertibles are among the most prized Fords of the era. Options affect price considerably.

Big-block Galaxie 500XLs are avidly sought by collectors.

Ford GALAXIE 500XL

When it came to racing, Ford always rolled up its sleeves and attacked the competition at full throttle. This 1963 lightweight Galaxie was one of 50 cars that clearly illustrated how seriously Ford took winning drag races.

Stripped out interior

All of the unnecessary items in the interior such as the radio, heater, all sound deadeners, carpeting and clock were removed. In addition, Econoline van seats replace the plush cushions.

427 V8 engine

Introduced halfway through 1963, the 427 ultimately emerged as Ford's most legendary and fearsome powerplant of the 1960s.

Fastback styling

The big Galaxies were also used for stock car racing. The fastback roof, in addition to looking stylish, helped to reduce aerodynamic drag on stock car oval tracks and increased the maximum speed by more than 10 mph.

Manual transmission

All lightweight Galaxies were only available with a 4-speed transmission. Since saving weight was a primary concern, the transmission casings and bell-housings were made of aluminum instead of steel.

Six-cylinder suspension

This car uses the lighter chassis found under the 300 Series Galaxies that used six cylinder motors. It is made of lighter gauge steel and weighs considerably less than the standard 500XL chassis.

The lightweight package

All lightweight Galaxies were designed for one purpose—drag racing. These cars are so radical that they weren't the least bit street-able.The drag cars came with a high 12.2:1 compression ratio, different 2nd and 3rd gears in the transmission and a 4.56:1 rear axle ratio.This car was not for the faint hearted.

The 700-lb. diet

All lightweight Galaxies used fiberglass fenders, doors, trunk lids and hoods, while the steel bumpers were replaced with aluminum parts.

Specifications

1963 Ford Galaxie 500XL

ENGINE

Type: V8

Construction: Cast-iron block and heads

Valve gear: Two valves per cylinder operated by pushrods and rockers

Bore and stroke: 4.23 in x 3.78 in

Displacement: 427 c.i.

Compression ratio: 12.2:1

Induction system: Twin reverse-mounted Holley 600 cfm four-barrel carburetors

Maximum power: 425 bhp at 6,000 rpm

Maximum torque: 480 lb-ft at 3,700 rpm

TRANSMISSION

Borg-Warner T-10 four-speed

BODY/CHASSIS

Lightweight perimeter steel chassis with two-door steel and fiberglass hardtop body

SPECIAL FEATURES

In true 1960s style, this Galaxie 500XL features a Borg-Warner T-10 four-speed transmission.

The gas cap is hidden by a flip-up lid in the taillight panel.

RUNNING GEAR

Steering: Recirculating ball

Front suspension: Unequal length wishbones with coil springs and telescopic shock absorbers

Rear suspension: Live rear axle fitted with 4.56:1 gears with semi-elliptical leaf springs and telescopic shock absorbers

Brakes: Drums (front and rear)

Wheels: Centerlines, 15-in. dia.

Tires: BFG radials (front), Mickey Thompson slicks (rear)

DIMENSIONS

Length: 199.3 in.   **Width:** 82.4 in.

Height: 54.3 in.   **Wheelbase:** 119.0 in.

Track: 63.6 in. (front), 62.7 in. (rear)

Weight: 3,772 lbs.

Ford MUSTANG

Following its 1964 launch, the Mustang was a massive hit. Creating a place in the pony car market, its sales continued to increase. A modification of a 1966 car was the next step for this almost perfect package.

"...no ordinary Mustang."

"Do not be fooled by its looks; this is no ordinary Mustang. Underneath there have been a multitude of changes. The supercharged engine delivers considerable power, and the modified chassis gives more stability and poise than the original. Great attention has been paid to the interior, which blends well with the orange exterior. You would be hard-pressed to find a better example of a 1966 Mustang."

The carpet of this car is taken from Mercedes and it certainly looks elegant.

Milestones

1961 Inspirational
Ford President Lee Iacocca decides that the company should produce a sporty-looking car. Prototypes are built using a German four-cylinder engine.

1966 Mustangs came as convertibles as well as hardtops.

1964 Six months
ahead of the 1965 calendar year, Ford releases the Mustang. It is an instant hit, sparking a host of imitators from other manufacturers as the pony car war heats up.

The Mustang's first major design changes were introduced on the 1967 model, a bigger car.

1974 After a series
of styling changes, the original Mustang is replaced by the Mustang II. Initially a strong seller, it falls victim to the impending oil crisis and becomes a bloated, underpowered version of its previous self. Sales suffer as a result.

UNDER THE SKIN

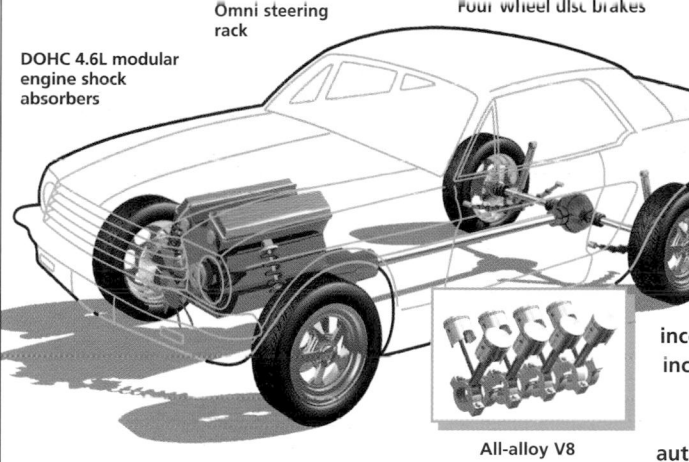

Ömni steering rack

DOHC 4.6L modular engine shock absorbers

Four wheel disc brakes

All-alloy V8

Uprated chassis

The original 1966 Mustang has a simple chassis layout that was adequate for the times, but feels its age now. Many changes have been made in the suspension. Up front, Mustang II parts have been incorporated and a chrome Ford 9-inch axle is in the rear. Disc brakes have been installed all around. Transmission is a Ford AOD-E automatic with a Lokar shifter. The rack-and-pinion steering is taken from a Dodge Omni.

THE POWER PACK

4.6 Liter "modular" V8

In 1966, the Mustang was available with a 200-c.i. inline six or a 289-c.i V8, in either 200 bhp or 225/271 bhp state of tune. The venerable cast-iron motor was considered too heavy for this Mustang and has been replaced by a 32-valve, 4.6 liter modular Ford V8 unit with all-alloy construction. From its relatively small displacement, 281 c.i., it produces 392 bhp with the aid of a Kenne Bell twin-screw whipplecharger running at 6 pounds of boost. This is in combination with a multipoint electronic fuel-injection system and a modern engine layout of four valves per cylinder operated by four chain-driven overhead camshafts.

Dynamite

For some people, the pre-1967 Mustangs are the best of the breed. The lines are uncluttered and classic. When mated with a stiff chassis and powerful engine, excellence is created—exactly what this 1966 example is.

Tasteful modifications have not betrayed the Mustang's good looks.

Ford MUSTANG

If you like the looks but not the performance, what can you do? Build your ideal car, of course. With nearly 400 bhp and a chassis that can handle the power, this Mustang would be your dream car.

Supercharged engine

To get phenomenal performance from the Mustang, a 32-valve, all-alloy 4.6 liter "modular" Ford V8 engine, from a late-model Mustang Cobra, has been fitted. The power has been upped to 392 bhp by the addition of a Kenne Bell supercharger running at 6 pounds of boost.

Tangerine dream

Completing the modified look is the tangerine pearl custom paint scheme. The side scallops are finished in a blend of gold pearl and candy root beer.

Billet grill

A lot of attention has been paid to the look of this car. This is illustrated by the six-bar chrome front grill and the five-bar rear fascia, which incorporates 900 LEDs.

Four-wheel disc brakes

To balance the enhanced performance, disc brakes have been installed. At the front these are 11 inches in diameter with 9-inch ones at the rear.

Custom interior

As much work has gone into customizing the interior as modifying the mechanicals of this car. There are two shades of leather upholstery, cream and biscuit. There is also a wool carpet from a Mercedes, as well as modified 1965 T-Bird front seats.

Upgraded suspension

As with many modified first-generation Mustangs, this car uses the coil-sprung front suspension from the Mustang II. A chrome 9-inch rear axle combines with a Global West stage III suspension system out back.

Specifications

1966 Ford Mustang

ENGINE

Type: V8

Construction: Alloy block and heads

Valve gear: Four valves per cylinder operated by four chain-driven overhead cams.

Bore and stroke: 3.61 in. x 3.60 in.

Displacement: 281 c.i.

Compression ratio: 9.8:1

Induction system: Multipoint fuel injection with Kenne Bell twin-screw whipple supercharger

Maximum power: 392 bhp at 5,800 rpm

Maximum torque: 405 lb-ft at 4,500 rpm

TRANSMISSION

Three-speed automatic

BODY/CHASSIS

Steel chassis with steel body

SPECIAL FEATURES

Even the trunk has been upholstered in matching fabrics.

Budnick alloy wheels are a fine addition to the car.

RUNNING GEAR

Steering: Rack-and-pinion

Front suspension: A-arms with coil springs and telescopic shock absorbers

Rear suspension: Live rear axle with leaf springs and telescopic shock absorbers

Brakes: Discs, 11-in. dia. (front), 9-in. dia. (rear)

Wheels: Alloy, 17 x 7 in. (front); 17 x 8 in. (rear)

Tires: Toyo 215/45ZR17 (front), 245/45ZR17 (rear)

DIMENSIONS

Length: 176.0 in.   **Width:** 71.0 in.

Height: 50.3 in.   **Wheelbase:** 108.0 in.

Track: 58.6 in. (front and rear)

Weight: 2,358 lbs.

Ford **MUSTANG BOSS 302**

Released as a limited production special in 1969, the Mustang Boss 302 proved highly successful both on the road and on the track. The owner of this car took the concept a stage further and transformed a tired Boss 302 into his interpretation of what a Trans Am racer should be.

"...goes where you want."

"Climb into the high-back bucket seat, strap yourself in and savor the competition-style interior. The highly-tuned 302 V8 is lumpy at idle, but on the move it propels the Mustang like a scalded cat, pulling hard in all four gears. Tug the thick steering wheel and the Boss responds instantly, going exactly where you want. There is virtually no body roll through corners and the huge brakes slow the Boss quickly and effectively."

Except for the equipment necessary for competition, the interior is mostly stock.

Milestones

1969 Ford releases

a larger, curvier Mustang with more emphasis on performance. A special limited edition Trans Am racer, the Boss 302, debuts mid-year. Ford enters race-prepared examples in the Trans Am Championship and they finish second to the Penske/Donohue Camaro Z28s.

First-generation Mustangs share components with the Falcon.

1970 All Mustangs

are given a mild facelift with single headlights and a revised tail panel, and road-going Boss 302s receive hydraulic valve lifters. On the track the cars prove more competitive than ever. Boss driver Parnelli Jones and Ford win the driver and constructor's championships.

Ford's main rival in the Trans Am wars was the Camaro Z28.

1971 A new Boss

351 replaces the 302. Ford decides to retire from racing mid-year and no Bosses are built after 1971.

UNDER THE SKIN

Unitary construction

Four-wheel disc brakes

Lowered suspension

Small-block V8

Born to race

Although larger than their predecessors, 1969 Mustangs still have a Ford Falcon chassis with independent front suspension and a live rear axle. This Boss 302 has lowered front and rear suspension for better cornering, plus a strut tower brace to improve rigidity. Four-wheel discs are fitted for safe braking during competition events.

THE POWER PACK

Exotic Boss

Available for only two seasons, the high-performance Boss 302 is perfectly suited to vintage road racing. This car has been tuned up considerably and features a roller camshaft, forged steel crank and connecting rods, ACCEL injection, braided hoses plus a special baffled oil pan and eight Autolite in-line carburetors atop a Doug Nash-modified Hilborn intake manifold. It has a power output of 400 bhp and 343 lb-ft of torque, making this Mustang a serious race contender.

Cast-iron block and cylinder heads

Eight carburetors

Two valves per cylinder

Tubular exhaust manifolds

Highly prized

Road racing is gaining in popularity in the U.S. The Boss 302 is a milestone Mustang in its own right and highly competitive in this form. Consequently, both street and racing versions are very much in demand by collectors and enthusiasts.

Boss 302s are still seen at road racing events across the U.S.

Ford MUSTANG BOSS 302

This one-of-a-kind, pristine Boss 302 road racer combines a high-tech chassis and suspension with some very exotic and rare engine and drivetrain components.

Reworked engine

Standard Boss 302s are rated at 290 bhp, but this one, with its multiple-carburetor free-flowing cylinder heads and exhaust manifolds, is rated at an impressive 400 bhp.

Interior alterations

Although this Boss retains the original high-back bucket seats, four-point harnesses, a Mallory tachometer and Grant steering wheel have been added.

Big wheels and tires

During the 1969 season the factory Boss 302s ran with Minilite wheels. A set of these classic wheels, which have been chromed and shod with modern Goodyear tires, are fitted to this racer.

Stock body

Despite the radical internal modifications the body remains fairly stock, with no spoilers or unnecessary additions.

Lowered suspension

For better handling and stability, this Boss has been lowered with relocated control arms and reversed-rolled rear leaf springs.

Original paint

The policy of keeping the exterior appearance of this 302 as original as possible even extends to the paintwork. It is painted in Calypso Coral, a factory available color on Boss 302s in 1969. The black stripes however, have been added by the owner.

Uprated transmission

A Ford 9-inch rear end with a 4.11:1 set of gears sends the power to the rear wheels. A 5.43:1 Detroit Locker rear end can be installed if required.

Specifications
1969 Ford Mustang Boss 302

ENGINE

Type: V8

Construction: Cast-iron block and heads

Valve gear: Two valves per cylinder operated by a single camshaft via pushrods and rockers

Bore and stroke: 4 in. x 3 in.

Displacement: 302 c.i.

Compression ratio: 10.5:1

Induction system: Eight Autolite carburetors giving 2,850 cfm

Maximum power: 400 bhp at 6,500 rpm

Maximum torque: 343 lb-ft at 4,300 rpm

TRANSMISSION

Borg-Warner T-10 four-speed manual

BODY/CHASSIS

Steel monocoque with two-door body

SPECIAL FEATURES

Eight carburetor stacks poke through the hood.

Chromed Minilite spoked wheels add a period look to this custom racer.

RUNNING GEAR

Steering: Recirculating ball

Front suspension: Unequal length wishbones with coil springs, telescopic shocks and anti-roll bar

Rear suspension: Live axle with multi-leaf springs, telescopic shocks and anti-roll bar

Brakes: Power discs (front and rear)

Wheels: Minilite spoked magnesium, 8 x 15 in.

Tires: Goodyear Gatorback P225/50 ZR15

DIMENSIONS

Length: 187 in. **Width:** 72 in.

Height: 47 in.   **Wheelbase:** 108 in.

Track: 66 in. (front), 61.8 in. (rear)

Weight: 3,209 lbs.

Ford MUSTANG MACH 1

1973 was the final year of the big, original-style Mustang. The pick of the range was the Mach 1. It looked sporty, had special interior trim, competition suspension and standard V8 power. It was one of the most popular of Ford's ponycar range.

"...sporty aspirations."

"A standard 1973 Mustang is a long way from the original 1964 model. It became known as the Mustang that was bigger, heavier and plusher but not really as sporty as its forebearer. The Mach I, with its 302-cubic inch V8 changed that myth. It may not have a sense of urgency to it, but the Mach 1 offers adequate acceleration compared to other 1973 muscle missiles. The com-petition suspension virtually eliminates body roll, while ride comfort remains soft for a car with sporty aspirations."

The Mach 1's sporty theme extends to the cabin, with extra gauges and tach as standard.

Milestones

1969 The very first Mach 1 performance
SportsRoof model is launched by Ford in response to demand.

A matte-black hood section with an aggressive hood scoop were typical trademarks of the 1969 Mach 1.

1971 The Mustang grows
in all dimensions, addressing previous criticisms of cramped passenger space on early ponycars. There is extra space under the hood, too. Among other options, the 429 Cobra Jet V8 is offered, packing all of 375 bhp.

By 1974, in Mustang II guise, the Mach 1 was built for an environmentally conscious market.

1973 In its last year before it was
replaced by the slimmer, more economical Mustang II (fitting, given the approaching fuel crisis), the Mustang is offered in a range of five variations topped by the sporty Mach 1.

UNDER THE SKIN

Front and rear anti-roll bars

Leaf-sprung rigid rear axle

Stiffened suspension

V8 varieties

Competition blas

The sporty Mach 1 boasted a number of tweaks under the skin to justify this description, including a competition suspension package, anti-roll bars front and rear and bias-belted E70 x 14 tires. Otherwise, it shares the standard 1973 Mustang specification: independent coil front suspension, leaf-sprung live rear axle and drum brakes. Options included power steering, power front disc brakes, Cruise-O-Matic or Hurst four-speed transmission and various rear axle ratios.

THE POWER PACK

Two-barrel terror

In the 1973 Mustang lineup, the Mach 1 was the only model to come with a standard V8. The base V8 was the 302-cubic inch overhead-valve unit, fitted with a Motorcraft two-barrel carburetor. It made 136 bhp. For an extra $128 you could choose the 351-cubic inch Windsor V8 with the two-barrel carb and 156 bhp, or the 351 Cleveland with a two-barrel carb and 154 bhp. Among further options was a four-barrel 351 V8. It made much more power and had large-port cylinder heads and a different intake manifold.

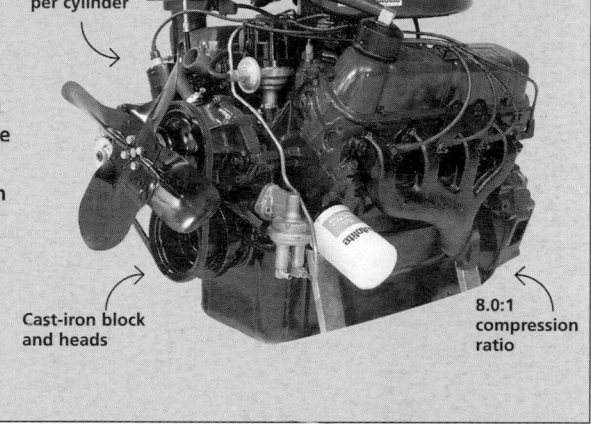

Two valves per cylinder

Two-barrel carburetor

Cast-iron block and heads

8.0:1 compression ratio

Best of breed

Although it was hardly recognizable as a first generation Mustang, the 1973 model, though restyled, was just that. While the Mach 1 isn't the most desirable of the early 1970 Mustangs—the earlier Boss 351 model takes the top honors here—it was still very fast and sporty.

Of all the 1973 Mustangs, the Mach 1 is the most collectable today.

101

Ford MUSTANG MACH 1

The Mach 1 line, which began in 1969, enhanced the sporty qualities of the Mustang, picking up on some of the themes of Carroll Shelby's modifications. The 1973 Mach 1 boasted a variety of enhancements.

Standard V8 power

All Mustangs for 1973 came with a six-cylinder engine as standard except the Mach 1, with its 302-cubic inch V8. Because it had an emissions-restricted output of 136 bhp, ordering one of the optional V8 engines was an attractive choice.

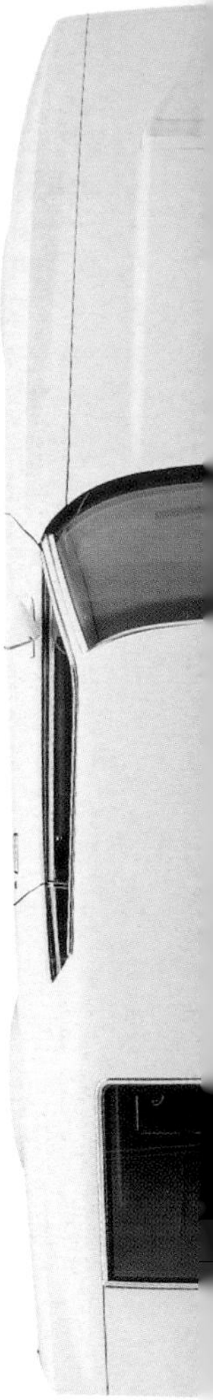

Competition suspension

Justifying its reputation as the sporty member of the Mustang group, the Mach 1 received a standard competition suspension, with heavy-duty front and rear springs and revalved shock absorbers.

SportsRoof style

The Mach 1 was offered in one body style only, a fastback coupe known as the SportsRoof. This is characterized by a near-horizontal rear roof line, in contrast to the cut-away style of the Mustang hardtop coupe. The rear window is tinted on the Mach 1 and a rear spoiler was optional.

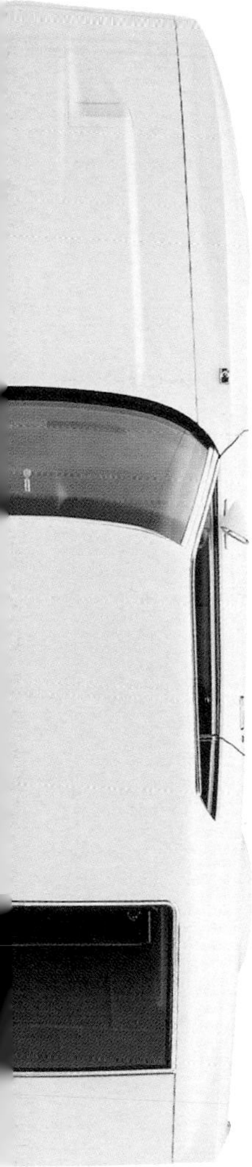

Specifications

1973 Ford Mustang Mach 1

ENGINE

Type: V8

Construction: Cast-iron block and heads

Valve gear: Two valves per cylinder operated by a single camshaft with pushrods and rocker arms

Bore and stroke: 4.00 in. x 3.00 in.

Displacement: 302 c.i.

Compression ratio: 8.5:1

Induction system: Single Motorcraft two-barrel carburetor

Maximum power: 136 bhp at 4,200 rpm

Maximum torque: 232 lb-ft at 2,200 rpm

TRANSMISSION

Three-speed automatic

BODY/CHASSIS

Unitary monocoque construction with steel two-door coupe body

SPECIAL FEATURES

Fold-down rear seats allow access to the trunk from inside. It also permits more room to carry unusually long items.

The hood scoops took different forms on Mach 1s, but they were always present on all models from 1969 on.

RUNNING GEAR

Steering: Recirculating ball

Front suspension: Wishbones with lower trailing links, coil springs, shock absorbers and anti-roll bar

Rear suspension: Live axle with semi-elliptic leaf springs, shock absorbers and anti-roll bar

Brakes: Discs (front), drums (rear)

Wheels: Steel, 14-in. dia.

Tires: E70 x 14

DIMENSIONS

Length: 189.0 in. **Width:** 74.1 in.

Height: 50.7 in. **Wheelbase:** 109.0 in.

Track: 61.5 in. (front), 59.5 in. (rear)

Weight: 3,090 lbs.

Impact bumpers

In 1973 it was federally mandated that all cars had to have 5-mph impact protection bumpers. To try and retain its sporty appearance, the Mach 1's bumpers were painted the same color as the rest of the car.

Choice of hoods

Two hood styles were offered for the Mach 1— one had functional NACA-type ducts the other had non functional duct work. Two-tone hood paint was an option on all Mach 1s.

Ford **THUNDERBIRD '55**

Although there's been a Thunderbird in the Ford lineup since 1955, the sporty two-seater convertible version only lasted until 1957. In those first three years, it had all the style—and almost the performance—to match the Chevrolet Corvette.

"...the real T-Bird."

"They're very rare now, so just seeing one of the original two-seat Thunderbirds is a treat. For true car enthusiasts, this is the only real T-Bird. Driving this 1956 model, one of the last off the line, instantly puts a smile on your face. Yes, it's a little loose and a little soft, but none of its faults matter: its looks and style make up for everything. With the V8 working hard, the T-Bird has the performance to match its style, easily exceeding 100 mph."

The Thunderbird's interior is typical of a 1950s American car—loud, brash and very stylized, a little like a jukebox of the period.

Milestones

1954 The T-Bird first appears at the Detroit Auto Show in February and goes on sale in October as a 1955 model. It's powered by a 292-cubic inch V8 with three-speed manual or three-speed automatic transmission.

After 1958 the Thunderbird became a four-seater.

1955 Changes for the 1956 model year are minor. Cooling flaps are added to the front fenders. To make more room in the trunk, the spare wheel is mounted vertically outside behind the body, making the whole car longer. A larger, 312-cubic inch V8 is also available with 215 or 225 bhp. Round 'porthole' windows are installed in the sides of the hardtop.

1956 Much more obvious changes are made for the 1957 model year with fins added at the rear. The car is also lengthened enough to allow the spare wheel back inside the trunk. The front grill and bumpers are also changed and smaller wheels added. Power increases to 270 bhp, but with a supercharger, the engine makes much more.

1957 The last 1957 model T-Birds are produced on December 13, replaced by a larger, four-seater car for 1958.

UNDER THE SKIN

Two-seater

The T-Bird has very simple construction, with a separate chassis and a live rear axle with leaf springs. Front suspension is independent wishbone and coil spring, with most parts coming from existing Ford sedans. The T-Bird had advanced features such as power brakes and steering.

Convertible or removable hardtop

'Continental' spare wheel kit

Leaf-sprung live rear axle

Traditional American V8

Power brakes

Coil spring front suspension

THE POWER PACK

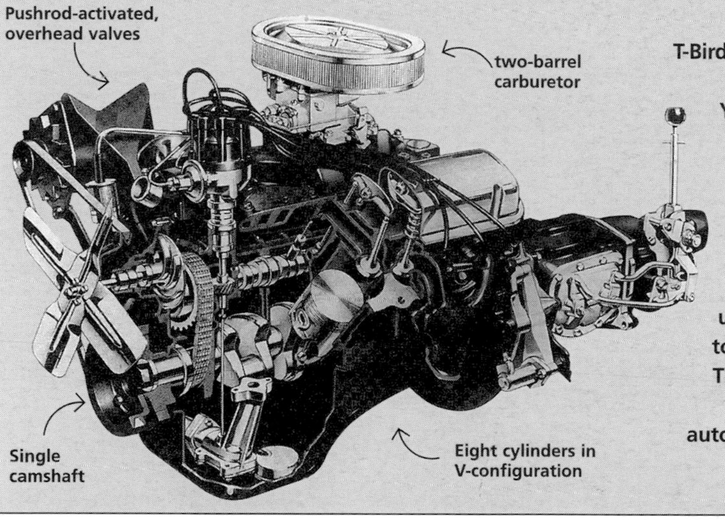

V8 power

Unlike the Corvette, the T-Bird was always only available with a V8: initially Ford's Y-block 256-cubic inch short stroke engine later enlarged to 312-cubic inches. Fed by a two- or four barrel carburetor, it is a classic pushrod, overhead-valve cast-iron unit designed more for lazy torque than outright power. This made up for the lack of gears on the three-speed automatic and the three-speed manual transmission.

Pushrod-activated, overhead valves

two-barrel carburetor

Single camshaft

Eight cylinders in V-configuration

Blown bird

The F-Bird, the Supercharged T-Bird, is the rarest, and now the most desirable, of all the early T-Birds. These are the supercharged 1957 models, with a Paxton-McCulloch supercharger added to a larger version (312 cubic inches) of the original V8 to give 300 bhp, or 340 bhp in race trim. Only 211 were sold.

Rare F-bird used 340-bhp, supercharged engine.

Ford THUNDERBIRD

The T-Bird was one of the smallest and most striking cars Ford built in the U.S. in many years. Ford called it a 'personal luxury' car rather than a sports car. It was never intended to be a serious rival to Jaguars or Ferraris.

Choice of transmissions

There was a choice of three different transmissions: a three-speed Fordomatic automatic or the three-speed manual; and perhaps the best option—a manual transmission with high overdrive ratios.

Cooling flaps

The 1955 models had poor ventilation, so Ford added a flap in the front fenders which could be opened to let cold air into the footwells.

Wrap-around windshield

Like the Chevy Corvette, which came out two years before it, the T-Bird has a wrap-around-type front windshield, a design which avoided the blind spot caused by conventional front windshield pillars.

V8 engine

From the beginning, the Thunderbird had a V8 engine. The prototype had only a 256-cubic inch engine with 160 bhp, but that was enlarged for production and became steadily more powerful year by year. By 1957, the most powerful engine—apart from the rare supercharged V8—was the 285-bhp, 312-cubic inch V8.

14/15-inch wheels

For its first two years, the Thunderbird ran on tall, 15-inch wheels. For the 1957 model year, they changed to 14-inch wheels which made the cars look sleeker.

Stretched rear

The original 1955 Thunderbird is very short, so the spare wheel had to be carried above the bumper. For 1957, Ford redesigned the back of the car to make the trunk longer so the spare wheel could be carried inside.

Open hardtop or convertible

As standard, the Thunderbird came with a bolt-on fiberglass hardtop. The car could also be ordered with a folding rayon convertible top instead of the hardtop, or in addition to it, for an extra $290.

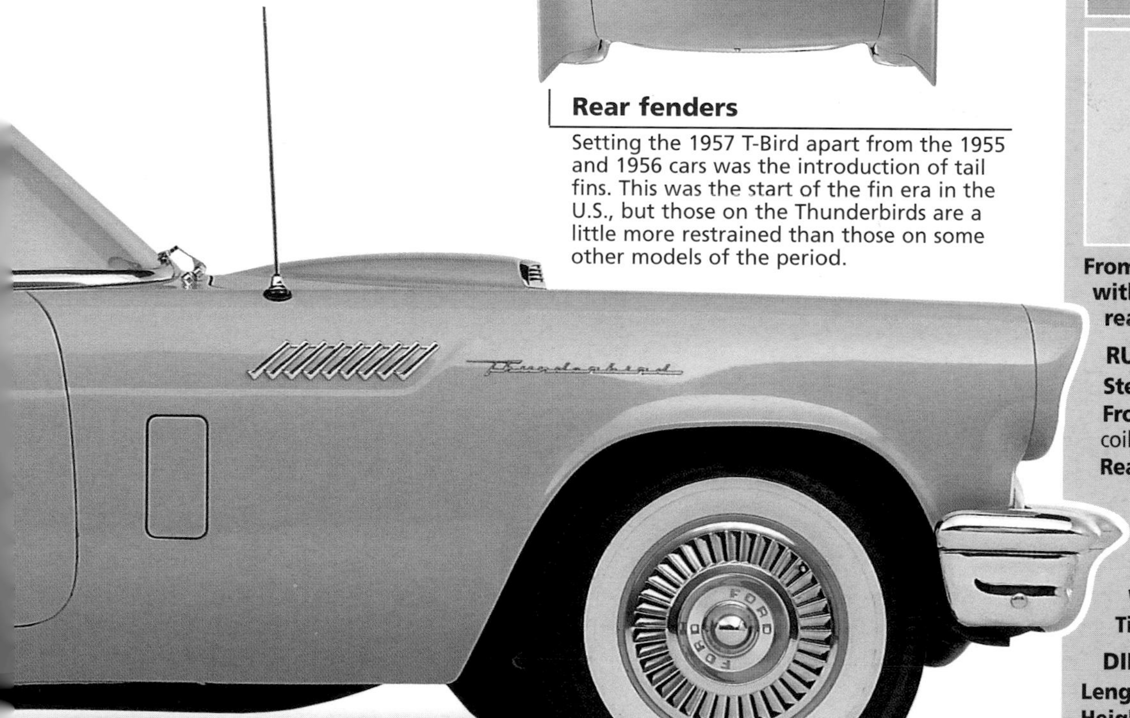

Specifications

1957 Ford Thunderbird

ENGINE
Type: V8
Construction: Cast-iron block and heads
Valve gear: Two valves per cylinder operated via pushrods and rockers from a single block-mounted camshaft
Bore and stroke: 3.74 in. x 3.31 in.
Displacement: 292 c.i.
Compression ratio: 8.1:1
Induction system: two- or four-barrel carburetor
Maximum power: 212 bhp at 4,400 rpm
Maximum torque: 297 lb-ft at 2,700 rpm

TRANSMISSION
Three-speed manual with optional overdrive or three-speed Fordomatic automatic

BODY/CHASSIS
Separate cruciform steel chassis with steel two-door body: choice of removable hardtop or convertible roof

SPECIAL FEATURES

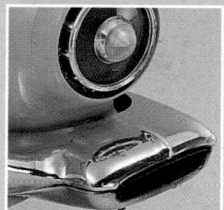

Exhausts exiting through holes in the bumper are a typical 1950s American styling feature.

From 1956, the hardtop was available with 'porthole' windows to improve rear three-quarter vision.

RUNNING GEAR
Steering: Power-assisted recirculating ball
Front suspension: Double wishbones, coil springs and telescopic shocks
Rear suspension: Live axle with semi-elliptic leaf springs and telescopic shocks
Brakes: Drums front and rear with optional power assistance
Wheels: Steel 14 in. dia.
Tires: Crossply, 7.5 in. x 14 in.

DIMENSIONS
Length: 181.4 in. **Width:** 70.3 in.
Height: 51.6 in. **Wheelbase:** 102 in.
Track: 56 in. (front and rear)
Weight: 3,050 lbs.

Rear fenders

Setting the 1957 T-Bird apart from the 1955 and 1956 cars was the introduction of tail fins. This was the start of the fin era in the U.S., but those on the Thunderbirds are a little more restrained than those on some other models of the period.

Ford **TORINO TALLADEGA**

In the late 1960s Ford and Chrysler were waging war in NASCAR. In 1969 Ford revealed its aero-styled Torinos, which cleaned up in the year's stock car racing by collecting 30 victories. To satisfy homologation rules at least 500 road-going versions had to be built. The result was the Ford Talladega.

"...the car was lethal."

"Though sedate looking, the Torino Talladega was the answer to watching the taillights of quicker Mopars and Chevrolets. Its nose was tapered and stretched five inches, and a flush mounted grill replaced the stock Torino piece. In street trim, the Talladega, named after NASCAR's fastest super-speedway, used a 335 bhp 428 Cobra Jet engine with a Drag Pack oil cooler. On the street the car was lethal, but in NASCAR trim it was deadly."

Talladegas have basic interiors, but they are equipped with full instrumentation.

Milestones

1968 Ford restyles

its Fairlane model with swoopier styling. A new top-of-the-line Torino, including a GT fastback and convertible, joins the line up. The latter can be ordered with a 390-or 428-cubic inch V8 big-block engine.

The Torino made its debut as a top-of-the-range Fairlane in 1968.

1969 In response to

the Dodge Charger 500 built for NASCAR racing, Ford releases the Talladega for NASCAR using the 427 engine at first, but switched to the semi-hemi Boss 429 engines after enough were homologated into the Mustang. Ford's aero-aces trounced the Charger 500 and the even more slippery winged Daytonas by winning 30 races that season.

Restyled 1970 Torinos had smoother styling.

1970 A redesigned

Talladega was disappointing in testing, so Ford retained the 1969 cars for NASCAR. Though successful the previous year, the Fords were no match to Plymouth's winged Superbirds.

UNDER THE SKIN

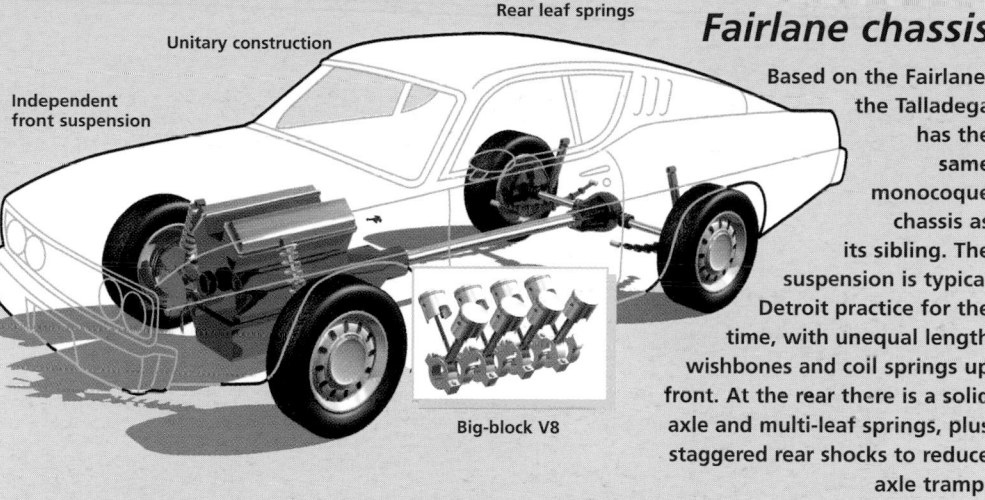

Unitary construction

Rear leaf springs

Independent front suspension

Big-block V8

Fairlane chassis

Based on the Fairlane, the Talladega has the same monocoque chassis as its sibling. The suspension is typical Detroit practice for the time, with unequal length wishbones and coil springs up front. At the rear there is a solid axle and multi-leaf springs, plus staggered rear shocks to reduce axle tramp.

THE POWER PACK

Motown muscle

All production Talladegas are powered by Ford's stout 428-cubic inch Cobra Jet big-block V8s. Underrated at 335 bhp, this engine was Ford's ace in the late 1960s horsepower race. The engines all had 10.6:1 compression, steel cranks, stronger con rods and received fuel from a Holley four-barrel 735-cfm carburetor. While this was the street engine, the NASCAR competition version used the sinister Boss 429 semi-hemi engine that was homologated the same year in the Boss 429 Mustang.

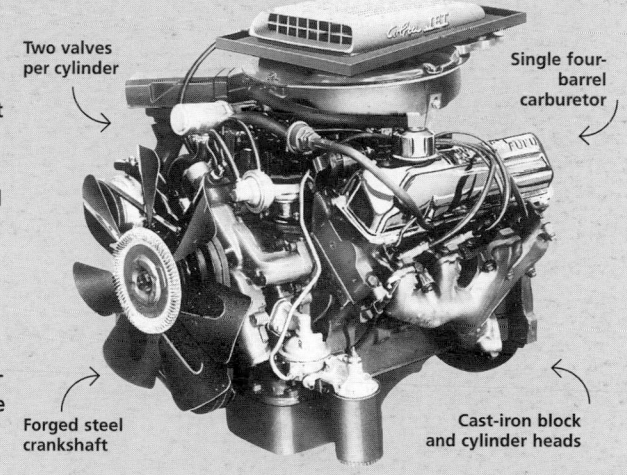

Two valves per cylinder

Single four-barrel carburetor

Forged steel crankshaft

Cast-iron block and cylinder heads

Two of a Kind

While Ford built only 745 Talladegas, its crosstown brother, Mercury, made similar modifications to 353 of its 1969 Cyclones and called it the Spoiler II. Its body was slightly longer and lower to the ground and included a rear spoiler and unique badging.

Cyclone IIs were offered with a 351 cubic inch V8 but a 428 was optional.

Ford TORINO TALLADEGA 🇺🇸

Through the use of aerodynamics and the Boss 429 engine, the purpose-built Talladegas accomplished its mission—to take the 1969 NASCAR championship. Once again, Ford's 'Total Performance' campaign shines through.

Cobra Jet power

The standard engine is the monster 428-cubic inch Cobra Jet unit. It was factory rated at 335 bhp for insurance reasons, but the true output is probably somewhere in the region of 450 bhp. In race trim the engine of choice was the Boss 429 that was homologated for racing in the Mustang Boss 429.

Handling suspension

All Talladegas are equipped with a 'handling' suspension, which basically consists of stiffer springs and shocks plus a thick front anti-roll bar.

Rocker Panel Modifications

The rocker panels were raised over an inch so the NASCAR prepared cars could be lowered while being in full compliance with the ride height requirements.

Traction-Lok rear

Ford's Traction-Lok differential, with a 3.25:1 final-drive ratio, was the only rear gearing available. It makes the Talladega surprisingly capable at high-speed cruising, although all-out acceleration suffers as a result.

Lack of ornamentation

The exterior of the Talladega is very plain and does not have any nameplates. Instead, it carries 'T' motifs on the fuel cap and above the door handles.

Nose modifications

The Talladega was based on the Fairlane SportsRoof but with some aerodynamic advantages. The nose was stretched more than five inches and brought closer to the ground. It also features a flush mounted grill and a narrowed Fairlane bumper.

Staggered rear shocks

Like many Detroit cars of the era, the Talladega has a solid axle and rear leaf springs. Staggered shocks are used to prevent severe axle tramp during hard acceleration.

Lightweight interior

To keep weight to a minimum, the Talladega uses a base interior, with a standard vinyl front bench seat and column shifter for the C6 automatic transmission.

Specifications

1969 Ford Torino Talladega

ENGINE
Type: V8

Construction: Cast-iron block and heads

Valve gear: Two valves per cylinder operated by a single camshaft via pushrods and rockers

Bore and stroke: 4.13 in. x 3.98 in.

Displacement: 428 c.i.

Compression ratio: 10.6:1

Induction system: Single Holley four-barrel carburetor

Maximum power: 335 bhp at 5,200 rpm

Maximum torque: 440 lb-ft at 3,400 rpm

TRANSMISSION
Ford C-6 Cruise-O-Matic

BODY/CHASSIS
Steel monocoque with two-door fastback body design

SPECIAL FEATURES

'T' (for Talladega) emblems are carried in the coach stripe on each side.

All Talladegas left the factory with 428 Cobra Jet V8 engines. In NASCAR-prepped cars they ran the notorious Boss 429.

RUNNING GEAR
Steering: Recirculating ball

Front suspension: Unequal length wishbones with coil springs, telescopic shocks and anti-roll bar

Rear suspension: Live axle with semi-elliptical multi-leaf springs and staggered telescopic shocks

Brakes: Discs (front), drums (rear)

Wheels: Ford slotted chrome steel, 14-in. dia.

Tires: Goodyear Polyglas F70-14

DIMENSIONS
Length: 209.8 in.   **Width:** 84.4 in.

Height: 59.1 in.   **Wheelbase:** 116 in.

Track: 64.7 in. (front), 62 in. (rear)

Weight: 3,536 lbs.

Mercury COUGAR GT-E

Introduced as a 1967 model, the Cougar was more of a refined boulevard cruiser than an all-out muscle car. However, for its sophomore year it turned into a real fire-breather when it was equipped with a 427-cubic inch V8.

"...tremendous torque."

"If you thought that early Cougars were little more than puffed-up Mustangs, the GT-E will undoubtedly change your mind. It does boast upscale appointments, but nail the throttle and be prepared to hold on for dear life. The big 427 packs a tremendous dose of torque and traction is good, thanks to a fairly substantial curbweight and long wheelbase. The Cougar isn't the handling champ of all time, but it won't disappoint."

As the GT-E was based on the XR-7 model, it has a fully loaded interior.

Milestones

1967 Mercury gets its own pony car, the Cougar. It shares many components with the Ford Mustang but rides on a longer 111-inch wheelbase and comes standard with V8 power. Offered in base, GT, or XR-7 form, a total of 150,893 Cougars is built.

The Eliminator supplanted the GT-E as the Hi-Po Cougar in 1969-1970.

1968 Changes are few, but the GT option is dropped. In its place is a special GT-E model, which is essentially an XR-7 with a 427 V8 and heavy-duty suspension. 358 are built before the 428 engine replaces the 427 midyear. In all, 602 GT-Es are built.

The last of the real muscle Cougars was the 1971 429 CJ.

1969 The Cougar is heavily facelifted and the performance model is now called the Eliminator.

UNDER THE SKIN

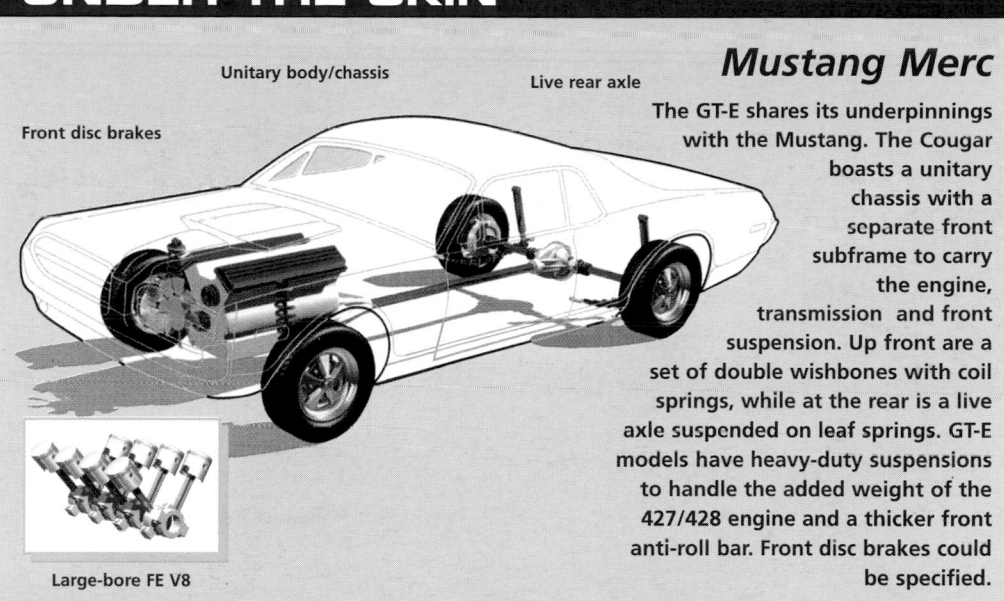

Front disc brakes

Unitary body/chassis

Live rear axle

Large-bore FE V8

Mustang Merc

The GT-E shares its underpinnings with the Mustang. The Cougar boasts a unitary chassis with a separate front subframe to carry the engine, transmission and front suspension. Up front are a set of double wishbones with coil springs, while at the rear is a live axle suspended on leaf springs. GT-E models have heavy-duty suspensions to handle the added weight of the 427/428 engine and a thicker front anti-roll bar. Front disc brakes could be specified.

THE POWER PACK

Fearsome 427

When the Cougar was launched in 1967, the mainstream performance model—the GT—was available with a 320-bhp, 390-cubic inch engine. But for 1968, things got even wilder. The magical number 427 appeared on the option sheet. This was the side-oiler engine, so named because it has a different block to the original 427 with the oil galley mounted on the left side to reduce engine wear. The cast-iron FE-series engine in the Cougar GT-E has a forged-steel crank, cross-bolted main-bearing caps, a 10.9:1 compression ratio and a dual-plane intake with a single four-barrel carburetor. Dual quad setups could be ordered.

Most power

The Cougar GT-E is among the most underrated 1960s muscle machines, but it also ranks as one of the most powerful Cougars ever built. Fitted with either the 427 or 428 engine, it is a terrific buy today and still has a lot of power.

The sultry though sinister Cougar GT-Es were only built in 1968.

Mercury **COUGAR GT-E**

It may have been almost indistinguishable from other Cougars, but the GT-E was in a different league altogether. With 427 cubes and 460 lb-ft of torque, it was arguably one of the quickest factory ponycars in 1968.

427 V8
It was the hallowed 427 that made the Cougar into a real screamer. Its 460 lb-ft of torque put the GT-E firmly in the true muscle car league.

Unitary chassis
Like most Ford Motor Company products of the time, the Cougar features unitary construction almost identical to the popular Mustang.

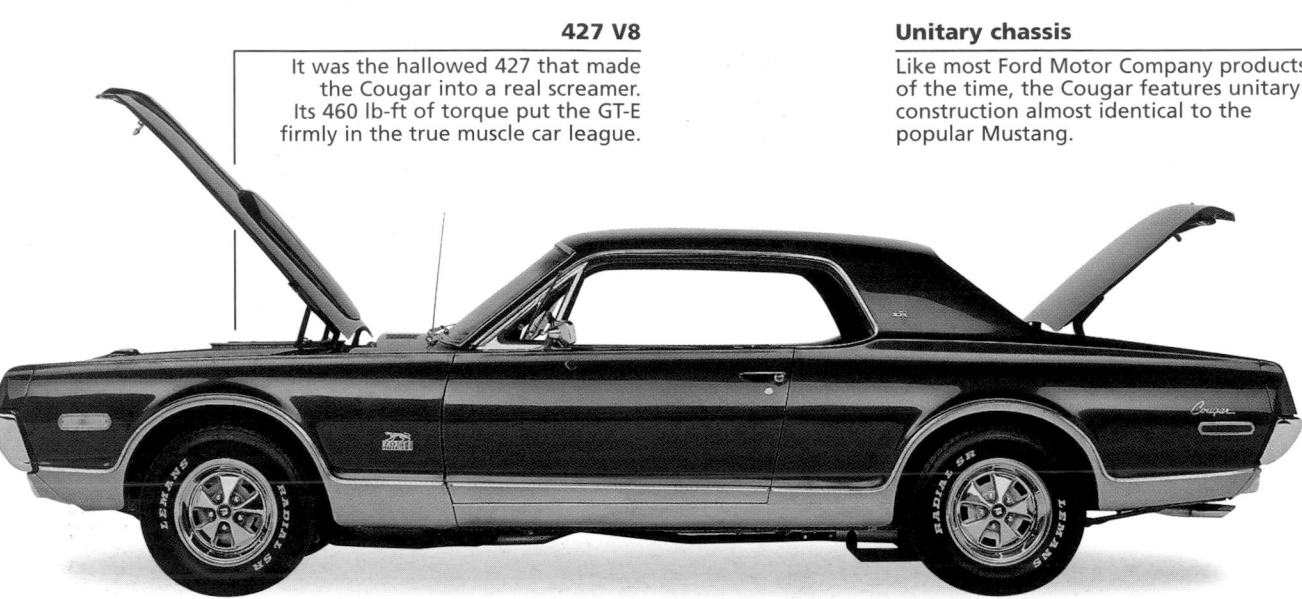

Automatic transmission
Unlike the 428 Mustangs, all Cougar GT-Es came with automatic transmissions in the shape of Ford's proven C6 Cruise-O-Matic unit. Even so, the car could run high 14s with a super tuning and an experienced drive behind the wheel.

Hardtop styling
Although its little brother—the Mustang—had a choice of bodystyles, all Cougars in 1967 and 1968 were exclusively two-door coupes. A convertible arrived for 1969.

Heavy-duty suspension

With so much performance on tap, the Cougar needed a heavy-duty suspension. However, with so much weight at the front, it can be a handful through the turns.

Improving traction

To get the most from the 427, it was wise to order a Traction-Lok rear end with a set of 3.91:1 gears. This car also has traction bars that help to reduce the car's ability to wheelhop during spells of overly aggressive acceleration.

Specifications

1968 Mercury Cougar GT-E

ENGINE
Type: V8

Construction: Cast-iron block and heads

Valve gear: Two valves per cylinder operated by a single V-mounted camshaft with pushrods and rockers

Bore and stroke: 4.23 in. x 3.78 in.

Displacement: 427 c.i.

Compression ratio: 10.9.1

Induction system: Two Holley 652-cfm four-barrel carburetors

Maximum power: 390 bhp at 5,600 rpm

Maximum torque: 460 lb-ft at 3,200 rpm

TRANSMISSION
C6 Cruise-O-Matic three-speed automatic

BODY/CHASSIS
Steel unitary chassis with two-door coupe body

SPECIAL FEATURES

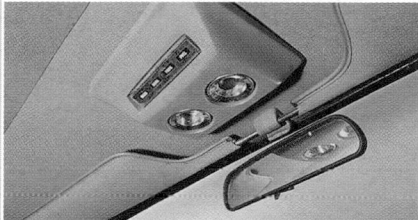

An overhead console with twin map lights could be ordered.

The hood scoop is a distinguishing feature of the GT-E.

RUNNING GEAR
Steering: Recirculating-ball

Front suspension: Unequal-length wishbones with coil springs, telescopic shock absorbers and anti-roll bar

Rear suspension: Live axle with semi-elliptic leaf springs and telescopic shock absorbers

Brakes: Discs (front), drums (rear)

Wheels: Styled steel, 14x6 in.

Tires: Goodyear Polyglas, G60-14

DIMENSIONS
Length: 190.3 in.   **Width:** 73.6 in.

Height: 54.6 in.   **Wheelbase:** 111.0 in.

Track: 61.2 in. (front), 60.3 in. (rear)

Weight: 3,174 lbs.

Mercury COUGAR ELIMINATOR

A true performance Cougar emerged in 1969 and continued through 1970. Available with a long list of sports options, it posed a considerable threat to the established muscle cars both on the street and at the drag strip. Despite its potential, the Eliminator is often overlooked by enthusiasts today.

"...a gentleman's muscle car."

"With its wood-rimmed steering wheel and full instrumentation, the Cougar appears to be a gentleman's muscle car. Starting up the monster 428 engine reveals a totally different character. The big engine demands high-octane fuel and concentration on the open road. Its greatest asset is the huge amount of mid-range torque. A drag racer's dream, it is enough to humble any would-be challenger. It's quick enough to run the ¼ mile in 14.1 seconds."

This Eliminator has base model trim and is fitted with vinyl seats instead of leather ones.

Milestones

1967 Two years after

Mustang, Mercury launches its own pony car, the Cougar. It features a distinctive front end with a razor-style grill and hidden headlights. Initially it is offered only as a hardtop.

Mercury's other 1969 muscle car was the Cyclone. This one is a Spoiler II.

1969 After minor updates

for 1968, the Cougar is restyled the following year and a convertible is now offered. A high performance model, the Eliminator, is launched mid-year and is available with a host of extra performance options, and was painted with 'high impact' exterior colors such as yellow blue, and orange.

The Cougar share the 302 and 428 engines with the Mustang.

1970 The Eliminator

returns for its second and final season. Its body restyling is more refined than the 1969 model. Just over 2,000 cars are sold and the model is dropped after only two years of production.

UNDER THE SKIN

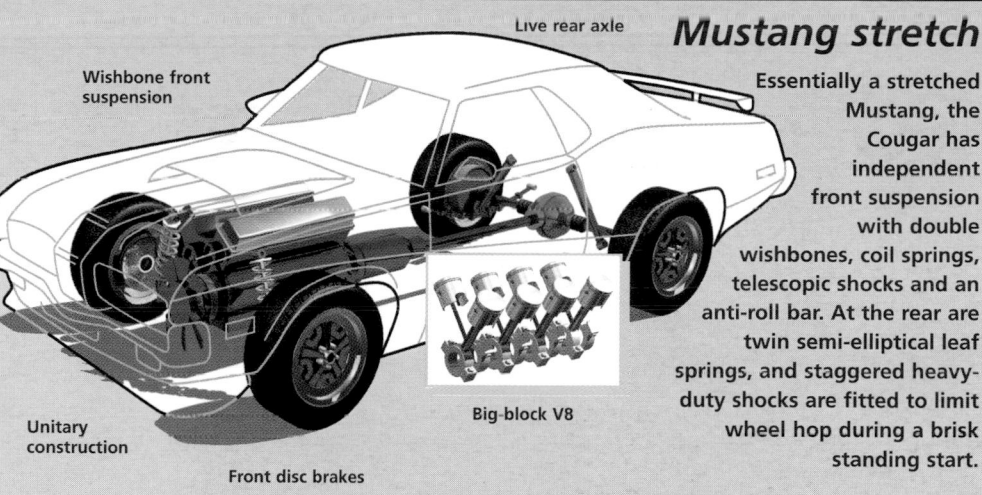

Wishbone front suspension

Live rear axle

Unitary construction

Front disc brakes

Big-block V8

Mustang stretch

Essentially a stretched Mustang, the Cougar has independent front suspension with double wishbones, coil springs, telescopic shocks and an anti-roll bar. At the rear are twin semi-elliptical leaf springs, and staggered heavy-duty shocks are fitted to limit wheel hop during a brisk standing start.

THE POWER PACK

Snake bite

The Eliminator was available with either a 302 V8 or a 428 Cobra Jet V8 (identical to the Mustang engine shown here). The 428 came with or without a ram air system. The engine benefits from a modified crankshaft, stronger connecting rods, and, if the Drag Pak was specified, the owner would receive an oil cooler and 4.30:1 gears. At the time, headers, dual quads, and quadruple Weber carbs could be ordered from dealer parts counters to make the Eliminator even more of a street terror than it already was.

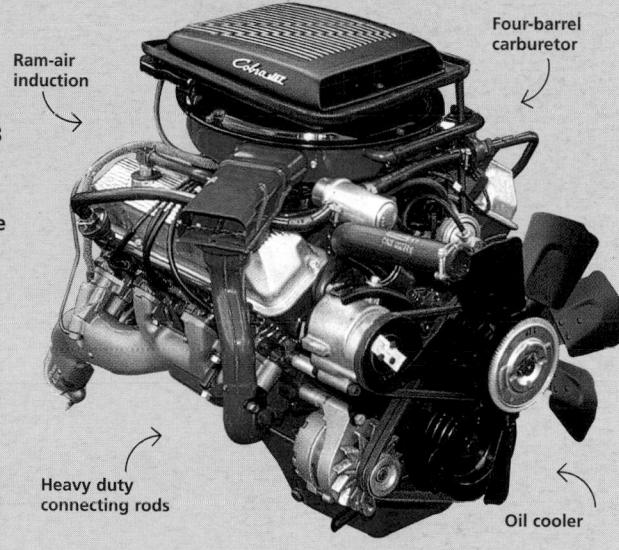

Ram-air induction

Four-barrel carburetor

Heavy duty connecting rods

Oil cooler

Street racer

Since the Eliminator is longer and heavier than the Mustang, it is able get more grip and harness the power from the mighty 428 V8. Though the engine had a factory rating of 335 bhp it actually made closer to 410. The lower rating was to fool insurance companies.

The 1970 Eliminator is offers more refined body panels than the 1969 car.

Mercury COUGAR ELIMINATOR

This is Mercury's version of the high-performance Mustang. More refined than its baby brother, it still keeps the Ford heritage with bright paint, side stripes, spoilers, a hood scoop, and big block power.

'High Impact' paintwork

'High Impact' exterior colors was the order of the day in 1970. The Cougar was available in bright blue, yellow and Competition Orange as seen here.

Staggered shocks

Axle tramp can be a serious problem with smaller-sized performance Fords from this era, especially those with big engines. The Cougar Eliminator has staggered rear shock absorbers to help overcome this problem.

Cobra Jet engine

The Eliminator is available with either the 290-bhp Boss 302 or the more stout 428 Cobra Jet with a conservatively rated 335 bhp. This example is powered by the larger 428, often thought of as one of the finest muscle car engines ever produced.

Interior trim

Although more luxurious than the Mustang, the Eliminator is a base model Cougar and has vinyl upholstery. Full instrumentation is standard and includes a tachometer.

Drag Pak

This Eliminator is garnished with the legendary 'Drag Pak' option, which includes the 428 Super Cobra Jet engine, an oil cooler, and ultra-low rear-end gearing (3.91:1 or 4.30:1). This makes the Cougar one of the fastest accelerating muscle cars.

Restyled front

For 1970 the Cougar received a revised front grill with vertical bars and a more pronounced nose. The tail panel was also slightly altered.

Sequential turn indicators

The rear indicators, which are also combined with the brake lights, flash in sequence when the driver flicks the lever. These are also found on contemporary Shelby Mustangs.

Specifications
1970 Mercury Cougar Eliminator

ENGINE

Type: V8

Construction: Cast-iron block and heads

Valve gear: Two valves per cylinder operated by pushrods and rockers

Bore and stroke: 4.0 in. x 3.5 in.

Displacement: 428 c.i.

Compression ratio: 10.6:1

Induction system: Four-barrel carburetor

Maximum power: 335 bhp at 5,200 rpm

Maximum torque: 440 lb-ft at 3,400 rpm

TRANSMISSION

C-6 Cruise-O-Matic

BODY/CHASSIS

Steel monocoque two-door coupe body

SPECIAL FEATURES

The headlights are concealed behind special 'flip-up' panels.

A rear Cougar spoiler is standard Eliminator equipment.

RUNNING GEAR

Steering: Recirculating ball

Front suspension: Unequal length wishbones with coil springs, telescopic shocks and anti-roll bar

Rear suspension: Semi-elliptical multi-leaf springs with staggered rear telescopic shocks

Brakes: Discs (front), drums (rear)

Wheels: Styled steel, 5 x 14 in.

Tires: F60-14 Goodyear Polyglas GT

DIMENSIONS

Length: 191.6 in.   **Width:** 77.6 in.

Height: 52.8 in.   **Wheelbase:** 111 in.

Track: 60 in. (front), 60 in. (rear)

Weight: 3,780 lbs.

Mercury MONTCLAIR

When most people think of Mercury customs, the 1949-1951 models come to mind. However, this unusual and individual 1955 Montclair illustrates that the later Mercurys have just as much potential for customizing into one-of-a-kind vehicles.

"...a comfortable ride."

"The blue dashboard and white tuck-and-roll upholstery evoke a feeling of spaciousness. Take your place on the comfortable bench seat and start the motor. On the highway the torquey V8 enables the Mercury to do better than just keep up with the traffic and the automatic transmission is perfectly suited to laid-back cruising. The air suspension also results in a more comfortable ride than that felt in many modern cars."

This 1955 Montclair has a number of period touches, like the tuck-and-roll upholstery.

Milestones

1954 Mercury
introduces its revolutionary Y-block V8 engine. Created in response to the modern GM V8s, it features overhead valves and produces 161 bhp, making for the fastest accelerating Mercurys yet seen.

Earlier model Mercurys are popular cars to customize.

1955 Retaining the
basic 1952 bodyshell, this year's Mercury has more angular styling and greater expanses of chrome. A new Montclair is introduced as the top-of-the-range model.

Mercurys were entirely redesigned for the 1957 model year. This is a top-of-the-line Turnpike Cruiser.

1956 Having
proved a success, the 1955 model receives a minor styling update. The Montclair returns and a four-door model is added to the range. An all-new Mercury debuts for 1957.

UNDER THE SKIN

Updated

In Detroit during the 1950s most cars featured a separate chassis and the 1955 Mercury was no exception. This car has been modified with an independent front suspension and a live rear axle taken from a 1981 Camaro. It also has airbags in place of the standard coil springs, and power front disc brakes are an additional safety feature.

Independent front suspension

Body-on-the-frame construction

Live rear axle

Small-block V8

Two valves per cylinder

THE POWER PACK

Holley four-barrel carburetor

Five main-bearing cast-iron crankshaft

Cast-iron block and cylinder heads

Venerable V8

Like many customized cars, this Mercury has been fitted with a late-model small- block Chevrolet V8. This particular unit, displacing 350 cubic inches, was taken from a 1983 C10 pickup. It is of cast-iron construction, with two valves per cylinder, and features a five main- bearing crankshaft. It has been fitted with an Edelbrock intake manifold and a 750-cfm Holley four-barrel carburetor. With these modifications it has a power output of 210 bhp at 4,000 rpm.

Top model

In 1955 the Montclair Sun Valley hardtop coupe was the top-of-the-range Mercury. Today, most of these cars are restored to stock specifications and, therefore, a custom version makes an interesting alternative to the popular 1949–1951 Mercurys.

The Montclair makes an interesting choice for a modern custom.

Mercury MONTCLAIR

The Montclair Sun Valley was eye-catching when it first appeared in the mid-1950s. And with its chopped roof and custom paint, this customized Mercury continues to make a statement wherever it goes.

Chevrolet V8 engine
For practicality and power output this Mercury has a small-block Chevrolet V8 installed in place of the original Y-block engine.

Tuck-and-roll upholstery
Despite the engine and running gear this car has a number of period custom features, including the 1950s-style tuck-and-roll upholstery.

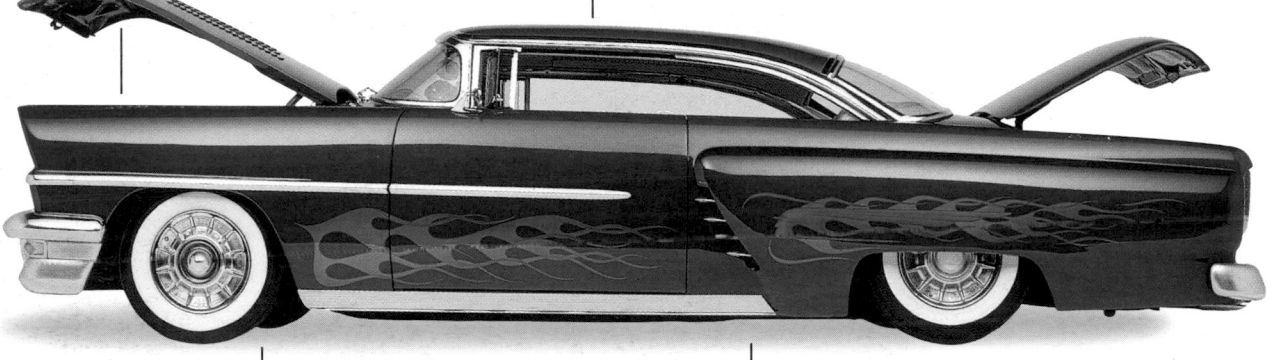

Modern running gear
A Camaro front subframe and suspension have been grafted onto the original chassis. The Salisbury rear axle was also taken from the same Camaro.

Smoothed body
Like most lead sleds the body has been smoothed out, with the headlights and taillights frenched into the body. The door handles and exterior badging have also been removed.

Air suspension
Air bags on the rear suspension give a smooth ride and also allow the car to be raised for driving or lowered for show purposes.

Modified grill

Although not obvious at first, the original bumper/grill has been reworked with additional chromed teeth.

MBT 546

Custom paint

As this car is driven regularly, the body has been coated in tough PPG blue acrylic urethane metallic paint. In true 1950s style, flames have been added below the beltline.

Specifications

1955 Mercury Montclair

ENGINE

Type: V8

Construction: Cast-iron block and heads

Valve gear: Two valves per cylinder operated by pushrods and rockers

Bore and stroke: 4 in. x 3.48 in.

Displacement: 350 c.i.

Compression ratio: 9.5:1

Induction system: Single Holley four-barrel carburetor

Maximum power: 210 bhp at 4,000 rpm

Maximum torque: 285 lb-ft at 2,800 rpm

TRANSMISSION

Three-speed GM TurboHydramatic

BODY/CHASSIS

Separate chassis with two-door steel hardtop body

SPECIAL FEATURES

In popular lead sled style, even the radio antenna has been frenched into the bodywork.

There is even a pair of fuzzy dice hanging from the rear-view mirror—a very period custom accessory.

RUNNING GEAR

Steering: Recirculating ball

Front suspension: Independent with unequal length wishbones, air bags, front stabilizer bar and telescopic shocks

Rear suspension: Live rear axle with airbags and telescopic shocks

Brakes: Power discs, 9.5-in. dia. (front), drums, 9-in. dia. (rear)

Wheels: Steel discs, 15-in. dia. (with 1957 Cadillac hub caps)

Tires: G78 x 15 Whitewalls

DIMENSIONS

Length: 198.6 in. **Width:** 82.7 in.

Height: 51.8 in. **Wheelbase:** 119 in.

Track: 62.5 in (front and rear)

Weight: 3,558 lbs.

Oldsmobile 4-4-2

While the 1968 4-4-2 had plenty of power with its 400-cubic inch V8 engine, this stock-looking Oldsmobile street machine has been modified with a massive 455 V8 that makes the kind of power found only in the limited edition Hurst-modified cars.

"...fast and fun street machine."

"The 1968 Oldsmobile 4-4-2 came with a W-30 360-bhp 400-cubic inch engine with the new, forced-air option. This custom example, however, has a full-size 455-cubic inch Rocket motor with added performance parts, similar to the Hurst/Olds introduced that same year. With a 410 bhp under the hood and a convertible top, this 4-4-2 is a fast and fun street machine. It accelerates like a rocket and handles better than most cars of its era. "

The interior remains relatively stock, but the engine under the hood is a different story.

Milestones

1964 The 4-4-2
nameplate debuts as a package option on the mid-size F-85™.

1965 The standard
4-4-2 engine is a destroked and debored 425 V8 creating the new 400-cubic inch V8.

Early 4-4-2s have more square bodywork than the later cars.

1967 Tri-power
induction is offered for one year and the engine makes 360 bhp.

1968 A restyled
body gives the 4-4-2 a more elegant look. 3,000 modified versions known as the Hurst/Olds are offered with 455 engines.

The 1970 W-30 came with a big 455 V8 and fiberglass hood.

1970 A 455-cubic
inch engine becomes available with Oldsmobile's "select fit" parts. The W-30 455 makes 370 bhp, but its 14.3 quarter mile time suggests this car made more power. These cars had fiberglass hoods and plastic fender liners.

UNDER THE SKIN

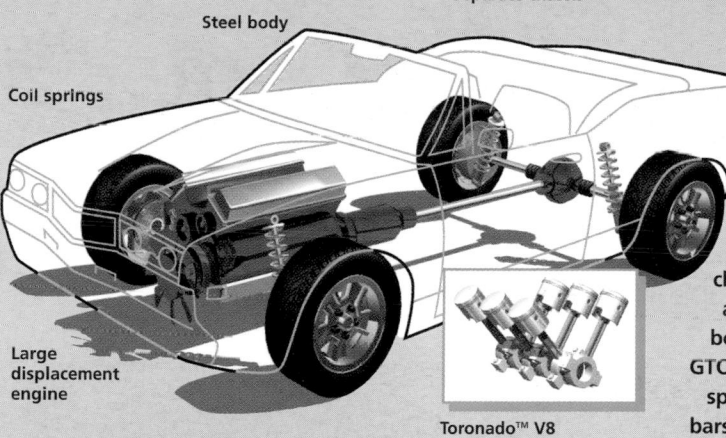

Separate chassis

Steel body

Coil springs

Large displacement engine

Toronado™ V8

One of the best muscle cars

The 1968 4-4-2 has something that many other auto manufacturers' hastily-conceived large-horsepower cars didn't have—a decent chassis. Although it still has a separate frame and steel body, like the Chevelle® and GTO®, the 4-4-2 offered better springs, and large anti-sway bars for an improved ride and handling.

THE POWER PACK

Full-size V8

After 1965 the first '4' in 4-4-2 stood for the size of the standard 400-cubic inch engine. Oldsmobile destroked and debored its full-size 425 V8 engine just for the 4-4-2. For 1966, Olds™ offered a tri-carburetors boosting power to 360 bhp (right). In 1970, its size was increased again to 455. It was the biggest and most powerful engine Olds ever offered. The owner of the model featured here has replaced the factory 400 V8 engine with a 455-cubic inch Rocket motor that makes 410 bhp thanks to special modifications.

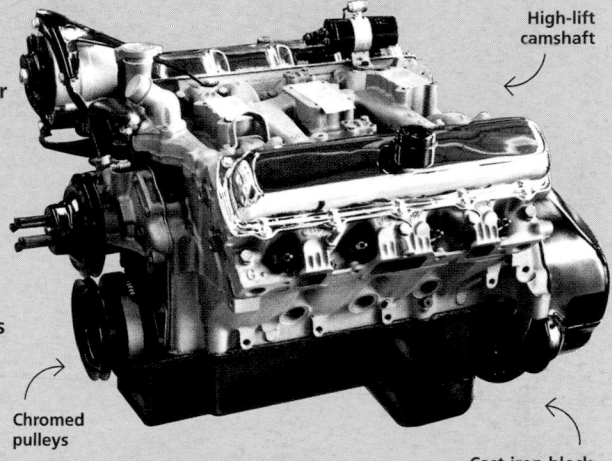

High-lift camshaft

Chromed pulleys

Cast-iron block

Convertible

The new 1968 range of 4-4-2 models updated the earlier cars. At the top of the new range, above the hardtop coupe, was the convertible. It offered incredible value for this type of car, not to mention loads of fun with the top down in the summer.

The convertible top and stock wheels give this 4-4-2 a stealth-like look.

Oldsmobile **4-4-2**

The 4-4-2 was one of the best muscle cars of the 1960s. It has incredible performance and, unlike many of its rivals, it also has the agility and braking to match the speed.

Custom paint

The bodywork has been sprayed with a base coat of Infinity White paint, followed by a clear coat to give a deep, high gloss finish.

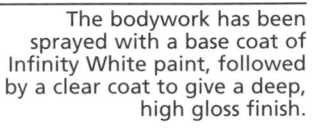

4-4-2 badging

By 1968 the 4-4-2 nameplate had become familiar and sought-after property. Badging in the grill announced that you were driving something special.

Uprated wheels and tires

The 1968 4-4-2 had 14-inch diameter wheels, but the owner of this car has chosen to upgrade to 15-inch Super Stock II rims, shod with Goodyear Eagle ST tires.

Improved cabin

As well as 1970 Gold Madrid interior, this particular car features full GM and AutoGauge instruments and a 'Rallye' steering wheel.

To improve handling, the owner installed a
This means the wheel has to be tur

Heavy-duty suspension

The rear end has been beefed up by replacing the stock coil springs with heavy-duty springs from a station wagon. Modern polyurethane bushings and $1^7/_8$-inch thick front and rear anti-roll bars have also been added to tighten the suspension further.

harp steering

ratio steering box.
when cornering.

Big 455 V8

Although the 455 V8 engine was not offered in the 1968 4-4-2, it was available in a special edition called the Hurst/Olds. It became standard for all 4-4-2 models in 1970.

Specifications
Oldsmobile 4-4-2 Convertible

ENGINE
Type: V8

Construction: Cast-iron cylinder block and cylinder heads

Valve gear: Two valves per cylinder operated by a single camshaft

Bore and stroke: 4.12 in. x 4.25 in.

Displacement: 455 c.i.

Compression ratio: 10.5:1

Induction system: Four-barrel carburetor

Maximum power: 410 bhp at 5,500 rpm

Maximum torque: 517 lb-ft at 3,500 rpm

TRANSMISSION
Turbo HydraMatic 350 three-speed automatic

BODY/CHASSIS
Separate chassis with two door convertible steel body

SPECIAL FEATURES

The interior has been taken from a 1970 Oldsmobile and features Gold Madrid vinyl upholstery.

On this modified car, the exhaust tips exit behind the rear tires rather than out of the back as on the standard 4-4-2s.

RUNNING GEAR
Steering: Recirculating ball

Front suspension: Wishbones with coil springs, shocks, and anti-roll bar

Rear suspension: Rigid axle with coil springs, shocks, and anti-roll bar

Brakes: Discs front, drums rear

Wheels: Super Stock II, 15-in. dia.

Tires: Goodyear Eagle ST

DIMENSIONS
Length: 201.6 in.   **Width:** 76.2 in.

Height: 52.8 in.   **Wheelbase:** 112 in.

Track: 59.1 in. (front), 59.1 in. (rear)

Curb weight: 3,890 lbs.

Oldsmobile TORONADO

Ultraconservative Oldsmobile produced one of the most innovative cars of the 1960s with its Toronado coupe. The bold styling was just a teaser, for underneath lay Detroit's first front-wheel drive layouts. This endowed the Toronado with first-rate handling finesse.

"...fantastic front wheeler."

"The Toronado was one of the most well balanced drivers that came out of Detroit in the 1960s. The first thing you'll notice about this fantastic front wheeler is the lack of any transmission tunnel. Fire up the engine and the muted Rocket V8 revs happily and is an eager performer on the road. The real revelation comes when you turn your first corner—the car really handles. The payoff is a rather hard ride, but its light steering and easy cruising keep you smiling."

Needles and rocker switches fill the dash-board, but it's all clear and accessible.

Milestones

1966 General Motors turns history on its head with its most radical car of the decade, the front-drive Oldsmobile Toronado.

1967 Optional front disc brakes and radial tires improve the package.

The second generation 1971-1978 Toronado was bigger and heavier.

1968 A semi-notchback rear end is grafted on. Under the hood the engine displacement grows to 455 cubic inches, although standard power output falls by 10 bhp.

E-bodies, including the Toronado, were downsized in 1979.

1970 In its final year before being replaced by an all-new Toronado, fixed headlights replace the pop-up ones.

UNDER THE SKIN

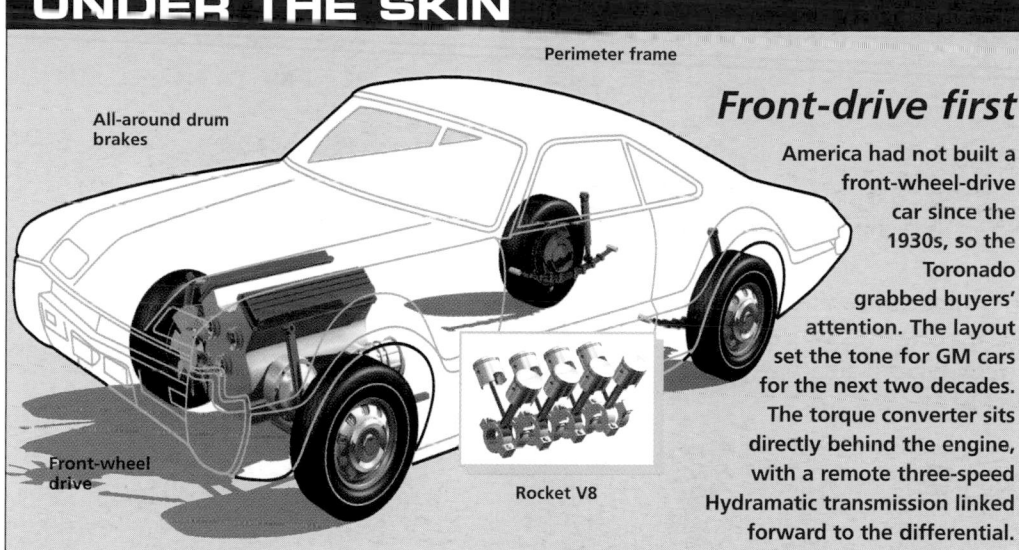

Perimeter frame

All-around drum brakes

Front-wheel drive

Rocket V8

Front-drive first

America had not built a front-wheel-drive car since the 1930s, so the Toronado grabbed buyers' attention. The layout set the tone for GM cars for the next two decades. The torque converter sits directly behind the engine, with a remote three-speed Hydramatic transmission linked forward to the differential.

THE POWER PACK

Full-size V8

Originally, chief engineer John Beltz requested an all-alloy transverse V6 engine in the Toronado, but the GM chiefs knew that the market wanted a V8 in a flagship model. So Oldsmobile turned to the familiar full-size Rocket V8. Standard in Olds' big cars, the 425-cubic inch, cast-iron engine was rated at 385 bhp in the Toronado. Engineers mounted it in a rubber-insulated subframe, resulting in less cabin noise and vibration. From 1968, the engine size grew to 455 cubic inches and, though power dropped to 375 bhp, there was an optional W-34 package with twin exhausts and a special cam, capable of 400 bhp.

'66 Toronado

The original is the best when it comes to Toronados, and the first fastback body-style is preferred over the semi-notchback form adopted for 1968. And unless you find a modified 400-bhp version, the original 1966 Toronado has more power than later cars.

Today, the earlier models are the most sought after.

Oldsmobile TORONADO

Front-wheel drive was one thing, but an innovative engine/transmission layout freed up a lot of space inside and allowed engineers to deliver class-leading handling.

Concealed headlights

In all but 1970 models, the quad headlights are hidden away in pods. These swing up at the press of a button, increasing the sense of drama around the car.

Split transmission

For packaging reasons, the transmission is not an all-in-one unit. Instead, there is a torque converter mounted behind the engine with a two-inch Morse chain running to the Turbohydramatic three-speed.

Beam rear axle

In contrast with the innovative front end, the rear is conventional. The beam axle is suspended on rudimentary single-leaf, semi-elliptic springs. Two sets of shock absorbers are fitted, one pair mounted horizontally.

Bold styling

The Toronado combines European and American styling influences. Its designer, David North, created a clean and dramatic shape dominated by swoopy rear pillars, smooth flanks and heavy chrome bumpers.

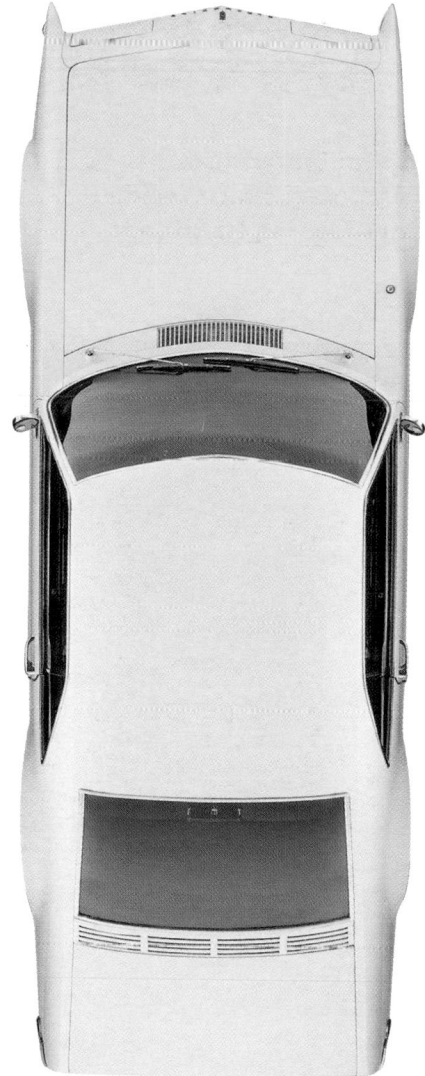

Big cabin
Enormous doors open wide to provide access to a very spacious six-passenger interior. A long, 119-inch wheelbase coupled with the compact drivetrain gives ample room for passengers.

Front-wheel drive
In 1966, front-wheel drive cars were unique to the U.S market. The Toronado was easily the world's biggest example.

Specifications

1966 Oldsmobile Toronado

ENGINE
Type: V8

Construction: Cast-iron block and heads

Valve gear: Two valves per cylinder operated by a single camshaft with pushrods and rockers

Bore and stroke: 4.13 in. x 3.98 in.

Displacement: 425 c.i.

Compression ratio: 10.5:1

Induction system: Single four-barrel carburetor

Maximum power: 385 bhp at 4,800 rpm

Maximum torque: 475 lb-ft at 3,200 rpm

TRANSMISSION
Turbohydramatic three-speed automatic

BODY/CHASSIS
Separate chassis with steel two-door coupe body

SPECIAL FEATURES

Cornering lights on the front fenders were an option on 1967 Toronados.

The heavily chromed rear bumper has cutouts for twin exhaust pipes.

RUNNING GEAR
Steering: Recirculating ball

Front suspension: Wishbones with longitudinal torsion bars, shock absorbers and anti-roll bar

Rear suspension: Beam axle with semi-elliptic springs and shock absorbers

Brakes: Drums, front and rear

Wheels: Steel 15-in. dia.

Tires: 8.85 x 15

DIMENSIONS
Length: 211.0 in.   **Width:** 78.5 in.

Height: 52.8 in.   **Wheelbase:** 119.0 in.

Track: 63.5 in. (front), 63.0 in. (rear)

Weight: 4,655 lbs.

Plymouth BARRACUDA

In 1970, Plymouth turned the Barracuda into one of the finest examples of American muscle and called it the 'Cuda. On the street, powered with the immortal 426 Hemi engine and four-speed transmission, 'Cudas were killers.

"...a brutal torque monster."

"The Hemi 'Cuda takes you by surprise—the interior is plain and dull (even a tachometer was an option). Only the steering wheel hints at anything out of the ordinary. But find a huge empty space and let it loose and you'll see what this car is all about. Thin tires spin furiously, smoke and then grip, hurling the 'Cuda down the strip in anything but a straight line, but at incredible speed and with a wonderful noise to match. The Hemi 'Cuda is a brutal torque monster."

The 'Cuda's dashboard is typically 1960s in style using fake wood vinyl.

Milestones

1964 Plymouth introduces the Barracuda as an answer to Ford's Mustang. The Valiant-based Barracuda looks plain and has little power. The biggest engine is the 273-cubic inch V8.

1967 The larger 383-cubic inch V8 is squeezed under a remodeled Barracuda's hood finally turning it into a real muscle car.

The 'Cuda was built to compete with the Ford Mustang but was not such a huge sales success.

1968 Chrysler finally adds the Hemi to race in NHRA but less than 100 are made.

The Plymouth Superbird showed the full capabilities of the Hemi engine.

1969 New E-bodied shape appears as a 1970 model with the Hemi engine as a production option: E74. The Hemi 'Cuda is the top of the model line which has five engine options.

1974 End of the road for the 'Cuda. The 1970 and 1971 models were among the best performing and nicest looking cars Plymouth ever built.

UNDER THE SKIN

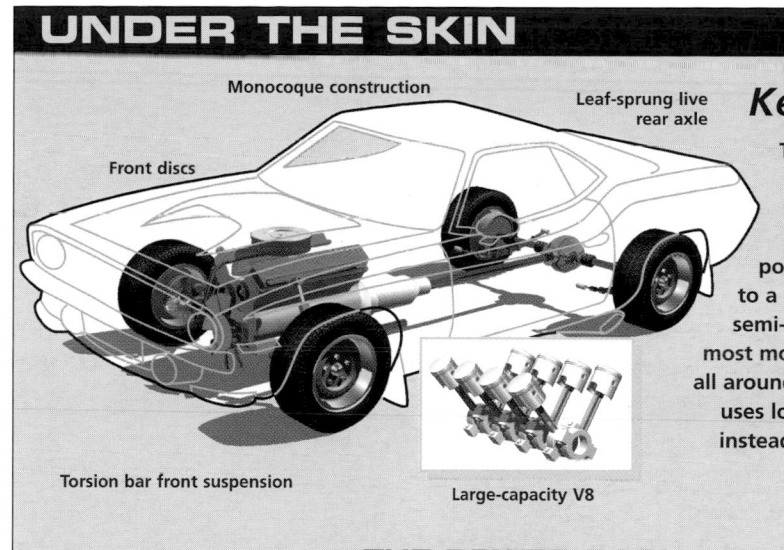

Monocoque construction

Front discs

Leaf-sprung live rear axle

Torsion bar front suspension

Large-capacity V8

Keep it simple

The 'Cuda was about as mechanically simple as you could get, but very tough. Its staggering power and torque are fed to a heavy duty live axle on semi-elliptic leaf springs and most models have drum brakes all around. The front suspension uses longitudinal torsion bars instead of coil springs to save space rather than for handling reasons.

THE POWER PACK

The greatest V8

One of Plymouth's signature options available in many of its performance cars was multiple carburetors. Since the AAR 'Cuda was just that, it received three two-barrels and an Edelbrock intake manifold mated to its 340-cubic inch engine and was referred to as 'Six Barrel' carburetion. The 340 also received a high-lift camshaft and large-valve cylinder heads. Though the SCCA put a maximum engine displacement of 305-cubic inches on competition cars, Plymouth installed a highly tuned 304-cubic inch V8 in its race cars.

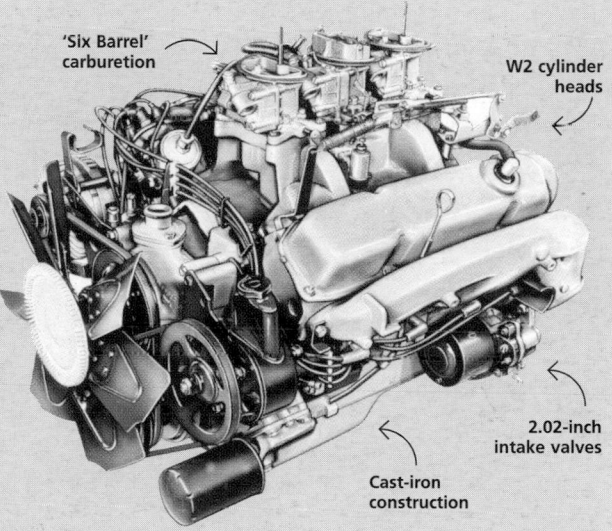

'Six Barrel' carburetion

W2 cylinder heads

2.02-inch intake valves

Cast-iron construction

SCCA racer

Plymouth went SCCA racing with the 'Cuda, building more than 2,500 units to homologate the car and producing the AAR 'Cuda 340. AAR stands for Dan Gurney's All American Racers. All cars had rear anti-roll bar, front discs and side-exiting exhausts.

The AAR 'Cuda was a rare homologation special to compete with the Z28.

Plymouth BARRACUDA

While the Hemi 'Cuda was king at the drag strip and on the street, Plymouth offered an SCCA road racer to compete with the Ford Mustang and called it the AAR 'Cuda.

Hood pin location

In addition to conventional hood latches all 'Cudas, including the Hemi 'Cuda, have the hood secured by two pins running through it. Smaller pins located by wires went through them to keep the hood secured, helping to give the race car look to all the models.

Powerful V8

Although the AAR 'Cuda looks the sportiest, it is not the most powerful. It was built to homologate the small-block engine for SCCA racing and was fitted with a 340-cubic inch V8 with three two-barrel carburetors called 'Six-Barrel' carburetion.

Rallye wheels

The 'Cuda got by with strong (but heavier) steel wheels. On the AAR, they are of the perforated 'Rallye' design.

Torsion bar suspension

Chrysler went for more space-efficient torsion bar suspension at the front where you would normally expect to find coil springs. Tuning this front suspension was difficult and was one of the reasons the race cars were not a success.

Live axle

Cars like the 'Cuda were made to go fast in a straight line, so it needed a heavy duty live axle to handle the power.

Side stripes

The AAR has black 'strobe' side stripes that give it a real race car look.

'Upside down' grill

The front grill is just deep enough to hold the single round headlights, with the chrome strip carrying the turn signals at the top.

Rear drums

Discs were never available for the rear, but because most of a car's braking was done by the front wheels, that was not a problem.

'Shaker' intake

On larger-engined 'Cudas, the air intake mounted on the carbs poked straight through a hole in the hood, moving with the engine to give rise to the 'shaker' name. The AAR has a fiberglass hood with a built-in scoop.

Specifications
1970 Plymouth 340 AAR 'Cuda

ENGINE
Type: V8
Construction: Cast-iron block and heads
Valve gear: Two valves per cylinder actuated by single block-mounted camshafts via pushrods, rocker and solid lifters
Bore and stroke: 4.04 in. x 3.31 in.
Displacement: 340 c.i.
Compression ratio: 10.5:1
Induction system: Three two-barrel carburetors, Edelbrock intake manifold
Maximum power: 290 bhp at 5,000 rpm
Maximum torque: 350 lb-ft at 2,800 rpm

TRANSMISSION
Chrysler TorqueFlite three-speed automatic. Optional four-speed manual

BODY/FRAME
Unitized with two-door coupe body

SPECIAL FEATURES

Flared-end, side-exiting exhausts are one of the AAR 'Cudas trademarks.

Large air cleaner hides three two-barrel carburetors on an Edelbrock manifold.

RUNNING GEAR
Steering: Recirculating ball
Front suspension: Double wishbones with longitudinal torsion bars, telescopic shock absorbers and anti-roll bar
Rear suspension: Live axle with semi-elliptic leaf springs, telescopic shock absorbers and anti-roll bar
Brakes: Discs (front), drums (rear)
Wheels: Pressed steel, 7 in. x 15 in.
Tires: E60 x 15 in. (front), G60 x 15 in. (rear)

DIMENSIONS
Length: 186.7 in. **Width:** 74.9 in.
Height: 50.9 in. **Wheelbase:** 108 in.
Track: 59.7 in. (front), 60.7 in. (rear)
Weight: 3,592 lbs.

Plymouth DUSTER 340

At the end of the 1960s the Chrysler Corporation attempted to create a new entry-level muscle car. This was achieved by combining the powerful 340-cubic inch V8 with a light, two-door version of the Plymouth Valiant bodyshell to create the high-performance Duster 340.

"...a budget street racer."

"The Duster 340, Plymouth's budget muscle machine, is in essence a down-sized Road Runner. The 340-cubic inch V8 provides smooth power delivery and is capable of embarrassing drivers of other high-performance cars. Combined with a Torqueflite automatic transmission, it makes the Duster a perfect low-cost street racer. Standard front disc brakes provide exceptional stopping power, and the torsion bar suspension is extremely rugged."

Like all Plymouth cars, the Duster's interior is simple but very functional.

Milestones

1970 Plymouth

division introduces its Valiant-based Duster 340, with a swoopy coupe body and a high-power V8. With 275 bhp and a $3,300 list price, it is one of the best muscle car bargains of the year.

In 1971 Dodge introduced a Duster clone, the Demon 340.

1971 Performance

is unchanged, but the appearance is updated with the addition of a vertical bar grill, vivid graphics and an optional hood with huge '340' script.

The Challenger T/A was also powered by a 340-cubic inch V8 but it used three two barrels.

1972 New power and

emissions regulations take their toll and power is at 230 bhp.

1974 The Duster

340 is replaced by the Duster 360 with a larger V8 producing 245 bhp. Performance Dusters are retired after 1976.

UNDER THE SKIN

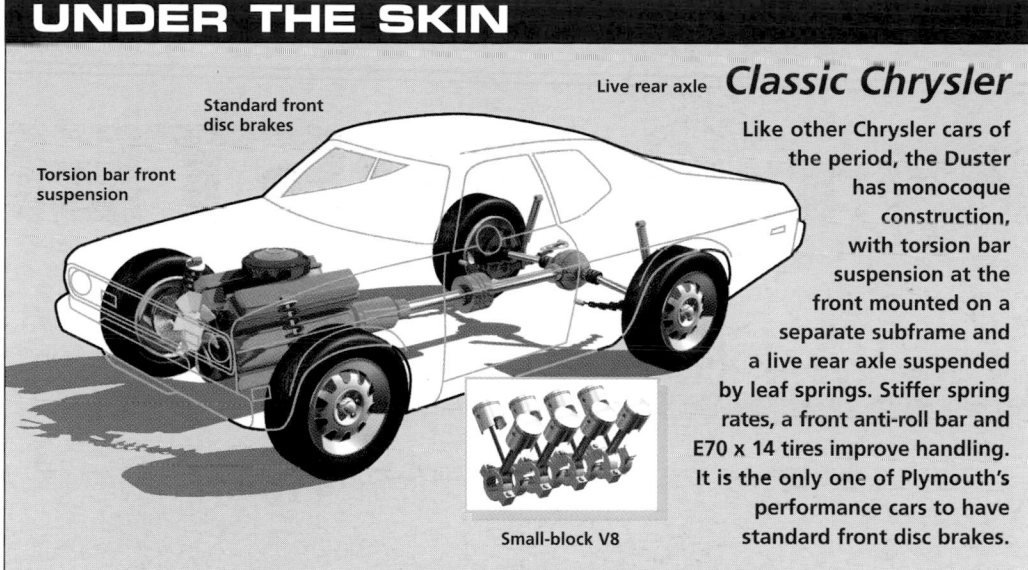

Live rear axle · Standard front disc brakes · Torsion bar front suspension · Small-block V8

Classic Chrysler

Like other Chrysler cars of the period, the Duster has monocoque construction, with torsion bar suspension at the front mounted on a separate subframe and a live rear axle suspended by leaf springs. Stiffer spring rates, a front anti-roll bar and E70 x 14 tires improve handling. It is the only one of Plymouth's performance cars to have standard front disc brakes.

THE POWER PACK

Hi-po exclusive

Unlike the 318-cubic inch V8, the high-revving 340 is exclusively a high perform-ance engine. For use in the Duster 340, it is fitted with a single Carter AVS four-barrel carburetor, has a high 10.5:1 compression ratio—requiring it to run on premium fuel—and a high-lift camshaft. Optional dual exhausts and more aggressive rear gears help to further enhance performance. Factory rated at 275 bhp, the V8 propels the Duster to 60 mph in just 6.0 seconds and gives elapsed times of 14.7 seconds at 94.3 mph.

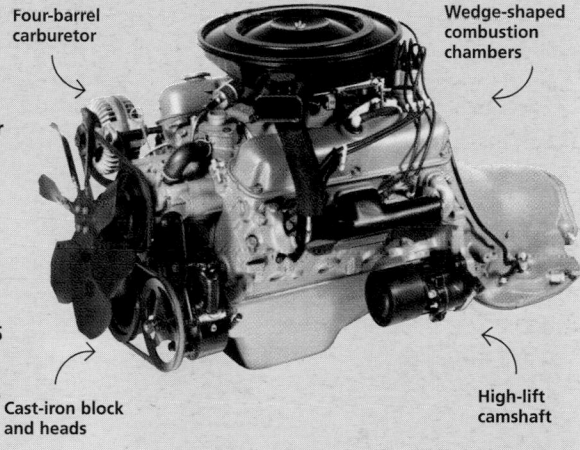

Four-barrel carburetor · Wedge-shaped combustion chambers · Cast-iron block and heads · High-lift camshaft

A good buy

The original Duster 340s are the most understated. 1971 editions retain all the performance credentials, but feature louder graphics. After 1971 performance is noticeably reduced, but today, at around $5,000 a good Duster 340 is an excellent buy.

In their day the Duster 340s were a good muscle car buy.

Plymouth **DUSTER 340**

Although sometimes viewed as little more than a coupe version of the Valiant, the Duster 340 combined light weight, Mopar V8 power and heavy-duty suspension at a very attractive price.

V8 engine

The 340-cubic inch V8 is one of Detroit's most tractable small-blocks of the muscle car era. With hydraulic lifters and a single four-barrel carburetor, it is easy to tune and its 275 bhp was more than adequate for street races.

Performance tires

The Duster 340 came with standard Goodyear Polyglas E70 x 14 tires and Rallye wheels, although this example has been fitted with period aftermarket wheels and later Jetzon Revenger 15-inch radials.

Optional transmissions

The standard transmission is a three-speed manual, but a four-speed or the excellent TorqueFlite automatic were available as options.

Loud graphics

From 1971 the Duster 340 was given larger side stripes with a 340 script carried on the rear quarter panels. Two different hoods were available—one with fake scoops and the other with a large 340 script.

Rear axle ratios

At the rear, the live axle is suspended by leaf springs. Standard rear gearing is 3.23:1, although shorter gears and a Sure Grip limited-slip differential were also available.

Power steering

In base form the Duster 340 has manual steering, although the optional power set-up at extra cost was a sensible choice. Very light by today standards, it nevertheless makes the Duster easy to maneuver, especially at lower speeds.

Specifications
1971 Plymouth Duster 340

ENGINE
Type: V8

Construction: Cast-iron block and heads

Valve gear: Two valves per cylinder operated by a single camshaft via pushrods, rockers and hydraulic lifters

Bore and stroke: 4.03 in. x 3.30 in.

Displacement: 340 c.i.

Compression ratio: 10.5:1

Induction system: Single Carter four-barrel carburetor

Maximum power: 275 bhp at 5,000 rpm

Maximum torque: 340 lb-ft at 3,200 rpm

TRANSMISSION
Three-speed TorqueFlite automatic

BODY/CHASSIS
Unitary steel construction with two-door coupe body

SPECIAL FEATURES

An optional matt-black hood introduced in 1971 includes '340' in large script.

The 340-cubic inch V8 was previously used in the Dart and the 'Cuda.

RUNNING GEAR
Steering: Recirculating ball

Front suspension: Double wishbones with longitudinal torsion bars, telescopic shocks and anti-roll bar

Rear suspension: Live axle with semi-elliptic leaf springs and telescopic shocks

Brakes: Ventilated discs, 10.5-in. dia. (front), drums, 9-in. dia. (rear)

Wheels: Cragar, 5.5 x 15 in.

Tires: Jetzon Revenger, 70 x 15

DIMENSIONS
Length: 192 in. **Width:** 71.6 in.

Height: 52.7 in. **Wheelbase:** 108 in.

Track: 57.5 in. (front), 55.5 (rear)

Weight: 3,500 lbs.

Plymouth HEMI 'CUDA

As a muscle car legend, there are few cars to rival a 1970 Hemi 'Cuda. It has classic, well-proportioned good looks and an engine that is just as famous as the car itself. Despite its relative rarity, some owners feel the need to build themselves a better Hemi 'Cuda.

"...the definitive Plymouth."

"The Hemi 'Cuda is the definitive Plymouth muscle car. It combines a great looking body style with the fearsome Hemi powerplant. Slip behind the steering wheel of this modified 'Cuda and prepare for an adventure. Off the line it is obvious that this engine has been modified. Next you notice that the huge modern tires grip fantastically. Power-shifting into second causing the rear tires to screach reveals this Hemi 'Cuda's explosive acceleration."

This 'Cuda retains a stock interior including a pistol grip shifter and multiple gauges.

Milestones

1964 The Barracuda is launched as Plymouth's retaliation to Ford's successful Mustang. It is built on the Valiant platform and has fastback coupe styling. Top engine option is the 273-cubic inch V8.

The 1967 GTX was just one of Plymouth's many Hemi powered muscle cars.

1967 A more powerful 383-cubic inch V8 gives the Barracuda more performance.

1968 The Hemi engine is finally fitted to a small number of 'Cudas.

The Duster was Plymouth's entry level muscle car for 1970.

1970 The 'Cuda is restyled with Chrysler's new E-body. The Hemi is now a real production option, and 652 hardtops and 14 convertibles are manufactured.

1971 The Hemi engine is retained for one final year. Power remains at 425 bhp and 490 lb-ft of torque.

UNDER THE SKIN

Solid as a rock

Based on Chrysler's E-body, the 'Cuda uses a steel monocoque. The front suspension uses double wishbones with torsion bar springing. The rear is more conventional with a semi-elliptic leaf-sprung live rear axle. This car has Koni adjustable shock absorbers in place of the standard Chrysler units. Disc brakes are in the front, while drums are in the rear.

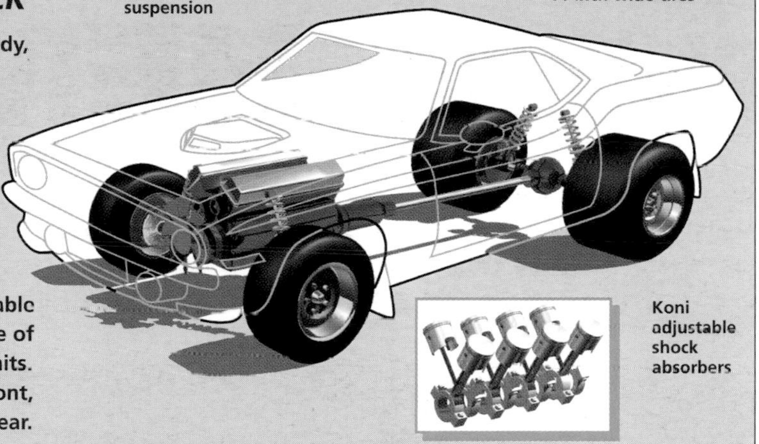

Torsion bar front suspension

14-inch wide tires

Koni adjustable shock absorbers

Rare Hemi V8

THE POWER PACK

Race-bred V8

The ultimate 'Cuda engine is the legendary 425-bhp 426-cubic inch Hemi V8. All cast-iron, the Hemi has two valves per cylinder in hemi-spherical combustion chambers, operated via pushrods and mechanical lifters from a single V-mounted cam. This modified car has a Dick Landy Industries-prepared motor which has been overbored to 432 cubic inches. A 3-inch exhaust system helps make even more power.

Hemispherical combustion chambers

Two valves per cylinder

Forged steel crankshaft

All cast-iron construction

King 'Cuda

Of all the Barracuda range, the 1970 Hemi 'Cuda is the pick of the bunch. Its race-bred engine and rarity make it a real collector's piece, popular with purists and performance freaks alike. Not many are modified as they command higher prices in stock condition.

This car is finished in the original factory color of Lime Light.

Plymouth **HEMI 'CUDA**

Lime Light green was only one of the factory optioned 'High Impact' colors available for the 1970 'Cuda. If you have an engine as powerful as this one, why not have a paint scheme that's equally outrageous?

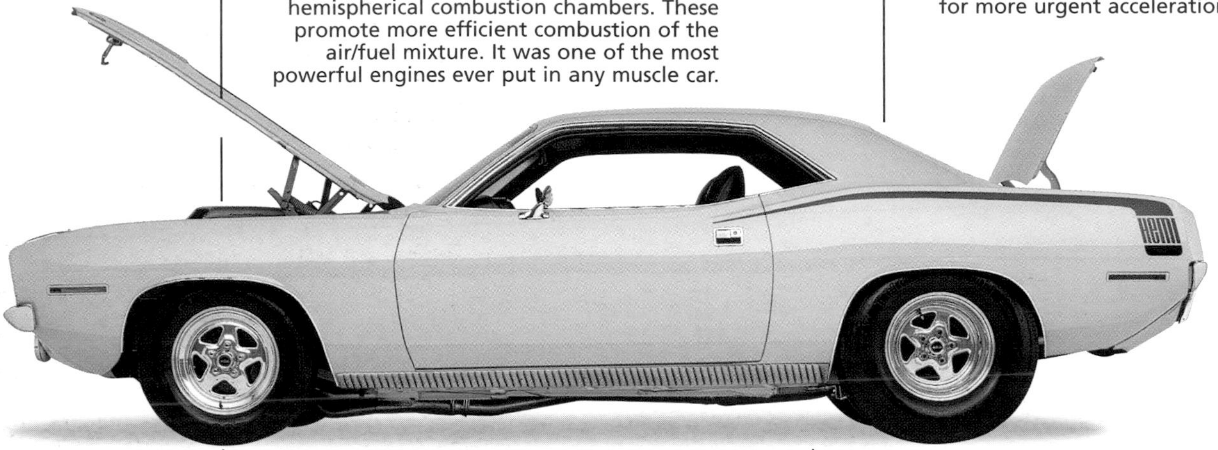

Hemi V8

The Hemi V8 was so called because of its hemispherical combustion chambers. These promote more efficient combustion of the air/fuel mixture. It was one of the most powerful engines ever put in any muscle car.

Low ratio back axle

The lowest standard axle ratio available was 4.10:1. This car has an even lower 4.56:1 ratio axle for more urgent acceleration.

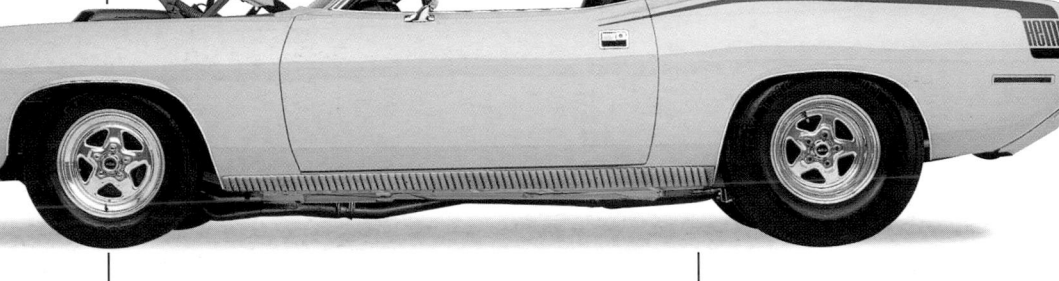

Torsion bar front suspension

The 'Cuda uses double wishbone front suspension sprung by longitudinally-mounted torsion bars. Adjustable Koni shock absorbers are used on this car.

Drag racing tires and wheels

For looks and performance, huge 14-inch wide Weld Racing Pro-Star alloy wheels and super-sticky Mickey Thompson tires have been added to this wild Hemi 'Cuda.

Hardtop body

This, like most Hemi 'Cudas, has a two-door hardtop body. There were only 14 Hemi convertibles made in 1970.

Hood-retaining pins

These race-style hood-retaining pins were actually factory fitted with the shaker hood which came as standard equipment on the Hemi 'Cuda.

Custom tail pipes

Even with the free-flow system fitted to this car, the owner has managed to retain the neat feature of having the twin tail pipes exiting through the rear valance.

Limited-slip differential

The 'Cuda has a Chrysler 'Sure-Grip' limited-slip differential as standard equipment.

Specifications
1971 Plymouth Hemi 'Cuda

ENGINE

Type: V8

Construction: Cast-iron block and heads

Valve gear: Two valves per cylinder actuated by a single camshaft via mechanical lifters and pushrods

Bore and stroke: 4.25 in. x 3.75 in.

Displacement: 432 c.i.

Compression ratio: 10.25:1

Induction system: Twin Carter AFB four-barrel carburetors

Maximum power: 620 bhp at 6,500 rpm

Maximum torque: 655 lb-ft at 5,100 rpm

TRANSMISSION

Chrysler A-833 four-speed manual

BODY/CHASSIS

Steel monocoque two-door coupe body

SPECIAL FEATURES

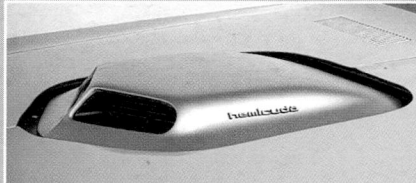

This Hemi 'Cuda has the popular shaker hood. The Shaker was often a different color from the bodywork.

The most obvious change from stock on this car is the enormous rear wheels and tires.

RUNNING GEAR

Steering: Recirculating ball

Front suspension: Double wishbones with longitudinal torsion bars, Koni adjustable telescopic shock absorbers and anti-roll bar

Rear suspension: Live axle with semi-elliptic leaf springs, Koni adjustable shock absorbers

Brakes: Discs (front), drums (rear)

Wheels: Weld Racing Pro-Star, 15 x 7 (front), 15 x 14 (rear)

Tires: P225/70R-15 General (front), 18.5-31 Mickey Thompson (rear)

DIMENSIONS

Length: 186.7 in.   **Width:** 74.9 in.

Height: 50.9 in.   **Wheelbase:** 108 in.

Track: 59.7 in. (front), 60.7 in. (rear)

Weight: 3,945 lbs.

Plymouth ROAD RUNNER

As a no-frills, budget-priced muscle car, the Road Runner was very successful, combining cartoon character personality and powerful engines. Expected to sell just 2,500 in its first year, nearly 45,000 Road Runners actually made it to the street.

"...neck-snapping assault."

"Although it is based on the stock model, this Road Runner feels fantastic. The instrumentation has been swapped for something straight out of Silicon Valley, priming you for an intergalactic performance experience. The soundtrack is really something special, with the V8 amplified through the huge three-inch exhaust. Put your foot down and you're catapulted to 60 mph in around five seconds, a neck-snapping assault that sees the tires smoking right down the asphalt."

This car has been refitted with a high-tech dashboard and digital instruments to give it a futuristic look.

Milestones

1968 The Road Runner is launched

in pillared coupe form. A pillarless hardtop coupe joins the range later in the year. The standard engine is the 383-cubic inch V8, but Chrysler's legendary 425-bhp 426-cubic inch Hemi is available as an option.

The Superbird was the rarest Road Runner variant and a successful NASCAR racer.

1969 More standard equipment is listed for

1969, and a new convertible body style is added as an option.

1971 Road Runners offered a more streamlined look.

1970 In the Road Runner's last year,

the 440 engine is offered as an option and with three two-barrel carbs would produce 375 bhp. The stunning 'winged warrior' Superbird, with Hemi engine and a special aerodynamic body kit, is also launched. The Road Runner name would live on in the next generation Satellite series, however. The most powerful 1971 model has the rare 426 Hemi and only a few were made.

UNDER THE SKIN

Simple but strong

The Road Runner was based on the 1968 Plymouth Belvedere which is built on the B-body platform. Other cars in this line included the stripped down Satellite and outrageous GTX. In standard form, the Road Runner was fairly conventional, but if optioned with a 426 or 440 V8 engine, four-speed transmission, and a performance axle ratio, these rather mundane cars became muscular street screamers.

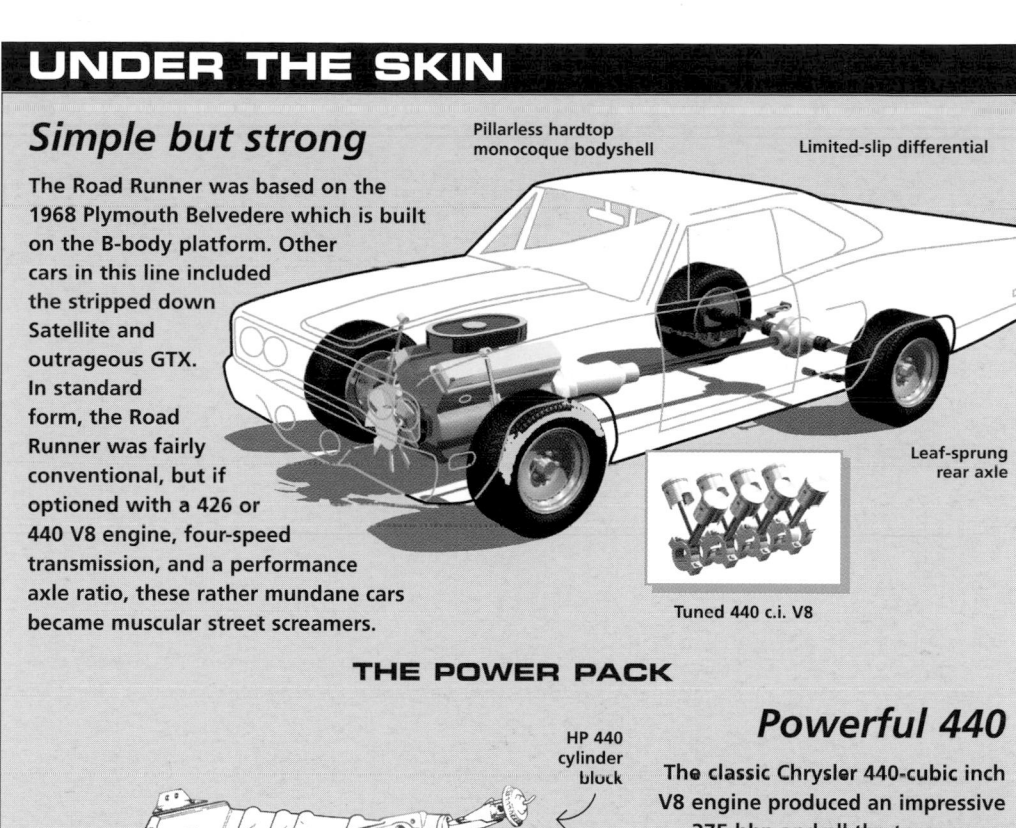

Pillarless hardtop monocoque bodyshell

Limited-slip differential

Leaf-sprung rear axle

Tuned 440 c.i. V8

THE POWER PACK

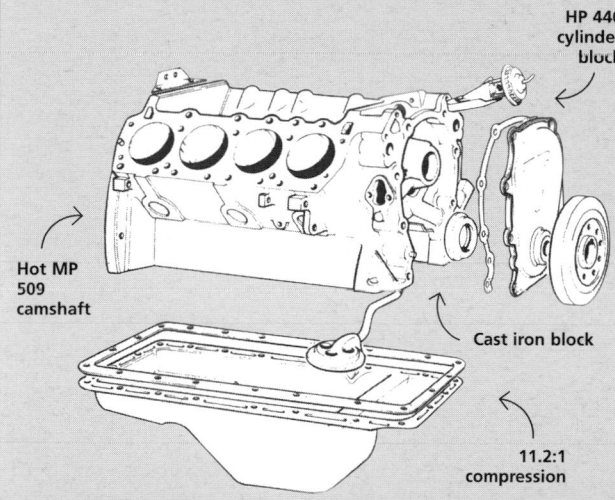

HP 440 cylinder block

Hot MP 509 camshaft

Cast iron block

11.2:1 compression

Powerful 440

The classic Chrysler 440-cubic inch V8 engine produced an impressive 375 bhp and all the torque you could ever need, even in standard form. This modified engine has 11.2:1 compression, a hot MP 509 camshaft, ported and polished 906 heads, high-flow headers and a three-inch exhaust. Other performance features include electronic ignition and an electric fuel pump. This all adds up to a big punch, delivered with the reliability that most exotic cars could only dream of.

Hemi hardtop

With the optional 425-bhp 426-Hemi engine, the Road Runner was a full-blooded icon from the era of muscle cars. With hemispherical combustion chambers, high-lift cam, and dual Carter four-barrel carbs, it is able to run the ¼ mile in a tire-shredding 13.5 seconds.

The ultimate Road Runner has a 425-bhp Hemi motor and a hardtop body.

Plymouth ROAD RUNNER

With a 'meep meep' from its horn and decorated with decals of the famous Warner Brothers cartoon character, the Road Runner had a touch of humor as well as extreme performance.

Upgraded transmission

Chrysler's 727 TorqueFlite transmission was one of the best automatics during the 1960s. It could handle the power of any engine Chrysler had. This Road Runner is equipped with one that has been upgraded even further.

Digital instrumentation

The Road Runner left the factory with stock gauges, but the owner of this car has replaced these with state-of-the-art digital electronics.

Raked suspension

The Road Runner had a torsion bar front end and leaf-sprung rear. The rear air shocks fitted to this car have been pumped up to raise the rear and the torsion bar front has been dropped to give an aggressive nose-down stance.

Crazy paint

The original factory color of this car was Plum Crazy. It has been resprayed in DuPont Centari, mixing yellow with DuPont clear coat. In addition, the 'dust trail' side decal has been deleted, the front grill has been blacked out, and all the windows have been dark-tinted.

Hardtop style

The pillarless hardtop was available from mid-1968, but a convertible option soon followed.

Wide wheels, fat rubber

Cornering power is improved by the addition of 8.5-inch wide wheels and matching high-performance tires.

Road Runner decals

In a tie-in with Warner Brothers, Plymouth decorated the car with decals of the Road Runner and Wile E. Coyote cartoon characters.

Specifications
1970 Plymouth Road Runner

ENGINE

Type: V8

Construction: Cast iron cylinder block and ported cylinder heads

Valve gear: Two in-line overhead valves per cylinder operated by a single camshaft via pushrods and rockers

Bore and stroke: 4.32 in. x 3.75 in.

Displacement: 440 c.i.

Compression ratio: 11.2:1

Induction system: Single four-barrel carburetor

Maximum power: 440 bhp at 5,500 rpm

Maximum torque: 500 lb-ft at 4,000 rpm

TRANSMISSION

727 TorqueFlite three-speed automatic

BODY/ CHASSIS

Monocoque two-door coupe body

SPECIAL FEATURES

The Road Runner's horn produces a 'meep meep' sound like the cartoon character after which it was named.

This modified 440-cubic inch V8 engine produces an extra 65 bhp.

RUNNING GEAR

Steering: Recirculating ball

Front suspension: Wishbones with longitudinal torsion bars, leaf springs and telescopic shocks

Rear suspension: Rigid axle with semi-elliptic springs and shocks

Brakes: Discs front, drums rear

Wheels: American Racing, 15-in. dia.

Tires: 295/50 R15

DIMENSIONS

Length: 202.7 in. **Width:** 76.4 in.

Height: 57.4 in. **Wheelbase:** 116 in.

Track: 59.5 in. (front), 59.2 in. (rear)

Weight: 3,475 lbs.

Plymouth SUPERBIRD

Developed from the budget Road Runner coupe, the Superbird was designed to defeat Ford's Talladegas in NASCAR superspeedway races. Shortly after Plymouth's powerful rocket appeared, NASCAR had changed the rules, and Superbirds were only allowed to race the 1970 season.

" ...NASCAR racing warrior."

"Plymouth built more than 1,935 Superbirds as a follow up to Dodge's less-than-victorious 1969 Daytonas that were designed to slaughter Ford's Talladegas. The strikingly similar looking Superbird proved to be a NASCAR racing warrior. The aluminum wing, flush mounted rear window, Hemi engine, and 18-inch metal nose cone all added up to victory in 1970. In race trim at speeds in excess of 190 mph, the Superbird's nose cone actually added more weight to the front wheels, while the rear wing had to be properly adjusted or the rear tires would wear prematurely."

Stock Superbirds had typical Plymouth interiors with only the necessary gauges, console and shifter.

Milestones

1963 Chrysler decides
to take on Ford in NASCAR. As owners of Plymouth and Dodge, they had the 426-cubic inch Hemi V8 engine, whose power should have been enough to guarantee supremacy.

1964–68 Power alone
is not enough. On stock car ovals, Ford's supremacy continues because their cars have better aerodynamics.

1969 Dodge Charger Daytona appears with a rear wing giving downforce to keep the car on the track at 200 mph speeds. They win 18 NASCAR races this year. Unfortunately, Ford takes home more than 30.

The Superbirds proved their worth on the superspeedways.

1970 Superbird has better aerodynamics than the Dodge Charger and wins 21 races (including the Daytona 500) and beating Ford. Not very many people liked its unusual styling, so many were stripped of their wings and nose cones and turned back into Road Runners just so Plymouth could sell them.

1971 NASCAR rules,
designed to keep racing equal, impose a 25 percent engine volume restriction on rear-winged cars, which spells the end of the Superbird in competition.

UNDER THE SKIN

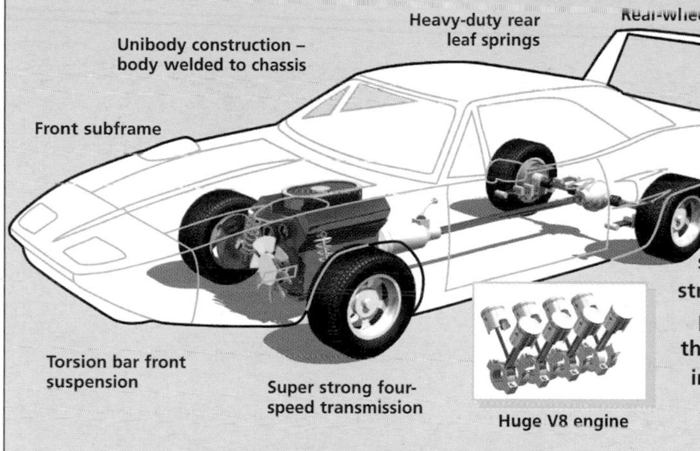

Heavy-duty rear leaf springs

Rear-wheel drive

Unibody construction – body welded to chassis

Front subframe

Torsion bar front suspension

Super strong four-speed transmission

Huge V8 engine

Beefed up

Racing Superbirds use the Chrysler 426 Hemi engine with close-ratio, four-speed manual transmission and Hurst shifter. All mechanical parts are strengthened to handle the extra power. Creative Industries built the aerodynamic nose and tail to improve the car's aerodynamics. It uses unibody construction—body welded to chassis.

THE POWER PACK

More horsepower inch for inch

The Hemi—so called because the combustion chamber (the area where the fuel is actually burned) is hemispherical—was the first mass-produced engine of its type in America. The Hemi head promoted even burning and more room for bigger valves (to get more fuel and air in). It also produced more horsepower per cubic inch than any other design, and forced Chevy and Ford to think about copies. Finally, it was the victim of NASCAR rule changes.

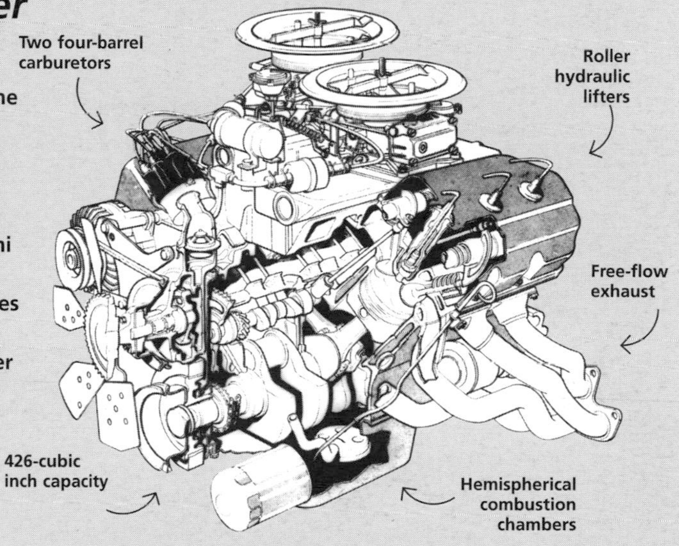

Two four-barrel carburetors

Roller hydraulic lifters

Free-flow exhaust

426-cubic inch capacity

Hemispherical combustion chambers

Vinyl Top

Did you ever notice that all Superbirds had vinyl tops? Plymouth was in a hurry to homologate these cars for NASCAR racing. Instead of properly doing the body work around the flush mounted rear window, it just hid the rough body work with a vinyl top.

The fender scoops cover a cut out giving better tire clearance at high speeds.

Plymouth SUPERBIRD

The Superbird could achieve over 200 mph on the race track using the vital downforce generated by the huge rear wing. Even the tamer street version could easily reach 140 mph.

Roll cage

The NASCAR version used a tubular roll cage welded to the frame that stiffened it tremendously as well as protected the driver at 200 mph.

Rear suspension

Asymmetric rear leaf springs (the front third was stiffer than the rear two-thirds) helped locate the rear axle.

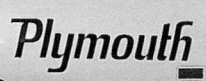

Four-speed transmission

Heavy-duty four-speed Chrysler model 883 was the strongest transmission available at the time.

Standard steel wheels

Steel wheels are still standard in NASCAR—wider 9.5 inch x 15 inch are used now, 15 inch x 7 inch when the Superbird ran. All NASCAR tires then were bias ply with inner tubes.

Live rear axle

Dana-built rear axle was originally intended for a medium-duty truck. Even in drag racing, the mighty Hemi could break it.

High-mounted rear wing

The rear wing provided downforce at the rear. Its angle was adjustable—too much and the increased force would shred the tires.

Front suspension

Front torsion bars resulted in better front suspension than competitors.

Cowl induction

Carburetor intake air was picked up from the high-pressure area at the base of the windshield—called cowl induction.

Aerodynamic nose

The nose was designed to lower drag and increase top speed while adding downforce—it actually put more weight on the front as speed increased.

Specifications
1970 Plymouth Superbird

ENGINE

Type: Hemi V8
Construction: Cast-iron block and heads; hemispherical combustion chambers
Valve gear: Two valves per cylinder operated by single block-mounted camshaft
Bore and stroke: 4.25 in. x 3.74 in.
Displacement: 426 c.i.
Compression ratio: 12:1
Induction system: Two four-barrel carbs, aluminum manifold
Maximum power: 425 bhp at 5,000 rpm
Maximum torque: 490 lb-ft at 4,000 rpm

TRANSMISSION

Torqueflite three-speed auto plus torque converter or Mopar 883 four-speed manual

BODY/CHASSIS

Steel channel chassis welded to body with bolted front subframe

SPECIAL FEATURES

Front spoiler overcomes front-end lift.

The rear wing's height means it operates in less-disturbed airflow.

RUNNING GEAR

Steering: Recirculating ball steering, power-assisted on road cars
Front suspension: Double wishbones with torsion bars and telescopic shocks
Rear suspension: Live axle with asymmetric leaf springs and telescopic shocks
Brakes: Vented discs 11 in. dia. (front), drums 11 in. dia. (rear)
Wheels: Steel disc, 7 in. x 15 in.
Tires: Goodyear 7.00/15

DIMENSIONS

Length: 218 in.   **Width:** 76.4 in.
Wheelbase: 116 in.
Height: 1159.4 in. (including rear wing)
Track: 59.7 in. (front), 58.7 in. (rear)
Weight: 3,841 lbs.

Pontiac **BONNEVILLE**

Traditionally, Pontiacs were reliable, dependable cars that suffered from a lackluster image. By 1959, the image started to change with the announcement of a new crop of lower, sleeker, full-size cars boasting up to 345 bhp and with a 'Wide Track' ride.

"...fast, relaxed cruising."

"The driving position is much lower than previous Ponchos and the visibility is better. Tractable in traffic, with incredible lower-end power, the V8 is also capable of blasting you to 60 mph in around 8 seconds. Although it boasts a wider track suspension, the car still has a tendency to pitch and wallow over uneven surfaces. Dive under hard braking is quite pronounced, too. However, for fast, relaxed cruising, a 1959 Bonneville is tough to beat."

The jazzy interior has a full-width bench seat upholstered in three different shades of vinyl.

Milestones

1957 A limited
production convertible joins the Pontiac lineup. Named Bonneville, after the famous salt flats, it has a fuel injected, 310-bhp V8 engine. Only 630 models were sold.

Bonneville got a shorter, narrower body for 1961.

1958 The
Bonneville becomes a full series on bigger, redesigned Pontiacs. It shares the 122-inch wheelbase with the Chieftain and is offered in hardtop and convertible form.

Even today, the Bonneville maintains a dash of sportiness.

1959 Pontiacs are
restyled with a longer, lower body. The Bonneville range is expanded to include a four-door Safari™ Wagon, Sport coupe and Vista hardtop sedan.

1960 Minor
changes include a new grill and taillights and a slightly altered interior.

UNDER THE SKIN

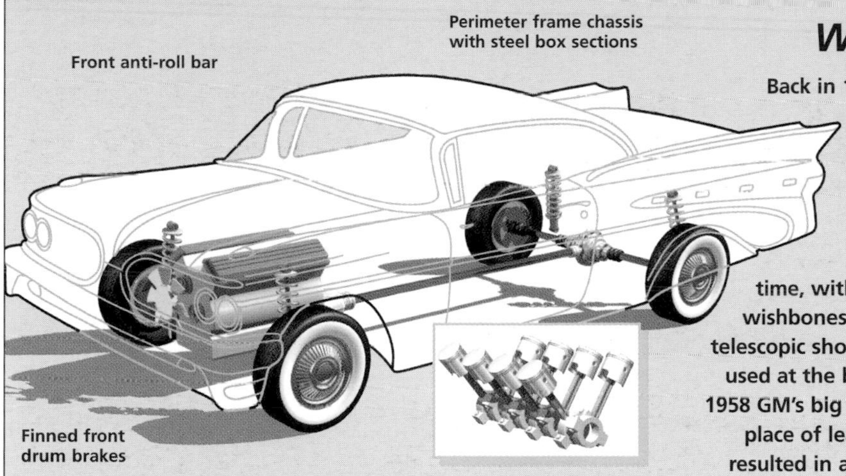

Front anti-roll bar

Perimeter frame chassis with steel box sections

Finned front drum brakes

Powerful V8

Wide track

Back in 1959, Bonnevilles were built from the 124-inch wheelbase Star Chief chassis. Front suspension is typical for the time, with unequal length wishbones, coil springs and telescopic shocks. A live axle is used at the back, although in 1958 GM's big cars used coils in place of leaf springs, which resulted in an improved ride.

THE POWER PACK

Pontiac power

Pontiac introduced its first V8 engine in 1955, and by 1959 the displacement had increased to 389 cubic inches. A variety of carburetor setups were offered. The base 389 has a four-barrel Rochester carburetor which results in 260 bhp (300 with automatic) in the Bonneville. Next up the ladder is a 389 that boasts 300/330 bhp. At the top is a Tri-Power setup with three two-barrel carburetors. With 345 bhp in top tune it makes the big Pontiac a real flyer, able to reach 60 mph in less than 7 seconds.

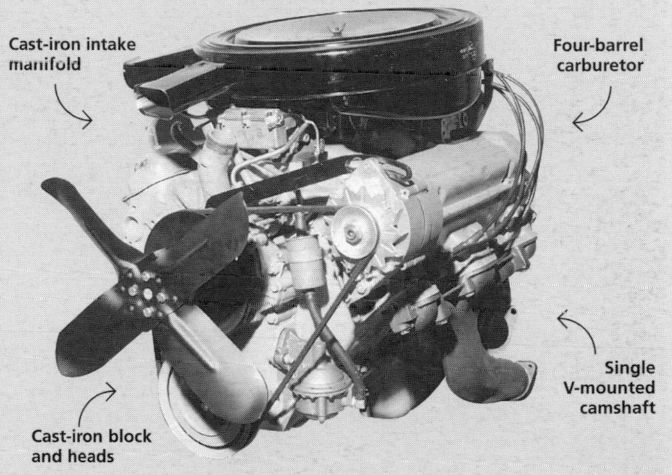

Cast-iron intake manifold

Four-barrel carburetor

Single V-mounted camshaft

Cast-iron block and heads

True classic

The 1959 Pontiac is one of the most attractive-looking cars of the glitzy 1950s. The most desirable are the Bonneville Sport coupe and convertible. Cars fitted with a 345-bhp Tri-Power V8 and a manual transmission have truly classic status.

The Sport Coupe is perhaps the best-looking 1959 Bonneville.

Pontiac BONNEVILLE

With its swoopy look, 'Wide Track' ride and powerful 389 V8, the 1959 Bonneville was the first of a new breed of mainstream Pontiacs which placed emphasis on performance and assured roadability.

Standard V8

In 1959, all Pontiacs came with 389-cubic inch V8s. This particular car has a 10.0:1 compression ratio, a four-barrel Rochester carburetor and a cast-iron dual-plane intake manifold. The advertised power output is 300 bhp at 4,600 rpm.

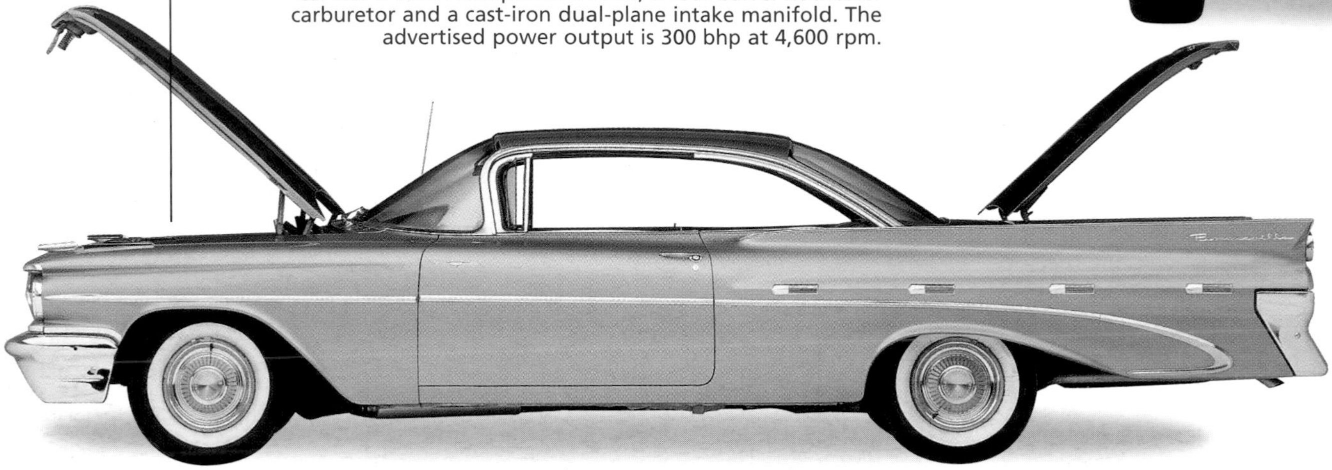

Wide Track

A big selling point in 1959 was the 'Wide Track' ride, which was claimed to improve handling and stability at speed. Compared to other big cars of the era, Pontiacs do feel more confident on the road.

Optional rear gearing

A variety of rear axle ratios were offered starting with a tall 3.08:1 for high-speed cruising and maximum fuel economy, through 3.23:1 and 3.64:1, and up to strip-storming 3.90:1 and 4.10:1 ratios. The last two were dealer installed.

Hardtop styling

The Bonneville Custom was the top-of-the-line series in 1959 and three different versions were available: four-door Vista hardtop, two-door Sport coupe and convertible. The sedan was by far the most popular, with 38,696 built. The hardtop coupe, seen here, was second, with 27,769 sold.

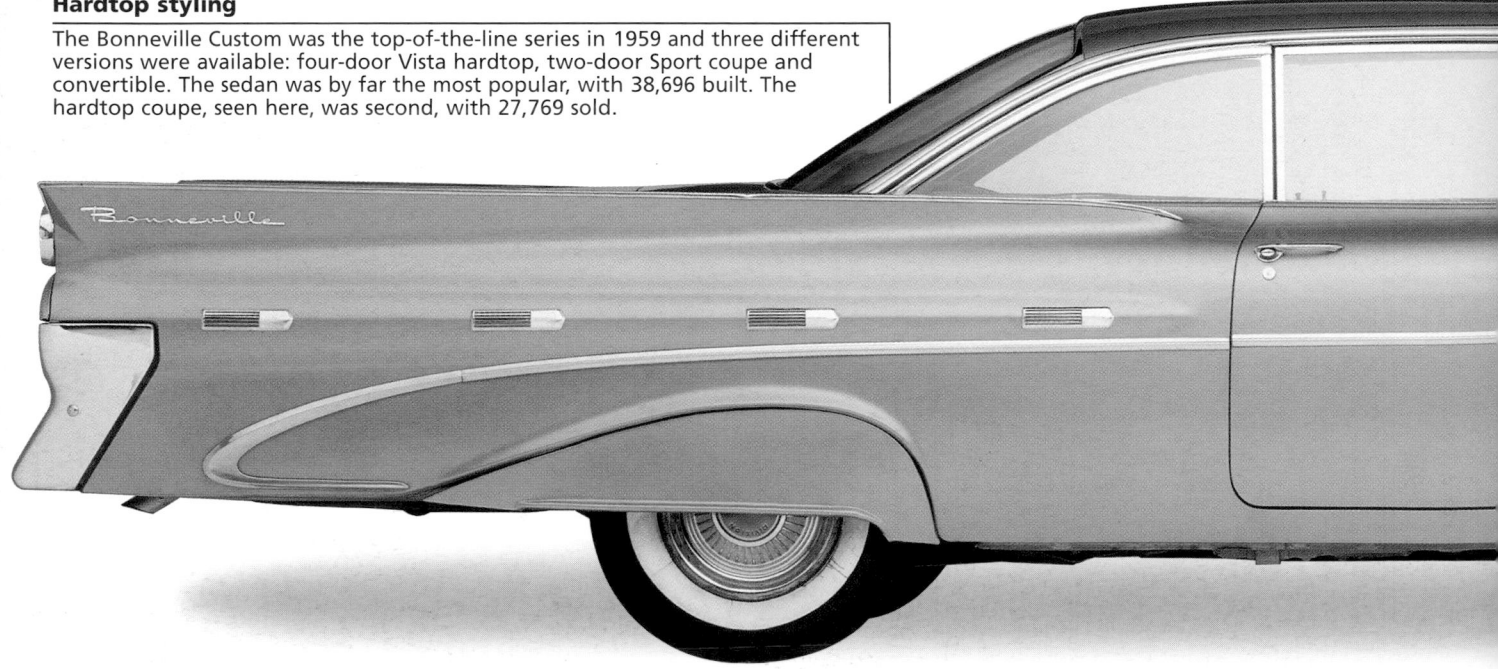

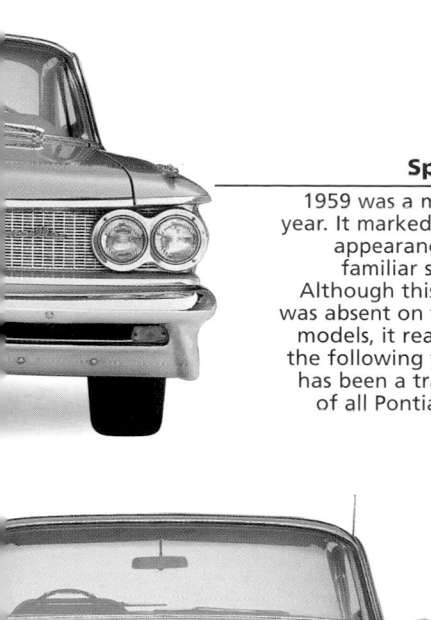

Split grill

1959 was a milestone year. It marked the first appearance of the familiar split grill. Although this feature was absent on the 1960 models, it reappeared the following year and has been a trademark of all Pontiacs since.

Smaller wheels and tires

To make the 1959 models appear even lower and longer, Pontiac switched to 14-inch wheels and tires.

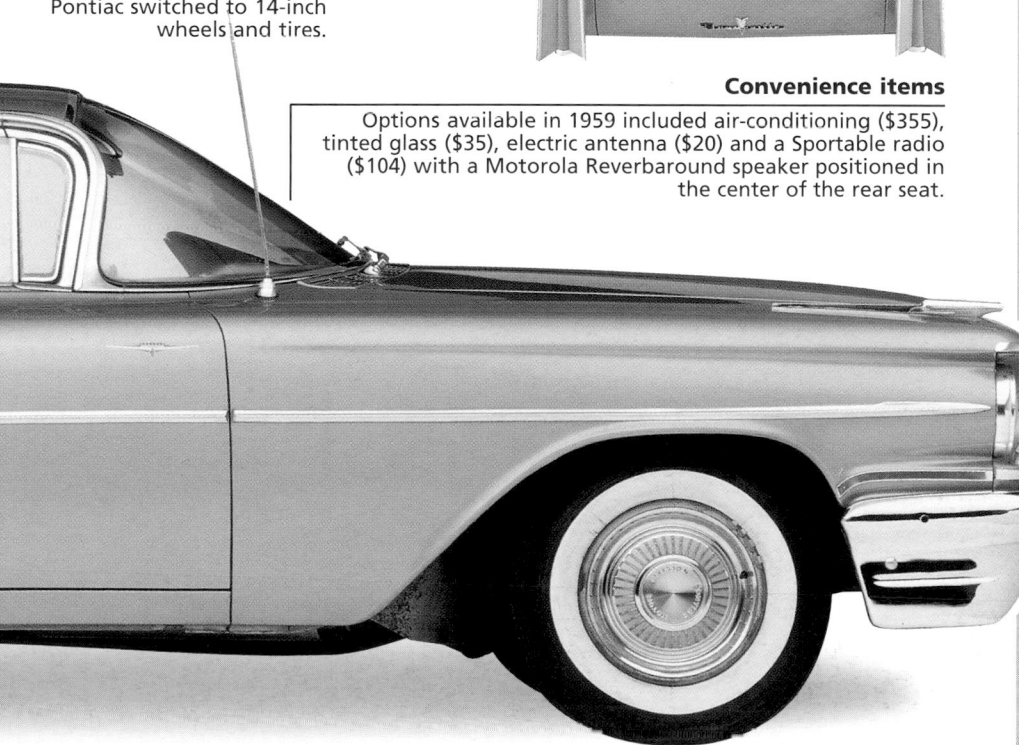

Convenience items

Options available in 1959 included air-conditioning ($355), tinted glass ($35), electric antenna ($20) and a Sportable radio ($104) with a Motorola Reverbaround speaker positioned in the center of the rear seat.

Specifications

1959 Pontiac Bonneville

ENGINE

Type: V8

Construction: Cast-iron block and heads

Valve gear: Two valves per cylinder operated by a single camshaft with pushrods and rockers

Bore and stroke: 4.06 in. x 3.75 in.

Displacement: 389 c.i.

Compression ratio: 10.0:1

Induction system: Rochester four-barrel carburetor

Maximum power: 300 bhp at 4,600 rpm

Maximum torque: 450 lb-ft at 2,800 rpm

TRANSMISSION

TurboHydramatic three-speed automatic

BODY/CHASSIS

Steel perimeter frame with separate hardtop two-door coupe body

SPECIAL FEATURES

Unusually, the reverse lights were mounted at the ends of the fins.

The Bonneville has optional fender skirts which are easily removed.

RUNNING GEAR

Steering: Recirculating ball

Front suspension: Unequal-length wishbones with coil springs, telescopic shock absorbers and anti-roll bar

Rear suspension: Live axle with coil springs and telescopic shock absorbers

Brakes: Drums (front and rear)

Wheels: Steel disc, 7.0 x 15 in.

Tires: 145/70 R14

DIMENSIONS

Length: 220.7 in.   **Width:** 75.4 in.

Height: 51.4 in.   **Wheelbase:** 124.0 in.

Track: 63.7 in. (front), 64.0 in. (rear)

Weight: 4,233 lbs

Pontiac **CAN AM**

Although it is often said that performance died during the 1970s, there were some bright spots. In 1977, Pontiac dropped a 400-cubic inch V8 into the LeMans™ to create the Can Am, a limited production sports coupe.

"...something different."

"Based on the mid-1970s LeMans, the Can Am has a low-set driving position and feels wide on the road. The interior may be bland, but the floor shifter at the end of your right hand indicates something different is going on. The 400 V8 works best at low rpm, and while not fast on paper, the Can Am still feels quick. A nice surprise is the handling—stiffer springs and anti-roll bars, along with radial tires give assuring grip."

Velour upholstery and every gauge one could imagine come standard in all Can Ams.

Milestones

1973 Pontiac fields a restyled
intermediate line, now called LeMans. Convertibles and hardtop coupes are not offered, but pillared sedans, coupes and wagons are. This is also the last year for the A-body GTO™.

Pontiac's popular Trans Am™ also used 400- or 403-cubic inch V8s.

1975 Pontiac drops its only
surviving performance intermediate, the Grand Am™, after sales reach only 10,769.

Pontiac's original muscle car, the GTO was also based on the midsize LeMans.

1977 In an attempt to inject
more performance into its lineup, Pontiac offers the Can Am, based on the LeMans Sport. It has big V8 power, handling suspension and white paint with orange and black graphics. A downsized LeMans arrives for 1978 on a 108.1-inch wheelbase. The sporty Can Am does not return.

UNDER THE SKIN

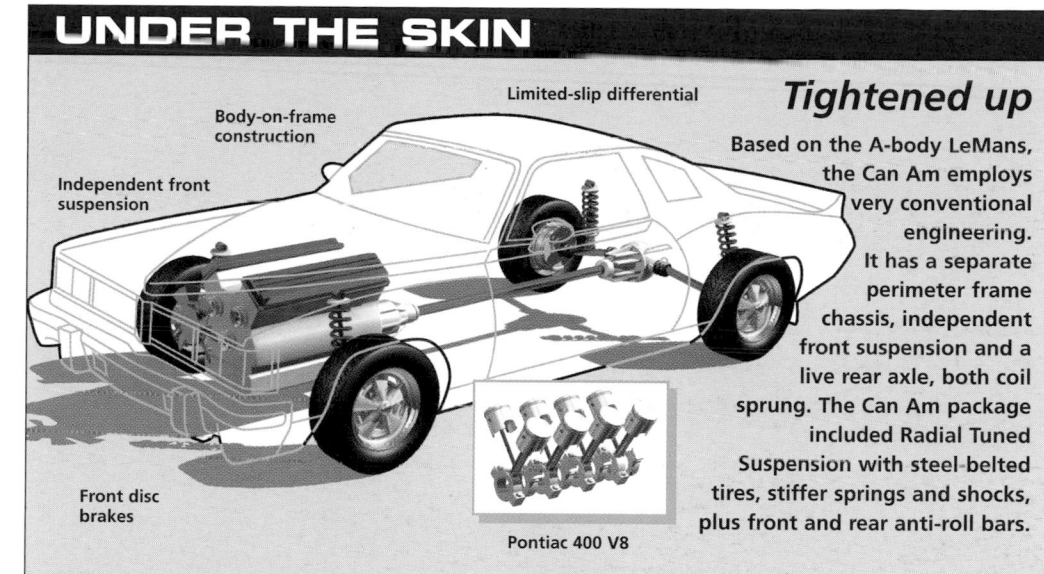

Body-on-frame construction

Limited-slip differential

Independent front suspension

Front disc brakes

Pontiac 400 V8

Tightened up

Based on the A-body LeMans, the Can Am employs very conventional engineering. It has a separate perimeter frame chassis, independent front suspension and a live rear axle, both coil sprung. The Can Am package included Radial Tuned Suspension with steel-belted tires, stiffer springs and shocks, plus front and rear anti-roll bars.

THE POWER PACK

High and low

The Can Am was intended to approach Firebird levels of performance, and so it was only natural to fit the ponycar's biggest engines in this over-achieving LeMans. In California and high altitude areas, a 185-bhp, 403-cubic inch Olds-mobile® V8 was standard. In all other states, the W-72 high-output 400-cubic inch Pontiac V8 was specified. It came with a dual-plane cast-iron intake and a four-barrel carburetor. With 200 bhp at a low 3,600 rpm and 325 lb-ft of torque, it made the Can Am a good performer.

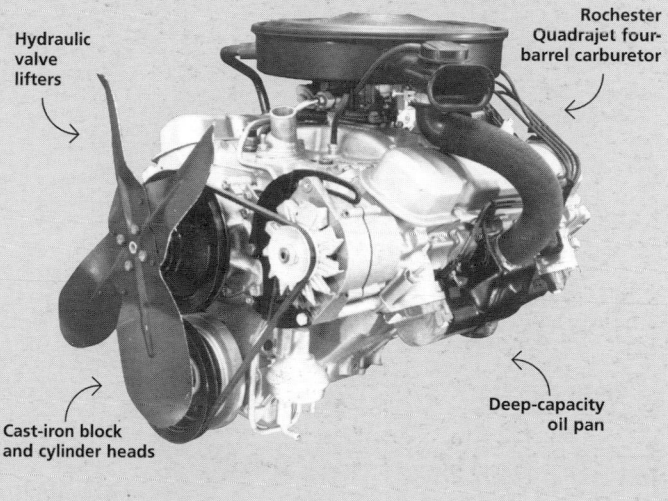

Hydraulic valve lifters

Rochester Quadrajet four-barrel carburetor

Cast-iron block and cylinder heads

Deep-capacity oil pan

White warrior

The Can Am was built only for 1977 and just 3,177 examples left the factory. It may be slower than its 1960s forebears, but thanks to a 400-cubic inch engine packing 200 bhp in top condition, it is undoubtedly a high performance bargain.

Today, good Can Ams can be bought for very a reasonable price.

Pontiac CAN AM

Fitting a huge engine in a mid-range coupe was the muscle car concept in its purest form. Although not the quickest, one road tester claimed the Can Am was "the strongest thing to come from Motown in years."

Biggest V8

In 1977, the 400 was the biggest engine offered by Pontiac. With a four-barrel carburetor and 200 bhp, it was potent too, and enabled Can Am drivers to flog their machines down the ¼-mile in a shade over 17 seconds.

Driver-oriented interior

Although it is essentially a LeMans, the Can Am has a driver-oriented Grand Prix instrument panel, with large circular gauges that are angled toward the driver.

Live axle

Most American production cars of the 1970s had front-mounted engines, with a live rear axle. Can Ams came with a 10-bolt rear end with a Safe-T-Track limited-slip differential. For economy, 3.23:1 was the shortest ratio offered.

Five-mph bumpers

Beginning in 1973, all manufacturers who sold cars in the U.S. had to comply with federal regulations which required heftier bumpers to withstand low-speed shunts. After a low-speed impact they bounce back to their original position.

All automatics

Though two different engines were available in the Can Am, only one transmission was available—a TH350 three speed automatic. The transmission included a 2.52 first gear for spirited standing starts.

Chassis enhancements

Stiffer coil springs, shocks with improved damping and front and rear anti-roll bars were offered as part of the RTS (Radial Tuned Suspension) package, along with 15-inch wheels.

Cosmetic enhancements

Because performance was a scarce commodity in the 1970s, Detroit dressed up its 'hot' offerings. This included a trunk spoiler, shaker hood scoop, plus a white body and wheels.

Specifications

1977 Pontiac Can Am

ENGINE

Type: V8

Construction: Cast-iron block and heads

Valve gear: Two valves per cylinder operated by a single camshaft with pushrods and hydraulic lifters

Bore and stroke: 4.12 in. x 3.75 in.

Displacement: 400 c.i.

Compression ratio: 8.0:1

Induction system: Rochester Quadrajet four-barrel carburetor

Maximum power: 200 bhp at 3,600 rpm

Maximum torque: 325 lb-ft at 2,400 rpm

TRANSMISSION

TurboHydramatic three speed automatic

BODY/CHASSIS

Steel perimeter chassis with separate two-door coupe body

SPECIAL FEATURES

Vents over the quarter windows add a sporty look to this 1970s hot rod.

Chrome-plated exhaust tips, as seen here, were a popular dealer option.

RUNNING GEAR

Steering: Recirculating ball

Front suspension: Unequal length A-arms with coil springs, telescopic shock absorbers and anti-roll bar

Rear suspension: Live axle with lower control arms, coil springs, telescopic shock absorbers and anti-roll bar

Brakes: Discs (front), drums (rear)

Wheels: Cast-steel, 7 x 15 in.

Tires: Goodyear Polysteel, GR70-15

DIMENSIONS

Length: 208.0 in. **Width:** 77.0 in.

Height: 52.7 in. **Wheelbase:** 112.0 in.

Track: 61.6 in. (front), 61.1 in. (rear)

Weight: 4,140 lbs.

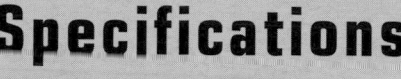

Pontiac FIREBIRD

The second-generation Firebird is one of Pontiac's most successful cars ever and it remained in production for 11 years. Perhaps the purest and best-performing cars are the early-1970s Firebird Formulas®.

"...plenty of low-end power."

"While most muscle cars were scrapped by 1972, Pontiac refused to let go. It continued to charge hard with the popular ponycar. Those who wanted attention bought the Trans Am®, but the more sedate looking Formula shared its power. The Formula has a 400-cubic inch V8 under its dual-scooped hood. Although power in the 1973 model is down because of the government's strict emissions regulations, this car is still very quick and has plenty of low-end power."

In 1973, Formulas had plush bucket seats and a sporty center console.

Milestones

1970 The second-generation
Firebird makes its debut in February. It is longer, lower and wider, with an Endura flexible nose. Four models are available: Firebird, Esprit®, Formula and Trans Am. The latter two are the performance models.

The first-generation Firebird made its debut in February 1967.

1973 The last of the
true muscle Firebirds appear as the 455 Super Duty Formula and the Trans Am.

1974 A facelift
for the second-generation Firebird introduces new front and rear styling to satisfy crash requirements.

The 1979 model was the most popular year, with 211,000 Firebirds being sold.

1979 This is the
last year for the 400- and 403-cubic inch V8s. The 400-cubic inch V8 was the more powerful engine and was used with a 4-speed transmission, while the lower performance 403 V8 was used with an automatic.

UNDER THE SKIN

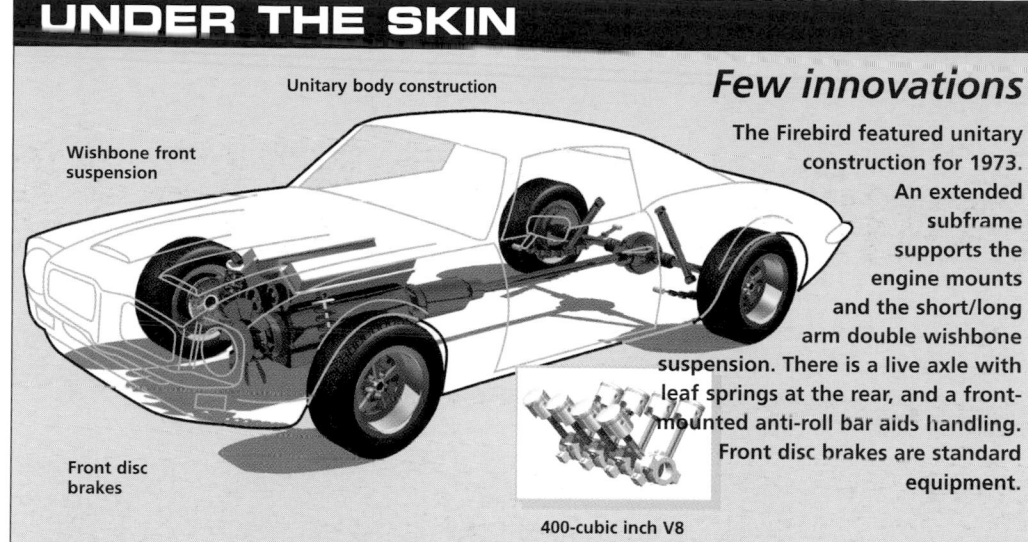

Unitary body construction

Wishbone front suspension

Front disc brakes

400-cubic inch V8

Few innovations

The Firebird featured unitary construction for 1973. An extended subframe supports the engine mounts and the short/long arm double wishbone suspension. There is a live axle with leaf springs at the rear, and a front-mounted anti-roll bar aids handling. Front disc brakes are standard equipment.

THE POWER PACK

Big and torquey

The second-generation Pontiac Firebird was available with a wide range of engines and power outputs, with everything from a lowly 110-bhp 250-cubic inch six to the mighty 455-cubic inch V8 with up to 335 bhp. In between there was the intermediate 230-bhp, 400-cubic inch Pontiac V8. The biggest 455 V8 catered to those who craved real muscle car performance. This brutal engine was only reserved for the outrageous Trans Am models, while a few Formula owners opted for the mighty engine in their cars.

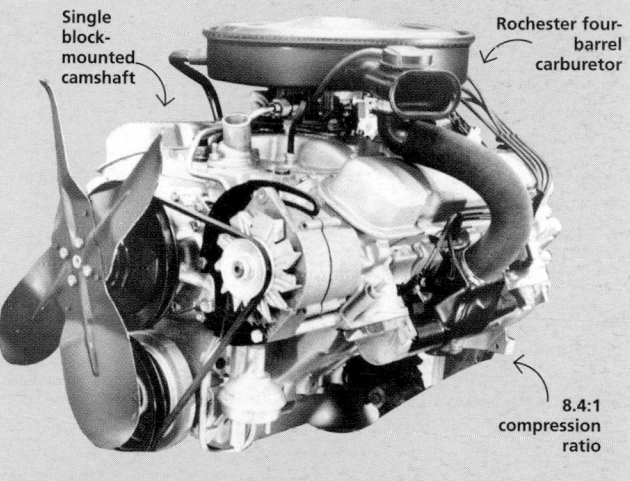

Single block-mounted camshaft

Rochester four-barrel carburetor

8.4:1 compression ratio

Fiery flagship

The flagship of the Firebird line in 1973 was the Trans Am. Apart from spoilers, decals and a shaker hood scoop, it is mechanically identical to the 455 Formula. The toughest engine available in 1973 was the 455-cubic inch Super Duty, with 310 bhp.

1970-1973 Firebirds are the cleanest-looking second-generation models.

161

Pontiac **FIREBIRD**

For those who did not have the money to buy the Trans Am but still wanted performance, the Formula was a good choice. It had the same mechanicals as its more renowned stablemate.

400-cubic inch engine

This large bore 400-cubic inch engine features 8.4:1 compression cast-iron pistons, large chamber D-port cylinder heads with 2.11-inch intake and 1.77-inch exhaust valves, a low lift hydraulic camshaft and a Rochester Quadrajet.

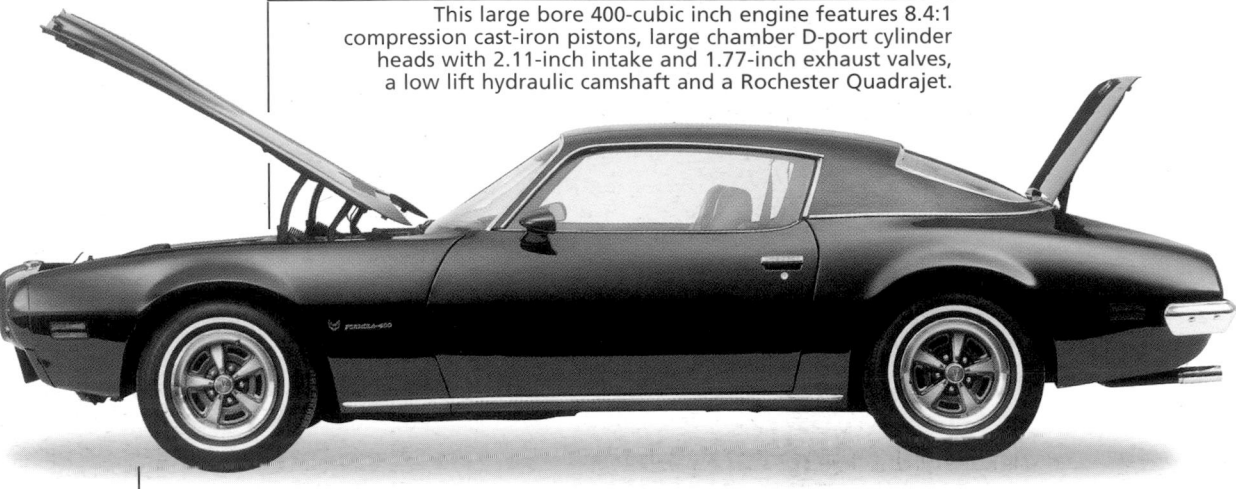

Steel wheels

Firebirds have steel Pontiac Rally wheels as standard, although special 'honeycomb' wheels were available at extra cost.

Limited-slip differential

Standard equipment with the four-speed manual transmission is the limited-slip differential. It was much easier to offer this as an aid to traction than to re-engineer the Firebird with independent rear suspension.

Separate rear bumper

In contrast to the front color-coded, impact-absorbing Endura nose, there is still a traditional-style chrome bumper at the rear. The last year for this very clean rear-end styling was 1973.

Optional air-conditioning

Unlike its import rivals, even the lowest model of the Firebird could be ordered with air-conditioning as an option.

Impact-absorbing nose

Pontiac was one of the first companies to introduce impact-absorbing bumpers. The Firebird has one of the cleanest nose profiles of any 1973 car.

Specifications

1973 Pontiac Firebird Formula 400

ENGINE

Type: V8

Construction: Cast-iron block and heads

Valve gear: Two valves per cylinder operated by a single block-mounted camshaft, pushrods and rockers

Bore and stroke: 4.13 in. x 3.74 in.

Displacement: 400 c.i.

Compression ratio: 8.4:1

Induction system: Single Rochester 7043263 four-barrel carburetor

Maximum power: 230 bhp at 4,400 rpm

Maximum torque: 177 lb-ft at 3,200 rpm

TRANSMISSION

Four-speed manual

BODY/CHASSIS

Steel monocoque with ladder-type front chassis rails and two-door coupe body

SPECIAL FEATURES

Twin hood scoops are unique to the high-performance Formula model.

Rally II wheels are standard equipment on the Formula and optional on lesser models.

RUNNING GEAR

Steering: Recirculating ball

Front suspension: Double unequal length wishbones, with coil springs, telescopic shocks and anti-roll bar

Rear suspension: Live axle with semi-elliptic leaf springs, telescopic shocks and anti-roll bar

Brakes: Discs, 11-in. dia. (front), drums (rear)

Wheels: Steel disc, 7 in. x 14 in.

Tires: F70-14

DIMENSIONS

Length: 191.5 in.   **Width:** 73.4 in.

Height: 50.4 in.   **Wheelbase:** 108.1 in.

Track: 61.6 in. (front), 61.6 in. (rear)

Weight: 3,766 lbs.

Pontiac GRAND PRIX

The top-of-the-line Grand Prix was a sales sensation for Pontiac. The 1967 model year was unique because there was a convertible and a hardtop model. Stylistically, this Grand Prix also stands out because of its bold, wraparound, front-end treatment.

"...Drives like a muscle car."

"Because of the sensational GTO, Pontiacs had a strong performance car image in the 1960s. The Grand Prix is certainly a big luxury car but it drives like a muscle car. Using a stout 350-bhp, 400-cubic inch engine, the GP has plenty of power. It leaps away from the lights defying its bulk for a 9.4 second 0-60 mph time. This is all easily handled by the automatic transmission. The all-coil suspension provides a supple ride and fine handling."

The combination of leather and wood in the cabin hides the GP's sporty potential.

Milestones

1962 Pontiac launches the first ever Grand Prix hardtop coupe.

The X400 was the 1963 Grand Prix show car.

1965 The Grand Prix wheelbase is increased by an inch.

1967 New front-end styling marks the Grand Prix, which is offered for this year only in convertible form as well. A 400-cubic inch V8 replaces the 389. A big 428 is optional.

The 1965 Catalina™ shared some mechanicals with the Grand Prix.

1968 Styling is altered with a more pronounced grill and a revised rear bumper.

1969 An all-new, neo-classic Grand Prix series is launched. It is built off the smaller A-body intermediate chassis and was known for having one of the biggest hoods at this time.

UNDER THE SKIN

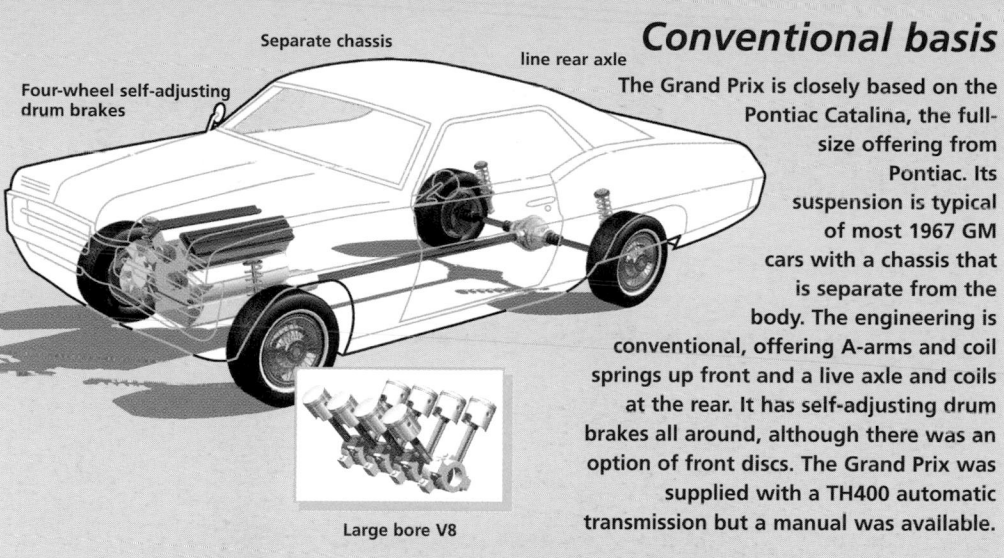

Four-wheel self-adjusting drum brakes

Separate chassis

line rear axle

Large bore V8

Conventional basis

The Grand Prix is closely based on the Pontiac Catalina, the full-size offering from Pontiac. Its suspension is typical of most 1967 GM cars with a chassis that is separate from the body. The engineering is conventional, offering A-arms and coil springs up front and a live axle and coils at the rear. It has self-adjusting drum brakes all around, although there was an option of front discs. The Grand Prix was supplied with a TH400 automatic transmission but a manual was available.

THE POWER PACK

Massive power

The 1967 Pontiac 400-cubic inch V8 engine is a bored-out version of the 389. This was a full-size engine and among the most powerful in Pontiac's 1967 lineup. Its high torque output meant that it was an ideal power plant for a street cruiser. Thanks to its semi-aggressive camshaft, the power rose from 325 bhp (as in the Bonneville™) to 350 bhp. During this era there seemed to be no limit to the size that the engines could grow. The Grand Prix could be ordered with a massive 428-cubic inch V8. This was available in two states of tune: 360 and 375 bhp.

Collectable

During the 1960s, Pontiac sold so many Grand Prix models that the car nearly became its best seller. Only one style was offered—a hardtop coupe—although the 1967 model year had a convertible option. Only 5,856 were made, and they are now collector's cars.

The convertible was only available in 1967 and has become quite collectable.

Pontiac GRAND PRIX

Occupying a place at the top of the Pontiac lineup, the Grand Prix encapsulated all the qualities of the marque: a wide, low stance; strong V8 power; luxurious trim and a performance edge.

Full-size V8

A 350 bhp, 400-cubic inch V8 was the standard Grand Prix engine in 1967. A larger 428-cubic inch HO (High Output) V8 was optional with as much as 375 bhp.

Convertible body

1967 was the only model year that the Grand Prix was offered as a convertible. This model is one of the more common hardtops.

Wedge-shaped fender tips

The front fenders jut forward with a strong wedge-shaped thrust mirroring the ridge along the hood that splits the grill in two pieces. It might not be very aerodynamic but it set a style that evolved through the 1970s.

Wasp-waist styling

A prominent downward-sliding body accent starts in the door and runs to the rear fender. This gives an impression of a slim midriff and chunky rear. The covers on the rear wheels are optional.

Hooded headlights

In contrast to the 1966 Pontiac lineup and the rest of the 1967 Pontiac range that feature stacked quad headlights, the 1967 Grand Prix has concealed headlights. This clean look has the parking lights hidden behind vacuum-operated headlight doors concealed in the grill.

Automatic or manual transmission

The majority of 1967 Grand Prix cars had TurboHydramatic three-speed automatic transmissions that were smooth-shifting and reliable. Fully synchronized four-speeds were offered as well, but only 760 cars were ordered with them.

Specifications

1967 Pontiac Grand Prix

ENGINE

Type: V8

Construction: Cast-iron block and heads

Valve gear: Two valves per cylinder operated by a single camshaft with pushrods and rocker arms

Bore and stroke: 4.125 in. x 3.75 in.

Displacement: 400 c.i.

Compression ratio: 10.5:1

Induction system: Single Carter four-barrel carburetor

Maximum power: 350 bhp at 5,000 rpm

Maximum torque: 440 lb-ft at 3,200 rpm

TRANSMISSION

TH400 automatic or four speed manual

BODY/CHASSIS

Separate chassis with steel two-door coupe body

SPECIAL FEATURES

The split front grill was a Pontiac trademark in the mid 1960s.

The concealed headlights make the Grand Prix instantly identifiable.

RUNNING GEAR

Steering: Recirculating ball

Front suspension: A-arms with coil springs and shock absorbers

Rear suspension: Live axle with coil springs and shock absorbers

Brakes: Drums (front and rear)

Wheels: Steel, 14-in. dia.

Tires: 8.55 x 14

DIMENSIONS

Length: 215.6 in.   **Width:** 79.4 in.

Height: 54.2 in.   **Wheelbase:** 121.0 in.

Track: 63.0 in. (front), 64.0 in. (rear)

Weight: 4,005 lbs.

Pontiac **GTO**

Generally acknowledged as the first factory-built muscle car, the name was borrowed from Ferrari where it stood for Gran Turisomo Omologato. Now its one of the top collectible cars of its era.

"...All attitude and performance."

"While many can argue which muscle car was the fastest, nicest or most powerful, only one can be the first—that's the Pontiac GTO. In 1964, when John Z. DeLorean installed a 389-cubic inch V8 in Pontiac's intermediate Tempest cars, he created a legend, not to mention an American automotive trend that would ripple for the next eight years. By 1971, the GTO was all about attitude as well as performance. Styled with the Judge™ option, and powered by a huge 455-cubic inch High Output engine with Ram-Air induction, the GTO had the sound and fury of real steel."

This GTO has the optional hood-mounted tachometer that is visible through the windshield.

Details apply to 1971 Judge model

Milestones

1968 The GTO receives another major restyling. The wheelbase is shortened from 115 to 112 inches. The new body uses rubber Endura bumpers and hidden headlights are a popular option. Its 400-cubic inch V8 retains 360 bhp in both the HO and Ram Air versions. Midyear, Pontiac replaces the Ram Air engine with a Ram Air II.

The 1965 GTO was a tough act to follow by 1971.

1969 The Judge is an attempt to revive GTO sales. It features a sharp rear spoiler, stripes and badging. Standard engine is the Ram Air III 400 V8 engine, but for and extra $390 the 370 bhp Ram Air IV engine becomes available.

1970 GTOs are again restyled. This is the most refined version yet. The Judge is still available and so is the Ram Air IV engine. A huge 455 V8 is also offered, but isn't popular.

1971 Poor sales, in 1970 force the Judge option to be dropped after selling 357 hardtops and 17 convertibles. The top engine is a 455 V8 with 355 bhp.

1972 GTO, becomes an option on the Le Mans.

UNDER THE SKIN

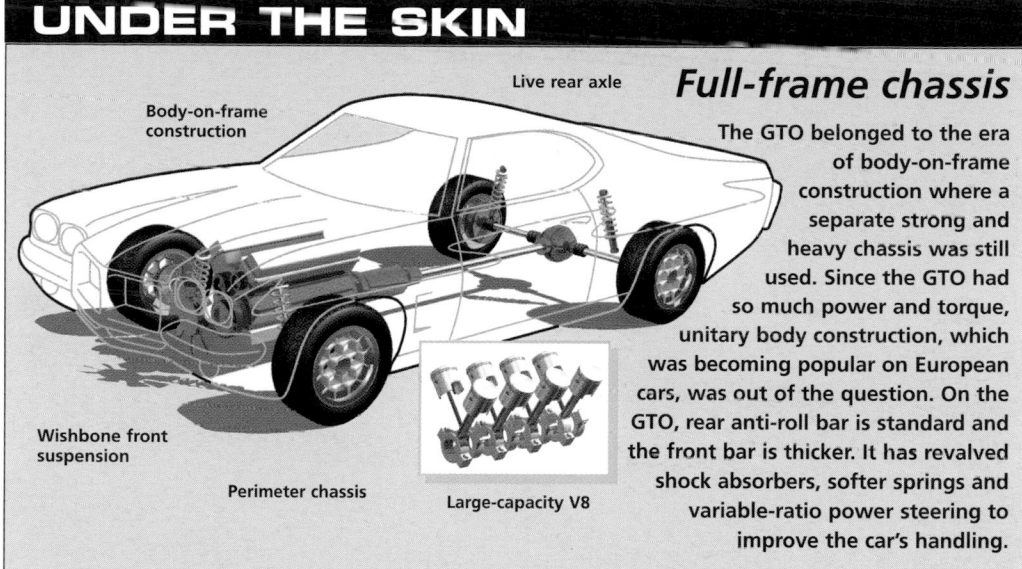

Live rear axle

Body-on-frame construction

Wishbone front suspension

Perimeter chassis

Large-capacity V8

Full-frame chassis

The GTO belonged to the era of body-on-frame construction where a separate strong and heavy chassis was still used. Since the GTO had so much power and torque, unitary body construction, which was becoming popular on European cars, was out of the question. On the GTO, rear anti-roll bar is standard and the front bar is thicker. It has revalved shock absorbers, softer springs and variable-ratio power steering to improve the car's handling.

THE POWER PACK

Easy power

By 1971, the GTO had lost the original 389-cubic inch tri-power V8 and the mighty Ram Air IV 400 V8 in favor of a big, but not as powerful 455-cubic inch V8. It has a 4.15-inch bore and 4.21-inch stroke but thanks to tough emissions standards, the big 455 only makes 355 bhp at 3,800 rpm and 412 lb-ft of torque at 3,200 rpm. The engine featured a small 8.4:1 compression ratio, round-port cylinder heads, a Rochester Quadrajet four-barrel carburetor and low-rise cast iron intake manifold.

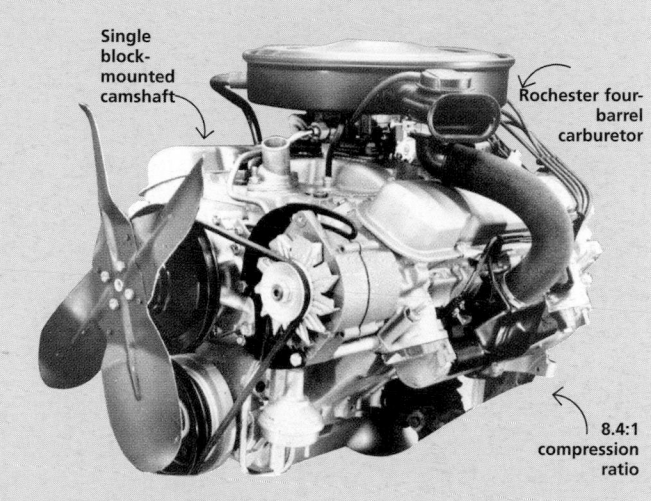

Single block-mounted camshaft

Rochester four-barrel carburetor

8.4:1 compression ratio

Rare Judge

One of the rarest GTOs is the 1971 Judge convertible. Unfortunately, the Judge option was dropped midway through the 1971 model year and only 17 convertibles were built. This pristine Judge is equipped with a High Output 455-cubic inch V8.

This rare GTO is one of only 17 Judge convertibles made in 1971.

Pontiac GTO

The GTO set the infamous John DeLorean on the road to success at GM and virtually invented the muscle car giving seemingly ordinary Tempests the performance to embarrass any sports car.

Ram Air

From 1965, all GTOs had an optional Ram Air system. By pulling a knob inside the cabin, hood vents would open and fed the carburetor with fresh, cool air.

High Output 455 V8

By 1971, the biggest and most powerful V8 you could order in the GTO was the High Output 455-cubic inch V8 with 355 bhp.

Servo front brakes

While the Le Mans range—which shared much of its hardware with the GTO—had unassisted drum brakes all around, the GTO models have front discs giving excellent results.

TH400 Automatic transmission

While the M-22 close-ratio manual four-speed was the racer's choice of transmissions, the TH400 automatic was easier in traffic and just as capable of delivering the power to the rear axles.

Positraction rear axle

Since these cars deliver a lot of power, a positraction rear axle was a popular option. For maximum acceleration, GTOs differentials were available with up to 4.33:1 gearing.

"Judge" graphics

If you wanted to get noticed, the Judge was the car to have. If the huge wing didn't make a loud enough statement, the multi-colored graphics sure did.

Wishbone front suspension

There are no surprises with the front suspension which features double wishbones with a thick anti-roll bar, coil springs and revalved shocks.

Wider wheels

To improve cornering and road holding, the GTO has wider wheels than the base Le Mans models. This car carries optional 'Honeycomb' wheels.

Rear anti-roll bar

The rear suspension needed all the help it could get to stop the car's body roll around corners. Its standard rear anti-roll bar greatly improve the way the GTO handles.

1971 Pontiac GTO Judge

ENGINE

Type: V8

Construction: Cast-iron block and heads

Valve gear: Two valves per cylinder operated by single block-mounted camshaft via pushrods, rockers and hydraulic lifters

Bore and stroke: 4.15 in. x 4.21 in.

Displacement: 455 c.i.

Compression ratio: 8.4:1

Induction system: Single Rochester four-barrel carburetor

Maximum power: 335 bhp at 4,800 rpm

Maximum torque: 412 lb-ft at 3,200 rpm

TRANSMISSION

Turbo 400 Hydra-Matic automatic

BODY/CHASSIS

Perimeter chassis with two-door coupe or two-door convertible bodywork

SPECIAL FEATURES

Optional hood-mounted, 8,000-rpm tachometer was first introduced in 1967.

The large vents on the hood are for the Ram Air system feeding fresh air to the four-barrel carburetor.

RUNNING GEAR

Steering: Variable-ratio power-assisted recirculating ball

Front suspension: Double wishbones with coil springs, revalved shocks and anti-roll bar

Rear suspension: Live axle with trailing radius arms, upper oblique torque arms, coil springs, revalved shocks and anti-roll bar

Brakes: Discs (front) and drums (rear)

Wheels: Honeycombs 14 in. x 7 in.

Tires: G60 x 14

DIMENSIONS

Length: 205.1 in.   **Width:** 76.7 in.

Height: 52 in.   **Wheelbase:** 112 in.

Track: 61 in. (front), 60 in. (rear)

Weight: 3,894 lbs.

Pontiac GTO JUDGE

Looking to boost sales of its muscle cars, Pontiac created The Judge option package for its 1969 model lineup and made it available on the tire-incinerating GTO. With its attention-getting paint scheme and outrageous graphics, a Ram Air-powered GTO Judge was a street-wise combination of flamboyance and force.

"...All rise for the GTO Judge."

"With its legendary Ram Air engines, the GTO is the quintessential muscle car. In 1969, a new option gave this powerful Poncho a new image—all rise for the GTO Judge. The Judge makes a statement even when it stands still. On the move its true intentions become evident. Push down on the throttle and feel its torque as your body sinks into its bucket seat. Bang second gear and listen to the tires chirp—now that's power. This honorable hot rod gives a very judicious jaunt."

A firm bucket seat, Hurst shifter and a hood mounted tach—what more do you need?

Milestones

1969 Although originally conceived as a single-color, bare-bones GTO at a low price, the Judge debuts as an option package on the Goat. It is equipped with the standard Ram III or optional Ram Air IV engines. The first 2,000 cars are painted Carousel Red, but later variants are available in any factory GTO color.

This 1968 GTO was one of the first cars to use a plastic Endura front bumper.

1970 GM A-bodies undergo a major restyle, and the GTO has more bulging lower sheet metal, plus new front and rear styling. Power-train choices on the Judge are unchanged, but there are new colors, and spring and suspension settings are altered. Late in the model year, a 455-cubic inch V8 becomes available.

The final, 1971 incarnation of the Judge is noticeably different from its predecessors.

1971 The Judge is retired due to a lack of consumer interest.

UNDER THE SKIN

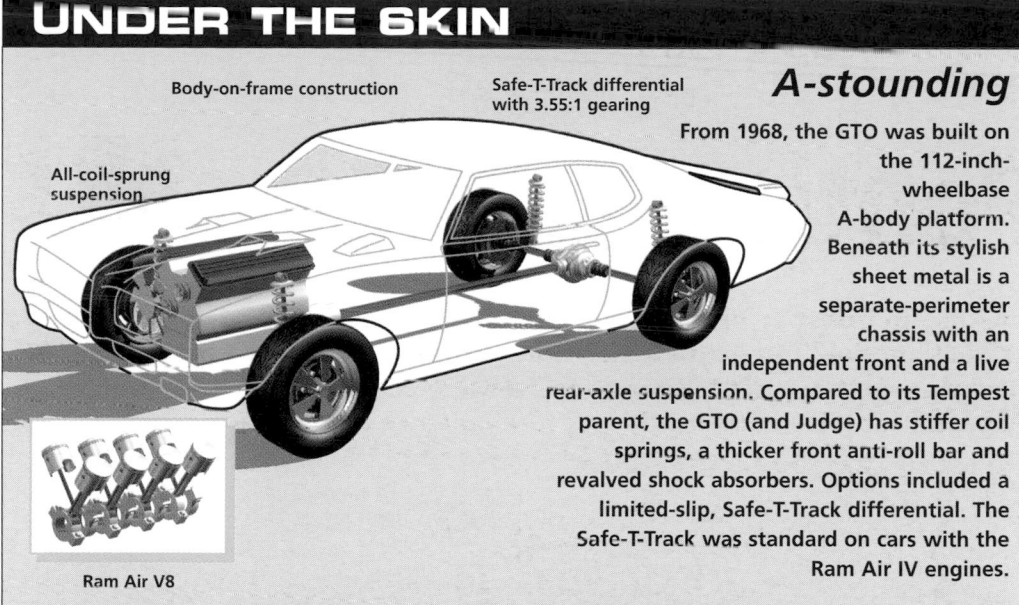

Body-on-frame construction

Safe-T-Track differential with 3.55:1 gearing

All-coil-sprung suspension

Ram Air V8

A-stounding

From 1968, the GTO was built on the 112-inch-wheelbase A-body platform. Beneath its stylish sheet metal is a separate-perimeter chassis with an independent front and a live rear-axle suspension. Compared to its Tempest parent, the GTO (and Judge) has stiffer coil springs, a thicker front anti-roll bar and revalved shock absorbers. Options included a limited-slip, Safe-T-Track differential. The Safe-T-Track was standard on cars with the Ram Air IV engines.

THE POWER PACK

Ramming air—III or IV

With outrageous styling, The Judge had to have the power to match. Its standard engine was a 400-cubic inch, Ram Air III, V8. This engine had D-port cylinder heads, a hydraulic camshaft, free-flowing exhaust manifolds and a Rochester Quadrajet 4-barrel carburetor. It made 366 bhp. Three is keen but with four you definitely get more. Owners who wanted to maximize performance ordered their Judge with the barely streetable Ram Air IV 400. It came with forged pistons, round-port cylinder heads and 1.65:1 rocker arms. According to the factory, this engine only made 4 more bhp than the III, but this figure was grossly underrated.

In session

Offered for sale for only three model years, the Judge has long been coveted by collectors. 1969 models boast cleaner styling, and Carousel Red is the definitive color. Due to high demand, buyers should be aware of GTO Judge imitations.

A Carousel Red Judge with the Ram Air IV is a highly desirable car.

Pontiac GTO JUDGE

Despite taking its name from the popular *Laugh-In* TV show, the Judge was no joke. Fitted with the Ram Air IV, it was one of the most respected muscle cars on the street.

Endura nose

One of the first cars to have energy-absorbing bumpers, the GTO's optional Endura nose could withstand parking lot shunts of up to four mph. Hidden headlights were a very popular option, however this GTO retains the fixed headlights.

III or IV for the road

Whereas regular GTOs came with a 350-bhp 400 as the standard V8, Judges got the 366-bhp Ram Air III. The hot setup, however, was the $389.68 Ram Air IV engine option with a 4-speed transmission. It was endowed with an aluminum intake manifold, 4-bolt mains and, of course, oval-port heads with 67cc combustion chambers. Only 34 buyers ordered their GTO Judges with the RA IV/4-speed option.

Standard Ram Air IV equipment

If you ordered your GTO with the Ram Air IV engine, you automatically received a heavy-duty cooling system. The standard gear ratio with this engine was a set of 3.90:1s and a Safe-T-Track limited slip differential. If these gears weren't steep enough, a set of 4.33:1s could be specified.

Heavy-duty suspension

Judges came with heavy-duty suspension, which includes stiff springs and shocks. Drum brakes were standard, but front discs were optional—and at a mere $64.25, highly advisable.

Eye-catching paint scheme

By 1969, image was everything in the muscle car stakes. The Judge was launched with one of the loudest schemes around, Carousel Red, set off by blue stripes outlined in yellow and with Judge logos on the front fenders and decklid spoiler.

Well-laid-out interior

The second-generation GTO had one of the best interiors of all its peers. All of the gauges were clearly visible, front bucket seats were very supportive and the floor-mounted Hurst shifter never missed a gear.

Specifications

1969 Pontiac GTO Judge

ENGINE
Type: V8

Construction: Cast-iron block and heads

Valve gear: Two valves per cylinder operated by a single camshaft with pushrods and rockers

Bore and stroke: 4.12 in. x 3.75 in.

Displacement: 400 c.i. (R/A III)

Compression ratio: 10.75:1

Induction system: GM Rochester Quadrajet four-barrel carburetor

Maximum power: 366 bhp at 5,400 rpm

Maximum torque: 445 lb-ft at 3,600 rpm

TRANSMISSION
Muncie M-21 four-speed manual

BODY/CHASSIS
Separate steel chassis with two-door coupe body

SPECIAL FEATURES

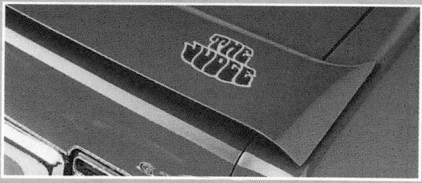

'The Judge' decals are prominently displayed all around the car.

The hood-mounted tachometer was not only stylish but very useful, too.

RUNNING GEAR
Steering: Recirculating ball

Front suspension: Unequal-length A-arms with coil springs, telescopic shock absorbers and anti-roll bar

Rear suspension: Live axle with coil springs, trailing arms and telescopic shock absorbers

Brakes: Discs (front), drums (rear)

Wheels: Steel Rally II, 14-in. dia.

Tires: Goodyear Polyglas, G-60 14

DIMENSIONS
Length: 195.0 in. **Width:** 75.0 in.

Height: 52.0 in. **Wheelbase:** 112.0 in.

Track: 64.0 in. (front and rear)

Weight: 3,503 lbs.

Pontiac TRANS AM

Since Pontiac only made eight Firebird® Trans Am convertibles in 1969, over the years many enthusiasts decided to build their own. The owner of this modified Trans Am drop-top decided to give it a modern touch by adding a late-model fuel injected 350-cubic inch engine and automatic transmission with overdrive.

"...an original stoplight warrior."

"This modified classic takes you back to cruising the boulevard in the summer of '69. But there's a twist—the 350 Chevy® engine puts out a serious rumble to ward off pretenders as you prepare for "The Stoplight Grand Prix." You're running fuel injection and a Positraction rear end to get all that power to the ground. Ready? Red...green...blast off! Light up the tires, and listen to the righteous sound of 250 horses slam you back in the seat and leave them all in a cloud of smoke! You're driving an original stoplight warrior."

The interior of this modified gem is perfect for cruisin'. There's lots of room to spread out and listen to old time rock 'n roll on the 8-Track.

Milestones

1967 Firebird is introduced
with a range of engines; the most powerful is the 400 c.i. V8, pumping out 325 bhp.

1969 Most sought after
of all the Firebirds becomes the Trans Am, named after the racing series.

1970 Shape is changed.
All Firebirds now look longer, lower and sleeker. The convertible Firebird is discontinued.

1974 facelift proved popular with buyers.

1974 A facelift gives
the Firebird a new lease on life.

1982 Third-generation
Firebird appears. It's smaller and lighter than before, but by this stage even the Trans Am produces only 155 bhp.

Camaro IROC Z28 lent its engine to the car featured overleaf.

1989 Power rises
steadily—the 350 c.i. V8 is available with 220 bhp in Camaro Z28 IROC trim. A modified version is transplanted into this 1969 Trans Am.

UNDER THE SKIN

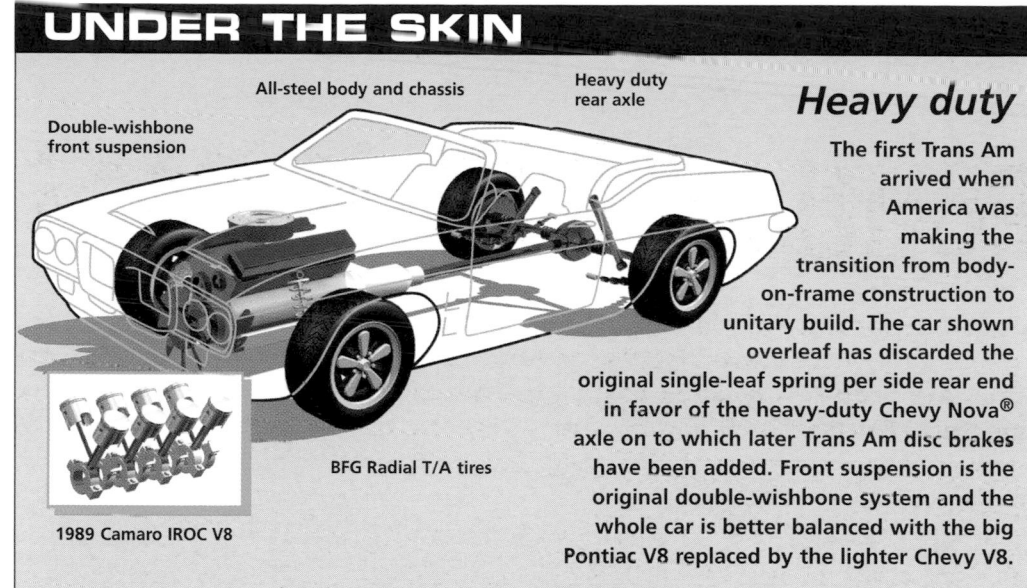

Double-wishbone front suspension

All-steel body and chassis

Heavy duty rear axle

BFG Radial T/A tires

1989 Camaro IROC V8

Heavy duty

The first Trans Am arrived when America was making the transition from body-on-frame construction to unitary build. The car shown overleaf has discarded the original single-leaf spring per side rear end in favor of the heavy-duty Chevy Nova® axle on to which later Trans Am disc brakes have been added. Front suspension is the original double-wishbone system and the whole car is better balanced with the big Pontiac V8 replaced by the lighter Chevy V8.

THE POWER PACK

Small-block power

Chevrolet's 350-cubic inch V8 is one of the all-time greats, fitted in various forms in everything from the Blazer® to the Corvette®. In the 1989 Camaro® IROC trim, it has cast-iron block and heads, roller rockers and fuel injection. Cast-iron headers were installed as standard, but tuners would replace those with freer-flowing steel headers to increase output. There's a vast number of other tuning parts for the 350—higher lift cams with longer overlap, and reworked ports, combustion chambers and valves. It's easy to tune to 300 bhp or beyond; it's just a question of how fast you want to go.

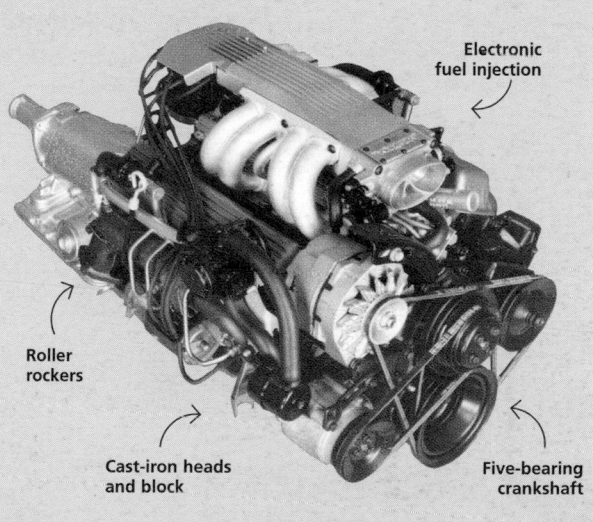

Electronic fuel injection

Roller rockers

Cast-iron heads and block

Five-bearing crankshaft

Plush Pontiac

Pontiac's answer to the Camaro Z28 appeared a year after its in-house rival. It was made a bit plusher in keeping with Pontiac's higher status in the GM hierarchy. In Trans Am form, it uses a bigger, 400-cubic inch V8, rather than the Z28's 302 cubic inch.

First-year Trans Ams were white with blue stripes.

Pontiac TRANS AM 🇺🇸

Why take a genuine collector's car and modify it? Why replace an immensely powerful 400-cubic inch V8 with a smaller 350? Look deeper at all the other modifications and improvements, and drive the car. Then it becomes obvious.

350-cubic inch V8

Pontiac's 400-cubic inch V8 was not one of America's greatest V8s, even though it produced plenty of power. Here it's been replaced by the superior, lighter and smaller 350 Chevrolet V8, as found in the Camaro Z28 and close to the specs found in the Corvette.

Taller wheels

The 1969 Trans Am ran on 14-inch wheels. They have been replaced by taller 15-inch wheels that fill the wheel arches to a greater extent and improve the car's overall look.

Power top

When the power convertible top was fitted to the Trans Am, all the effort was taken out of raising and lowering the top.

Positraction limited slip

The Nova axle is complemented by the Positraction limited slip differential with its 3.42:1 final drive ratio, taken from the 1979 Camaro Z28. This combination means the car can put its power down far more effectively than the original 1969 model.

Rear disc brakes

In the late-1960s, even front disc brakes were only an option on Firebirds and the rears were always drums. To help deal with the car's performance in the modern world, it's been fitted with the rear discs taken from a 1979 model Trans Am.

Hood scoops

The two hood scoops look impressive, but their function was to force air to the intake of the appropriately named Ram Air engine.

Rear spoiler

Part of the Trans Am package on the early Firebirds was the rear spoiler. It wasn't huge, but it was big enough to provide some downforce and, just as important, to make the car stand out from other Firebirds.

Chevy Nova rear end

Chevrolet produced Novas for Police Departments across the country. They have a heavy-duty rear suspension designed to cope with lots of power and sustained chases and abuse. This suspension has been incorporated into this Trans Am.

Specifications
1969 Modified Pontiac Trans Am

ENGINE

Type: Chevrolet small-block V8
Construction: Cast-iron block and heads
Valve gear: Two valves per cylinder operated by single block-mounted camshaft via pushrods, rockers and hydraulic tappets
Bore and stroke: 4 in. x 3.48 in.
Displacement: 350 c.i.
Compression ratio: 10:1
Induction system: Throttle body electronic fuel injection
Maximum power: 250 bhp at 5,000 rpm
Maximum torque: 295 lb-ft at 3,650 rpm

TRANSMISSION

1989 700R4 automatic transmission with overdrive

BODY/CHASSIS

Semi-unitary body/chassis with two-door convertible body

SPECIAL FEATURES

Rear disc brakes installed on this car come from a 1979 model Trans Am.

Fuel injection on IROC Z28 engine gives cleaner emissions and smoother pick-up.

RUNNING GEAR

Steering: Recirculating ball
Front suspension: Double wishbones with coil springs, telescopic shocks and anti-roll bar
Rear suspension: Live axle from 1979 Chevrolet Nova Police specification with semi-elliptic leaf springs and telescopic shocks
Brakes: Discs (front), with discs from a 1979 model Trans Am (rear)
Wheels: Steel 15 in. x 6 in.
Tires: BF Goodrich 235/60R15

DIMENSIONS

Length: 191.1 in.   **Width:** 173.9 in.
Height: 49.6 in.   **Wheelbase:** 108.1 in.
Track: 60 in. (front and rear)
Weight: 3,649 lbs.

Pontiac TRANS AM SD

By 1974, only GM could offer anything even vaguely approaching the performance machines of the late 1960s and early 1970s, with the Chevrolet Corvette and the more powerful Pontiac Trans Am SD-455.

"...raucous takeoffs."

"The 1974 Trans Am was strictly 'old school' American muscle in the performance and handling departments. Like its predecessors a decade earlier, it was great in a straight line. The massive 455-cubic inch engine plays a part in the car's front-heavy handling, although it gives fantastic midrange acceleration. Standard disc brakes up front and a limited-slip differential for raucous takeoffs are major plus points."

There is a comfortable feel to the interior, which is unmistakably 1970s.

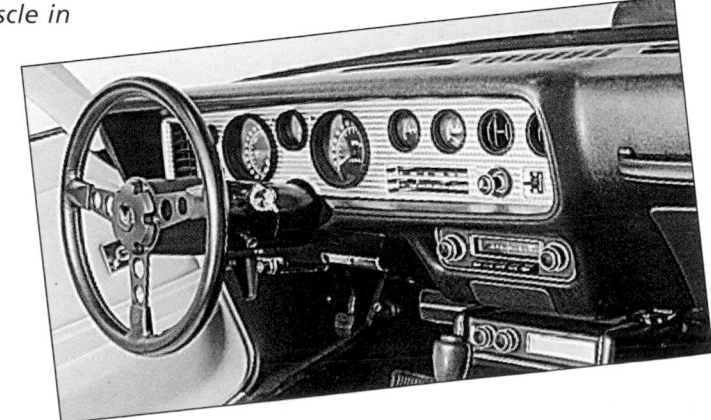

Milestones

1967 Pontiac
introduces the Firebird, it shares its basic shell with the Chevrolet Camaro, which debuted a few months earlier. Both are aimed at the 'pony market' created by the Mustang.

Chevrolet dropped the Camaro in 1975, leaving the Trans Am as GM's only muscle car.

1969 The Trans Am
is offered for the first time in the Firebird lineup as the top-of-the-line performance Firebird. Standard was the Ram Air III, 335 bhp 400 HO engine.

The Trans Am had a bold redesign for 1979.

1974 First major
body and engineering restyle for the Firebird/Trans Am series.

1976 Last year of
the Pontiac 455-c.i. engine, only available in the Trans Am as a limited edition.

UNDER THE SKIN

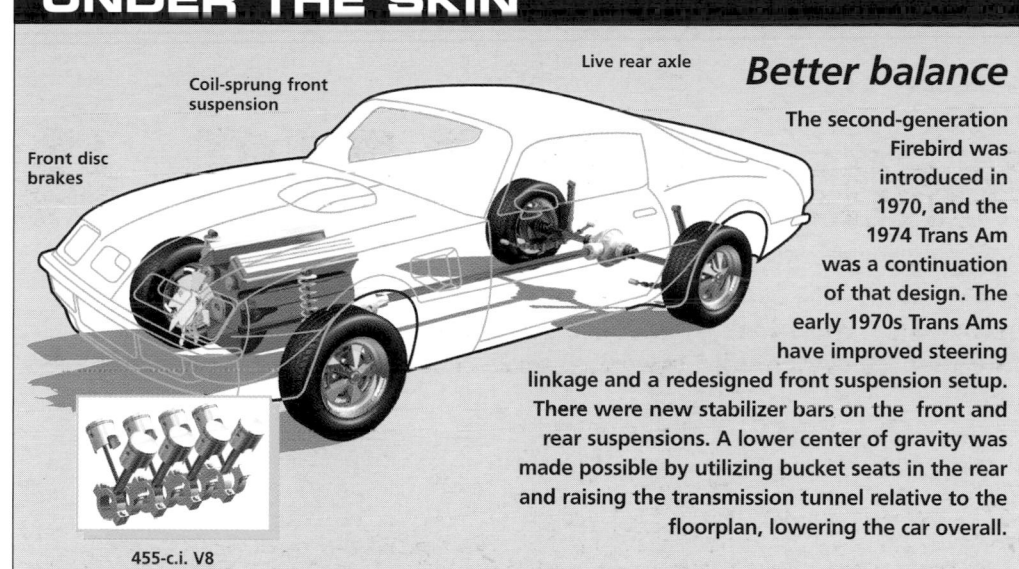

Coil-sprung front suspension

Live rear axle

Front disc brakes

455-c.i. V8

Better balance

The second-generation Firebird was introduced in 1970, and the 1974 Trans Am was a continuation of that design. The early 1970s Trans Ams have improved steering linkage and a redesigned front suspension setup. There were new stabilizer bars on the front and rear suspensions. A lower center of gravity was made possible by utilizing bucket seats in the rear and raising the transmission tunnel relative to the floorplan, lowering the car overall.

THE POWER PACK

Super-Duty punch

Pontiac's Super Duty 455 was the last bastion of big-cube power for the performance enthusiast. With a compression ratio of 8.4:1, output was down as the first of the mandatory emissions controls began to sap power. Nonetheless, the engine still sported all the performance features of the soon-to-be-gone muscle car era. This includes a lot of displacement, four-bolt mains, forged-aluminum pistons and an 800-cfm Quadrajet carb. There was even built-in provision for dry-sump lubrication. Earlier 1974 cars make use of the Ram IV camshaft and are capable of 310 bhp; later 1974 cars do not and are rated at 290 bhp.

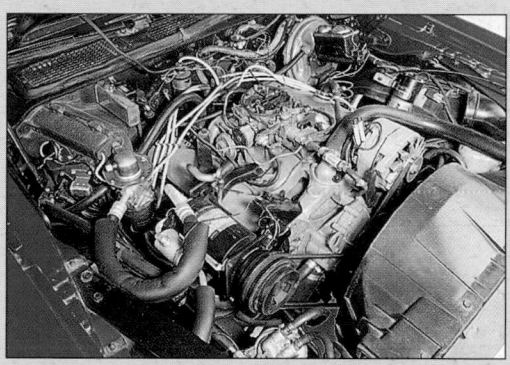

Last of its kind

If you wanted a muscle car in 1974, there was only one choice: the Trans Am SD-455. Big-block Camaros had been discontinued and MOPAR, the purveyor of some of the hot muscle car property, had pulled the plug on performance.

For 1974, Pontiac gave the Trans Am new front-end treatment.

Pontiac **TRANS AM** 🇺🇸

Pontiac Firebirds were offered in four series for 1974: Firebird, Esprit, Formula and Trans Am. The 455-SD engine could be ordered only in the Formula and the Trans Am. Super-Duty equipped Formulas are the rarest.

Special dash

Trans Ams featured a special steering wheel, a faux metal dash and a rally gauge cluster, which included a clock and dash-mounted tachometer. As a sign of the times, a new 'fuel economy' gauge was introduced later in the year.

LSD

Standard on the Trans Am was a limited-slip differential, ensuring minimal wheelspin and consistent launches.

New tires

For 1974, all General Motors cars had to use steel-belted radials. Hence, the old Firestone Wide-Oval F60-15 bias-belted tires were replaced with new Firestone 500 F60 x 15 steel-belted radials.

'Soft' bumpers

New for 1974 was a soft bumper treatment front and rear, utilizing molded urethane foam. These were faced with black rubber front bars to absorb parking bumps.

Scoops galore

Pontiac made sure that the Trans Am looked aggressive and powerful with flared wheel arches and front fender air extractors. The menacing-looking, rear-facing Shaker hood scoop finishes off the whole effect with SD-455 decals on the side.

Restyled rear end

The rear-end treatment includes a full-width rear spoiler. Taillights are wider, in a horizontal casing, giving a more integrated appearance.

Specifications

1974 Trans Am SD455

ENGINE

Type: V8

Construction: Cast-iron cylinder block and cylinder head

Valve gear: Two valves per cylinder

Bore and stroke: 4.15 in. x 4.21 in.

Displacement: 455 c.i.

Compression ratio: 8.4:1

Induction system: 800-cfm Quadrajet four-barrel carburetor

Maximum power: 310 bhp at 4,000 rpm

Maximum torque: 390 lb-ft at 3,600 rpm

TRANSMISSION

Three-speed automatic M40 Turbo Hydramatic

BODY/CHASSIS

Steel unibody construction

SPECIAL FEATURES

The SD-455 logos are seen only on Trans Ams and Formulas.

A holographic applique on the dash perfectly reflects mid-1970s style.

RUNNING GEAR

Steering: Variable-ratio, ball-nut

Front suspension: A-arms with coil springs and telescopic shock absorbers

Rear suspension: Live rear axle with leaf springs and telescopic shock absorbers

Brakes: Discs (front), drums (rear)

Wheels: Steel, 15-in. Rally II

Tires: F60 x 15 (raised white letters) Firestone steel belted

DIMENSIONS

Length: 196.0 in. **Width:** 73.4 in.

Height: 50.4 in. **Wheelbase:** 108.0 in.

Track: 61.6 in. (front), 60.3 in. (rear)

Weight: 3,655 lbs.

Shelby CHARGER GLH-S

As performance started to become important again in the 1980s, Carroll Shelby, in cooperation with Chrysler, began building limited-production sports cars based on the stock, performance-deprived 1986–1987 Charger.

"...Shelby muscle missile."

"An angular interior with shades of black and gray are typical styling cues of many cars built in the 1980s. The Shelby Charger GLH-S is no different. With its underhood modifications, however, performance is more like a 1960s muscle car. With your foot hard on the gas, this Shelby-modified muscle missile rockets down the road, though a firm hand is needed on the steering wheel. Suspension modifications really make this car handle, but its ride is still comfortable enough to be a daily driver."

Twin Auto Meter gauges are the sole deviation from the stock interior in this GLH-S.

Milestones

1982 The Charger nameplate is resurrected as a top-level version of the Omni-based Turismo coupe. It is powered by a 2.2-liter four-cylinder engine with 84 bhp. 14,420 examples are built.

Shelby's first effort in the 1980s centered on the Omni GLH.

1984 Dodge gets serious with the Charger. It now boasts meaner looks. A Shelby version is released, packing a High Output 2.2 liter, normally aspirated 110-bhp engine, a body kit and a stiff suspension with 50-series Goodyear tires.

For 1985, the GLH Turbo Charger got a 146-bhp turbo engine.

1985 A turbo 2.2 liter engine with a Bosch-fuel injection system is fitted to the Shelby. It now packs a whopping 146 bhp.

1986 Hottest Charger of all, the GLH-S enters limited production. Just 1,000 are eventually built.

UNDER THE SKIN

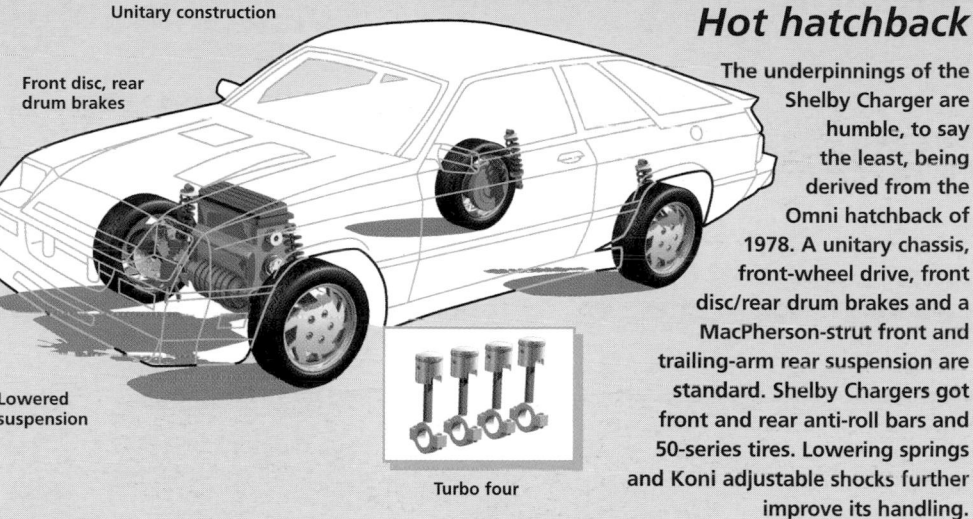

Unitary construction

Front disc, rear drum brakes

Lowered suspension

Turbo four

Hot hatchback

The underpinnings of the Shelby Charger are humble, to say the least, being derived from the Omni hatchback of 1978. A unitary chassis, front-wheel drive, front disc/rear drum brakes and a MacPherson-strut front and trailing-arm rear suspension are standard. Shelby Chargers got front and rear anti-roll bars and 50-series tires. Lowering springs and Koni adjustable shocks further improve its handling.

THE POWER PACK

A 4 that runs like an 8

Big-block muscle car owners, eat your heart out. This little GLH-S has a turbo four cylinder that will outrun muscle cars with engines three times its size. In 1987, Dodge Shelby Chargers were powered by a 146-bhp, 2.2-liter four. When Shelby started building his own cars again in 1986, the little four-cylinders were modified with an air-to-air intercooler and equal-length intake runners—good for 175 bhp. The engine in this car has been radically reworked with JE pistons, stainless-steel con rods and a ported, high-flow cylinder head. Combined with larger valves, a bigger 57mm throttle body, four extra injectors, twin intercoolers and other changes, it kicks out 289 bhp.

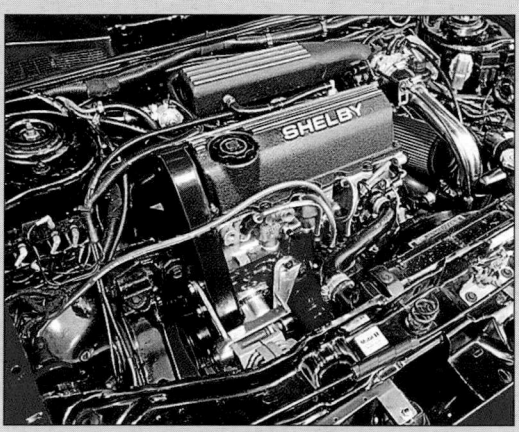

Acro-name

While some car companies use the acronyms GT or LM to signify racing classes, Shelby decided to take a similar though lighter approach in naming these Chargers. The original car—the GLH—stands for 'Goes Like Hell.' The faster GLH-S was name so because it 'Goes Like Hell-Some more.'

It may look stock, but this Charger is quicker than many sports and muscle cars.

Shelby **CHARGER GLH-S**

Fast, even in stock trim, the Charger GLH-S can be made faster still. With this kind of turbocharged performance, the GLH-S is a fun street performer. Its hatchback design makes it practical, too.

Hood bulge

When the Charger first got a turbocharger and fuel injection in 1985, a new hood was fitted with an offset bulge and scoop to clear the fuel injection's intake plenum.

Highly tuned engine

The many modifications to the 2.2-liter four include oversize valves and a high-lift cam to improve upper rpm power. There's also a hybrid turbocharger and even a fuel pump pirated from a Porsche 944 Turbo.

Monster exhaust

A low-restriction exhaust is essential for a powerful engine. This Charger has a three-inch stainless steel system with a high-flow catalytic convertor.

Hatchback design

Based on the Omni-derived O24 hatchback coupe, the 1984 Charger was restyled to include bigger C-pillars, a new front end with a simpler grill and integral airdam, rocker panel extensions and a decklid spoiler.

Specifications

1987 Shelby Charger GLH-S

ENGINE

Type: In-line four

Construction: Cast-iron block with alloy cylinder head

Valve gear: Two valves per cylinder operated by a single camshaft

Bore and stroke: 3.44 in. x 3.62 in.

Displacement: 2.2 liter

Compression ratio: 8.5:1

Induction system: Electronic fuel injection

Maximum power: 289 bhp at 6,200 rpm

Maximum torque: 274 lb-ft at 3,700 rpm

TRANSMISSION

Five-speed manual

BODY/CHASSIS

Unitary monocoque construction with steel three-door hatchback body

SPECIAL FEATURES

A hood vent feeds fresh air to the sequential intercoolers.

The battery has been relocated to the trunk to improve weight distribution.

RUNNING GEAR

Steering: Rack-and-pinion

Front suspension: MacPherson struts, lower control arms, telescopic shock absorbers and anti-roll bar

Rear suspension: Beam axle, semi trailing arms, coil springs, telescopic shock absorbers and anti-roll bar

Brakes: Discs (front), drums (rear)

Wheels: 7 x 16 in. cast aluminum

Tires: Goodyear Eagle GT P205/50VR15

DIMENSIONS

Length: 174.8 in. **Width:** 66.7 in.

Height: 48.2 in.   **Wheelbase:** 96.5 in.

Track: 56.1 in. (front), 55.7 in. (rear)

Weight: 2,483 lbs.

Lowered suspension

Fully adjustable Koni front and rear shocks, ¾-inch lowering springs and urethane bushings are subtle alterations that result in notably better handling than a stock Charger can deliver.

High-mounted brake light

From 1986, all cars were required to have a center high-mounted brake light. On Chargers, it is simply attached to the top of the spoiler.

Shelby **MUSTANG GT350**

When dynamic Texan, Carroll Shelby worked his magic on the best-selling Ford Mustang, he created a classic. The rare top-of-the-line 350-bhp Shelby Mustang GT350 was a great champion—and you could rent the street-legal 306-bhp version from Hertz for $35 a day!

"…tons of upper end power."

"'Rough…nasty…noisy…hard steering…I love it!' were the comments most testers made back in 1965, and it hasn't changed since. The special Detroit Locker limited slip differential makes loud ratcheting noises on slow corners, then locks with a bang when you hit the accelerator. The engine is smaller than most other American muscle cars of the time, but the GT350 is a winner at the track or on the street. Suspension is stiffer than the stock Mustang and really helps the car negotiate sharp turns. The high-performance 289 offers lots of torque and tons of upper end power."

With full instrumentation and a stripped-out interior, it is obvious that the GT350 means business.

Milestones

1964 Mustang introduced in April

and showrooms are mobbed. The first V8 comes slightly later, followed by a bigger V8, then a 271-bhp version (code name 'K'), which is the basis for the GT350.

The Mustang was launched in 1964 as a 'pony' car.

1965 Shelby American takes time out

from building Cobras to produce 100 GT350s and qualifying them to run as SCCA sports cars. They win four out of five of the B-Production regional wins in 1965, and take the overall championship that year and in 1966 and 1967.

1966 Hertz Rent-a-Car

buys about 1,000 GT350Hs (for Hertz), painted with gold stripes—most have automatic transmissions. There are stories about people renting them, racing them, then returning the Rent-a-Racers with brakes smoking and tires worn out.

Hertz gained publicity from renting Shelby Mustangs.

UNDER THE SKIN

New suspension

Engine is mounted in the front, driving through a special Borg Warner T-10 four-speed transmission to a heavy-duty rear axle, taken from a Ford Galaxie station wagon. The Mustang monocoque is steel with Shelby adding a rear seat replacement panel and fiberglass hood (with air scoop). Shelby added a wooden steering wheel—a sports car must-have at the time.

Koni adjustable shocks

Spare tire on fiberglass rear seat panel

Optional alloy wheels

Braces from cowl to suspension towers

Front-mounted V8

THE POWER PACK

Two valves per cylinder

Holley 4-barrel carburetor

10.5:1 Compression ratio

high-lift camshaft

Aluminum oil pan

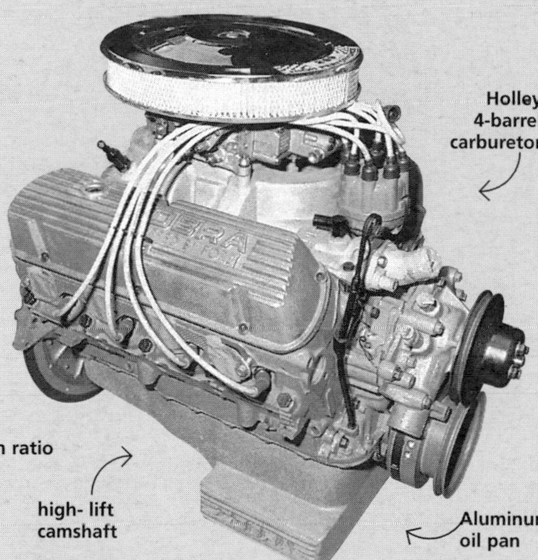

Ford 'Hi-Po' 289

Basically a Mustang GT unit, the high-performance 289-cubic inch Ford small block started at 271 bhp before Shelby began working on it, a substantial improvement on the 101 bhp of the first six-cylinder Mustangs. The engine of the GT350 street car with a Holley four-barrel carburetor developed 306 bhp, and the mighty GT350R had another 44 bhp. The main modifications were a higher compression ratio, high-lift cam, larger valves, and improved breathing with the performance carburetor.

The GT350R

Only 37 examples of the 'R' (for race) version were built. With a stout 350-bhp engine and stripped interior, it won championships in the Sports Car Club of America's (SCCA) hot B-Production class against Corvettes, Ferraris, Cobras, Lotuses and E-type Jaguars.

GT350R has a fiberglass apron which increased airflow to the radiator.

Shelby MUSTANG GT350

Ford's Mustang was selling well, but it lacked the high-performance image of the Corvette. So Ford asked Carroll Shelby to develop the GT350, which beat the Corvette on the race track and outperformed it on the road.

High performance 289 V8

Shelby modified Ford's 'Hi-Po' version of the small-block V8 with 10.5:1 compression ratio, improved valve timing and better breathing. This gave 306 bhp at 6,000 rpm.

Rear-exiting exhaust system

The original GT350s had side-exiting exhausts which were noisy and not permitted in some states. 1966 models were given a conventional rear-exiting exhaust system.

Improved front suspension

The standard Mustang front suspension was improved for the GT350 with stiffer springs, revalved Koni shocks and relocated control arms.

Optional Cragar alloy wheels

Conventional steel wheels were standard wear on the GT350, but many owners opted for the lighter Cragar alloys approved by Shelby.

Functional side scoops

The 1966 GT350 had side scoops which fed air to the rear brakes, distinguishing it from the standard fastback Mustang.

Rear drum brakes

The GT350's extra performance dictated the use of Kelsey-Hayes front discs, but drums were retained at the rear.

Acrylic rear quarter windows

On the 1966 models the standard Mustang fastback louvers were replaced by acrylic windows to make the car lighter.

Custom fuel cap

The 1966-model GT350s were given their very own fuel cap in the middle of the rear of the car, carrying the Cobra logo.

Limited slip differential

Early Shelbys were fitted with the Detroit Locker limited slip differential to improve cornering traction and eliminate wheelspin.

Specifications
1966 Shelby Mustang GT350

ENGINE

Type: V8

Construction: Cast-iron block and heads, aluminum intake manifold, tubular steel exhaust manifolds

Valve gear: Two valves per cylinder operated by single block-mounted camshaft via pushrods and rockers

Bore and stroke: 4.02 in. x 2.87 in.

Displacement: 289 c.i.

Compression ratio: 10.5:1

Induction system: Holley four-barrel carburetor

Maximum power: 306 bhp at 6,000 rpm

Maximum torque: 329 lb-ft at 4,200 rpm

TRANSMISSION

Borg Warner T-10 four-speed with close-ratio gears and aluminum case

BODY/CHASSIS

Standard steel Mustang fastback body with Shelby grill; fiberglass hood, removed rear seat, Mustang monocoque with subframes

SPECIAL FEATURES

Goodyear tires were the performance rubber to have on your 1960s muscle car.

Shelby Mustang ID plate is mounted on left fenderwell.

RUNNING GEAR

Front suspension: Wishbones, coil springs, Koni shocks and anti-roll bar

Rear suspension: Live axle with semi-elliptic leaf springs, Koni shocks and traction control arms

Brakes: Kelsey-Hayes disc brakes 11.3 in. dia. (front), drums (rear)

Wheels: Steel 6 in. x 14 in. or magnesium alloy 7 in. x 14 in.

Tires: Goodyear crossply Blue Dot 775-14

DIMENSIONS

Length: 181.6 in. **Width:** 68.2 in.

Height: 55 in. **Wheelbase:** 108 in.

Track: 56.5 in. (front), 57 in. (rear)

Weight: 2,792 lbs.

Index